Oskar Schindler Saved My Life

Oskar Schindler Saved My Life

CARL FREEDMAN

(as edited by Shelli Frydman Brosh)

Copyright © 2009 by Carl Freedman.

Library of Congress Control Number: 2009902082
ISBN: Hardcover   978-1-4415-1718-0
               Softcover   978-1-4415-1717-3

All rights reserved. No part of this book may be reproduced or transmitted in any form or by any means, electronic or mechanical, including photocopying, recording, or by any information storage and retrieval system, without permission in writing from the copyright owner.

This book was printed in the United States of America.

To order additional copies of this book, contact:
Xlibris Corporation
1-888-795-4274
www.Xlibris.com
Orders@Xlibris.com

To my beloved wife Ruth.
She is always by my side and my greatest inspiration.

And
In loving memory of our parents and family who perished.

Acknowledgements

Many people had a part in this life's tale becoming a book. First and foremost, our father, Carl Freedman, who vowed to uphold the promise to never forget and wrote every day (once he had retired). He wrote by hand in Yiddish, his mother tongue. Then with the help of some friends, he translated it to English so that his children and grandchildren would be able to know his story. This was a long and arduous process, the original handwritten English manuscript is over 670 pages long.

Huge thanks are due to Ann Dougherty who not only typed this handwritten manuscript into recognizable characters, but disentangled phrases, identified misspelled words, figured out many of the Yiddish and Polish words and made them legible—in short, miraculously brought this manuscript closer to accessibility. This first edition is in fact still a work in progress.

Many hours were volunteered. Thanks to my husband Dov Brosh for patient copying of various versions, the historian Leonard Rogoff for reading the manuscript and his valuable suggestions, our mother Ruth Freedman for inspiring and moving us to action, ideas and additional help from my brother Mel Freedman and my sister Rosalie Freedman Ofer and last but definitely not least, my dear sister-in-law Shelley Higgins Freedman for her invaluable organizational assistance and who nudged everybody to the finish line.

Shelli Frydman Brosh
February 2009
West Orange, New Jersey

Contents

Where I Came From 13

The Year 1939, September 16

The First Yom Kippur with the Nazis 19

Leaving the City 23

Life in Krakow in 1940 under the Germans 25

Opening the Ghetto 29

Life in the Shul (Beth Midrash) 38

I Work at My Profession 44

The Story About David Schwarzbaum and Us....................47

Moshke the Bad Messenger 53

A Day With the Dula Family 56

Typhus Fever in the Shul 65

The "Aussiedlung"—Finishing the Jews in Dzialoszyce...72

The First Night in a Concentration Camp 79

The First Day in a Concentration Camp 81

The First Day in a Place for Poor Guests 97

The First Day on my Job at SS Viking 134

The First Day in Plaszow Camp 146

Who Was Oskar Schindler? 164

The First Day at Work	165
The First Night at the Barracks	167
Commandant Goeth from Plaszow	173
Christmas Time 1944	175
The Liquidation of Schindler's Factories	185
The Burned Airplane	188
The Last Transport	190
They took us to Schiowitz	192
The Hospital at Schiowitz	200
The Americans Bombard the Factory	204
We March to Theresienstadt	209
My Time in the Hospital	216
Life at Landsberg Camp	221
My Brother Remains	227
The Girl from Stuttgart	234

Where I Came From

I grew up as Chaim Kalmen Frydman. Many years later in 1954 when I became a U.S. citizen, I changed my name to Carl Freedman. I was born in Krakow, Poland on January 11, 1920 on Krakowska Street 28, in a Jewish area called "The Kuzmark" or Kazimierz part of the city. Miodowa 39 was the last address where my family and I lived in Poland. We lived across from a very old cemetery. Lying to rest there were Tsadikim, righteous people, and a great Rabbi, the Remuh.

My father was Rabbi Symcha Frydman. My mother's name was Beila Ruchel Schumacher. I had four sisters and one brother. My half-sister, Sara, was the oldest. Next came my brother Moshe. I am the third and then my sisters, Chana, Ryvka and Mira was fifth and youngest.

My father, he should rest in peace, was Rabbi Symcha Frydman. He was studying to be a Rabbi when World War I broke out, but he was going blind. Although he was extremely knowledgeable and knew the whole Bible and the Talmud, he couldn't practice the profession because, for example, he couldn't write things down. Fortunately, he had a very good memory, which became his real profession and from which he made a living.

My father became a Badchen, an entertainer, an emcee at Jewish weddings and parties. He would create songs and poems about the bride and the groom, their families and guests which he composed on the spot. He was a poet and a singer and composed over 400 Jewish songs, five of which were published. His name was known all over Poland.

He was a genius, a born intellect. He could remember most of the bible. He had all the prayers from all year round in his mind. He remembered his melodies and they are also still in my ears. I remember his melodramas, monologs and humorous stories.

Every day my talented father was composing a new song with melodies and lyrics. He composed most of his songs at night. He would wake my brother Moshe and me up at two o'clock in the morning to help him. Moshe wrote the music notes and I had to write the words (lines). It took him about an hour and when he was finished, we went back to sleep. In the morning he didn't remember anything of what he had created. We had to read the whole composition back to him. He then was very satisfied with what he had done. He published songs that were sold to stores, libraries and private people. It brought in money for the house.

My mother, Beila Ruchel, was always worried about her children. Physically she was very weak and suffered from a heart condition. I was always so happy when I saw my mother in a healthy and good mood especially when she was without pain.

When I was five years old, my father sent me to a good private Hebrew school called "Talmud Torah" on Estera Street not far from my home. I still remember some of my teachers' names like Shimon Redner, Abele Birnbaum, and Hershel Pechman. The main director, Luzer Pancer, came every month to examine us and at the end of the year, he gave us our school certificates. We also had to go to public school from two o'clock until four o'clock. For one and a half hours until three thirty, we learned almost the same thing as in the public school, but spent only one and a half hours for the Talmud Torah studies. We had the same assignments as the public schools.

When I had my Bar Mitzvah on January 11th of 1933, we had a beautiful party at our house. We invited the boys from my Hebrew class and gave them all cigarettes, that was the fashion in Europe at that time. The evening after the party, my father called to me and said, "Please sit down with me, I want to talk to you."

I sat down with my father and he said, "look my son, when I saw the cigarettes at your party that you gave the young boys, I was upset. I know you could not do it any differently because that's the way they are doing things now. But I want you to promise me that you will not start to smoke cigarettes. I will tell you my experience. I smoke two packs of cigarettes every day and I can't stop. I am addicted to it. I went to the doctor and he told me that my lungs are black. I definitely should stop smoking. It will shorten my life if I don't stop. So, my dear son, I want to prevent you from starting to smoke. You will be very thankful to me, my son. Please promise me that and give me your right hand as a symbol to remember to keep your promise" and I did that. Thank God for this. I did not smoke and I am now alive. [Ed. As my father told us, it saved his life in concentration camp.]

When I was 14 years old, I went to the Belzer Yeshiva, studying Torah and Gemarah. After a year there, I felt that it was time to look for a job. At fifteen, I wanted to learn a profession. My father knew a lot of people and we found a place where they made all kinds of leather goods like briefcases, school bags and luggage. It was a family business with a mother, father, two daughters, and a son. The father was very Orthodox but the son and daughter were traditional. The son was the manager. His name was Shlomo Wiesenfeld. It was a small factory and had a store that sold to private people. When my father came in with me, they knew him and my father told Shlomo the story about me looking to learn a profession so he hired me on the spot for ten zloty a month. He promised my father that he would treat me nicely and teach me his profession.

I started two days later. For the first five weeks, I was the cleaning boy sweeping the floor. After that he let me go to some customers in the city with luggage. He packed three pieces of luggage sized 30-40-50 inside each other and then into one size 60 piece. I had 8 pieces of luggage to carry everyday on the streetcar to the city. It was a big place called Sukiennice. It was like Florida.

I was like a bellboy. After three months, I reminded the boss, Shlomo, that he promised my father he would teach me a profession and until now I only swept the floors, cleaned the shelves and was sent to the city. He told me that at first I had to do those things. I had to be patient, but I saw what was going on so I started to concentrate on the luggage. When I was in the shop doing my cleaning, I especially watched the guy who made the luggage and how he did it. But once, my boss saw that I was watching the worker. He asked me why I was watching him instead of doing my job. I didn't answer him, but I decided to start my own business. When they sent me to town with eight different sized luggages, I would go home and take the measurements. Each trip I would measure a different one until I had all the measurements for each size.

It took me one month to copy them and I bought all the equipment that I needed to start work. After two months of preparation, I made the first piece of luggage. It was done crooked but it was still a piece of luggage. I sold it for four zloty and I made one zloty and seventy-five groszen. I still worked at my job. I had saved about 80 zloty because I had also had received tips when I delivered luggage to the customers.

The guy who worked on the machine making schoolbooks was a friend of my brother's. One night he came to our house to play music with my brother. He saw what I was doing. Three days later I was fired from my job, so I now worked full time at home. Gradually, my sister Chana started to help me with the work.

After two years of working from home, I was starting to look for more customers. I rented a store and opened a workshop on Prsemyska Street. I hired two workers along with my sister Chana. I had a wonderful shop and people came in with repair items. I had quite a beautiful clientele. On Tuesday and Friday I took merchandise to the market where I sold luggage and handbags.

It was 1937, I was 17 years old and the business was growing. I hired another worker. I now had four workers and my sister Chana. She was almost 15 years old at the time and very smart. She did everything; she was a saleslady, worker and manager. My business was worth 10,000 zloty. This was a lot of money, the equivalent of about forty thousand dollars today. I was able to help our parents with money until 1939.

The Year 1939, September

The Second World War broke out on September 1, 1939. The Germans attacked Poland in the early morning. German airplanes attacked many Polish cities. Planes were flying over the main cities in Poland. We got up at six o'clock in the morning and saw people rushing into the street. I couldn't sleep all night because of the airplanes. I was standing at the window and saw whole families walking together with bundles in their hands. I called to my brother to see what was going on outside, and he said that we should also start packing to leave. I asked him where were we to go? The Germans were all over Poland. We went out to see what our neighbors were doing and we saw them with their suitcases in order to go to Lemberg (Lvov), which was near the Russian border. With a heavy heart, the whole family with father, mother, and six children, big and small left with enough food for one day in order to get away from the big cities.

We also started to pack. We knew what the Germans had done to the Jewish people in Germany. Before we left and after we finished packing, the whole family ate breakfast together. My mother prepared a package for each to carry and we left our home. All the neighbors from our building left and we started to walk together. I was holding my father's hand, my brother was holding our mother's hand and Sara (Sala) was taking care of the two little girls, Rivka and Mira. Our sister Chana was walking with a bitter heart.

We walked through the Krakow streets. We didn't even know where we were going. We went to Starowisina Street to the Podgorska Bridge. We came to the bridge and saw the German soldiers standing and watching thousands of people marching through. There were whole families. Some of them had large wagons on four wheels and they pushed the wagon together through the streets. They had all their belongings on the wagon. On the bridge we saw dead people lying on the ground and we were scared. We heard all the news from the people walking with us. They were carrying radios and they told us what was going on. They told us that the Germans were occupying all of Warsaw. They were in Tarnow, but we also heard that the Russians were occupying Lemberg. We heard that they occupied Rzeszow. We marched together but it was very hard with small children, a blind father and my mother was a very sick woman.

We marched quite a few hours through Krakow. We were in a small village and we sat down under a tree to rest. We ate what our mother had prepared for us. We looked around and saw that we were among Polish farmers and not one Jew. We got scared and we started discussing what we had to do. Night was falling and we did not have a place to sleep so we discussed whether we should go back home or continue walking. We asked our mother. She was a very smart woman but no one could be smart enough to know which way would be better. My brother felt that the best way was to continue to walk to Lemberg, but our mother wanted to keep us together and she wanted to go back home. She felt we should believe in destiny. She said that walking further would be dangerous. We could get killed not only from the Germans but also from the Poles. They will rob and kill us because we are Jews and some are anti Semitic. Also bandits were roaming around. The best thing for us would be to go back home and to pray to God that the war would come to an end soon. My father was a religious person. He said that we had to leave the whole situation to God. He will help us to overcome the war and remain together. God will be good to us. We all got up from our resting place and started to walk back home. It was almost two o'clock in the morning. We walked back home and met thousands of people also going back home. I was very satisfied that we were going back home.

During the five-hour walk, we passed small towns and villages and we saw more and more German soldiers coming on motorcycles. Big autos passed by and we saw hundreds or maybe thousands of people going back to Krakow. We thanked God as we approached Krakow. As we passed Podgorze and we walked on the streets we came to the Stazowytnia Bridge, we saw Polish officers with the mourners on the bridge with their dead. Many people were killed. Our hearts started to shiver. We were afraid. We walked through Starowisina Street and thank God, we came to Miodova 39, our building where we lived for so many years. We came back to our home sweet home and the house was not touched. Everything in the home was scattered all over the place because we all packed our own clothing.

We started anew. We didn't have enough bread. I went out to look around for a bakery. I found one and I saw a line with maybe a hundred people. I knew I couldn't come home empty handed. It took one and a half hours. I could only get one loaf of bread and paid double the price. I came home and we were happy to have bread in the house. Every day we had to go to the bakery and stand in line. One time my brother went with me and we got two loaves of bread, so we were very, very happy.

On a Wednesday morning we heard shots from the streets. We looked through the window and saw people moving with wagons and packages in their hands. They were running through the street to the Stazowytnia Bridge. Our neighbors were leaving the house and we were left alone in the whole building except for Mr. Bomba, the manager. We also started to pack the second time and mother prepared sandwiches. The whole family left together again. We started to walk with our packages along with hundreds of families. We again come to the Stazowytnia Bridge. At about 8:30 in the morning, we saw three German patrols stopping people and asking for identification. They didn't let everybody through. We were about 100 meters from them. The Germans asked them to stand aside and we saw that until now we didn't know what was happening to those people. We got scared and our mother said we were not to go forward but that we were going back home. What was happening to all the Jewish people would happen to us. We stopped walking and looked at each other. We decided to go back home, and we again were happy, kissed each other, and gave thanks that we were still together.

We walked back to our home where the building manager was standing in the doorway. He didn't say anything to us but he looked so angry. We went up to our apartment on the fourth floor, we were very tired from walking. We sat down and reviewed what had happened that day. We looked outside and saw there was no one in the street not even one person. It was empty. We heard noise from the tanks coming through the streets and a lot of German soldiers marching through. For 24-hours the Jewish people didn't show their heads on the streets. The sky was covered with black clouds. That was the start of the execution of the Jewish people.

The first proclamation from the German government was that all businesses such as stores, factories, and offices belonging to a Jewish person had to have that indicated with a Star of David on their windows and doors. Each Jewish family possessing more than two thousand zloty had to inform the German government. This was terrible for the Jewish people, but it was only the beginning. Even though we didn't want to obey, we had no choice.

The second proclamation was a shame for the Jewish people. Every Jew from 12 years old had to wear on his or her arm a white star. Little by little they took away all businesses from Jewish hands and all the Jewish professionals in high government jobs were thrown out.

On all the streets in Krakow, we saw the SS Commandos roaming around with big trucks. They blocked all the streets with their trucks. They picked up about 20 or 30 young men and women and took them to work 20 kilometers away from the city. Some of those people never came back. When I saw what was going on and I had to walk in the street, I started to limp on one foot when they began picking up people. Sometimes they looked at me and I was scared but they let me get by. I did it all the time. When I saw the SS trucks from far away I started to limp.

The First Yom Kippur with the Nazis

We were scared to death to walk or to talk on the first Yom Kippur under the occupation. We couldn't work but we were a family of eight people at the table. There was not much to eat and not much money left. Everything went sky high in price. The price of bread was running up and up. It was before Rosh Hashanah when a small group of Jewish people from Miodowa and Szeroka Streets got together and decided to have services in somebody's house. We organized a place at one of our good neighbor's four houses away from us for prayers and to keep our traditions. We had twenty two people but we did it secretly so the neighbors wouldn't see us coming together. We lived together with the Polish people in the same building. We called the manager and the people from the house the "Strus" because they were Poles. We were afraid they would call the Germans. We had to arrive slowly but we got together for Rosh Hashanah. Two days was not bad. My father was asked to lead the service and he prayed, as a Cantor. He prayed very sweet and good. We said prayers slowly and quietly. Everything was all right but my father was very nervous. On Yom Kippur, we came to "daven", to recite "Kol Nidrei" in the evening, we were also fasting. The next morning we gathered for prayers at nine o'clock.

Only the men went to prayers. At about 12:30 and in the middle of prayers, we heard a knock on the door. The door was locked and we stopped praying. They knocked again but we didn't answer. They broke the door down and about ten SS came in hollering at us. They took us out wearing the tallises (prayer shawls). They took us to the trucks. I went to one of the SS and told him my father was a blind man and I had to go with him. He looked at my father and me and told me to take my father home and to stay away from here. That's what I did and I was very happy when I walked with my father down the steps. The place was on the Third Floor. Later on we found out that they took the people with the tallises to the German police. They recorded their names and gave them a warning but they let them go back home.

After the SS left the place and all the people came back from the police with a warning, everyone was afraid. People prayed in their own homes. My father got very scared, nervous and panicky when I took him home. He was in bed for five days until he felt better.

We had a radio that my brother, Moshe, was taking care of. He was a mechanic and knew how to get the station from the other side where the Russians occupied Lvov. He was standing at the radio that day and suddenly he picked up Yiddish music! They were playing "oif'n pripitch'l brennt a feier'l..." He called us, the whole family to hear the music and we were astonished. But then he said "I have to leave as quickly as possible from here. I must leave here my dear parents, there will be a destruction of the Jewish population". And he came to me and said "My dear brother, Kalmen, you see what is going on. The Germans have given us a death sentence. They will kill us all and who knows if anybody from us will remain alive. I can't stand to see what is going on outside. I will be prepared if an SS man comes to take me to work. I will kill him first. I know they later will kill me too." That is what he said to me in front of our parents. He told our parents that we had to work out a plan on how to get to the other side, to Lvov where the Russians were because there, we Jewish, would have a chance to remain alive. We all began to cry. We knew that he was right but how could we take our blind father and small children when we would have to go through a deep lake wandering for days or even weeks. We looked at each other and didn't give him an answer. My dear mother said, "Let's think it over. Don't be so harsh. First let's see what other people are doing and then we will decide what to do. To leave everything and to break up a home is not very easy. What will happen if we can't go through this whole thing? If we could go and then come back, that would be different. But if we can't come back and we are locked in the middle, what is going to happen to us, to your father, to the little kids? Let's think first before we act so fast. There is a war outside telling us that our life is in danger here. Also there in Lvov". My brother said that there, for Jews there would be a new life, was no question that if we stayed here it would be a death sentence. My mother was crying and could not answer any more.

My brother Moshe ran from the Third Floor down to the street. His blood was cooking in his body. He wanted to find out how other people who wanted to do the same thing, to go to the Russian side were going to do it. He took information about everything on how to get there. He even made himself a map showing the route from Krakow to Lvov. He came home and showed us the map. The next day he went to our father and talked to him about how whole families were smuggling over to the other side. But my father was still sick from the Yom Kippur disturbance at prayers. In a weak voice, he told my brother "do whatever your heart tells you but talk it over with our mother. She is very smart. You know that whenever anyone in the family needs some advice, they come to mother. God should help you, you know we love you very much. We would like to keep the family together." So Moshe went to mother and told her the whole story and what was going onHe told her, "we are sitting on a volcano and it will bust one day. We have no other choice but to leave if we want to stay together"

. Mother didn't answer yes or no but she said, "Let's go to the Rabbi and find out what he thinks. He might know better." When my father was feeling better, we went to the Rabbi from Dzialoszyce, who lived on Detlowska Ulica. He knew my father very well and we talked with him for more than an hour. He told us that in wartime we never know who is going to be the winner. Today it is very bad here. Tomorrow it could be better. It is changing with the Russians. We told him that the whole family wanted to leave for the Russian side, especially my brother, Moshe. The Rabbi told us that when you try to get to the other side you have to hide, go through a deep lake where you may also have to swim. This was a big risk for us especially with a blind person, but he told us to do what we feel and wish. We left the Rabbi still feeling in question.

When we came home from visiting the Rabbi, we shared what the Rabbi had said. My brother was sitting and listening, not saying anything to us, he was not scared by what the Rabbi had said. He felt we should not listen to the Rabbi and that we should hurry to leave because we were in great danger from Hitler's evil people. They were mistreating us, hitting us and forcing work on us. Some of the workers didn't come back home. Everyday is worse than the last. My brother wanted us both to leave as fast as possible. We could prepare a place in Lvov for the whole family. One of us or both could come back to sell or liquidate the home and the merchandise from the little luggage factory I still had in order to get money. The factory was worth almost 10,000 zloty. For 10,000 zloty we could buy gold or diamonds because money was loosing its worth. He kept talking to me over the course of five days till we came to an understanding that we both had to leave together.

I let my brother talk me into going with him. I told him that as soon as we reached Lvov, we had to rent a place for our whole family, to prepare a home and then one or both of us must come back to get the family. We then would have the experience of knowing the shortest and best way to get to Lvov. We told our mother and father about what we'd decided to do. My father got very sad, we saw it on his face, mother didn't say anything. We started to prepare things to take with us. My brother bought large backpacks for both of us. Our mother prepared our laundry for us. She washed everything by hand because there were no washing machines in those days. She prepared heavy underwear, sweaters, winter coats; winter shoes and socks, a shawl, gloves, a warm hat because it was starting to get cold. It was a day before the Succoth holiday [which is usually in October, 5 days after Yom Kippur]. We decided to leave home, to leave Krakow, after the holiday. There was a nervous atmosphere on the faces of our mother, father and the other children. My oldest sister Sara said "you are both leaving and the whole responsibility will be on me!" would. My brother said to her "don't worry, we will be right back." We knew very well that the Germans, the SS had made the situation here very hard for Jews. They were catching Jewish people on the streets and sending them to forced labor and we knew that many didn't come back.

The weather was getting very cold. Posters were put up on walls from the German government ordering Jews to bring all their furs, new or old to the school across the street from us. If they found out that people didn't comply, the owner of the furs would be taken from their home and jailed, including the children. We had to give away our father's furs and also our mother's fur collars. They gave us ten days time. We collected all the furs from the house and brought them to the school. We didn't even get a receipt for them. My father was very depressed. He didn't know what to do, to give us his blessing and to tell us to go with good luck or not to let us go at all.

Five days later the German government ordered that all radios in Jewish homes had to be brought to the same school across the street. They gave us two weeks to comply. We had a radio in our house and with a bitter heart my brother took the radio to the school. He used to sit for hours listening to the radio and was able to find out what was happening in Lvov on the Russian side. Now he would miss getting all the news. After about ten days, not even the two weeks, the SS went from building to building looking for furs or radios. They even came to our building into our home looking and checking. In some homes, they found a radio or fur, and took this person out of the house with them and put him in jail. Some of them didn't come back home. We spent our Succoth holiday together but with a horrible feeling. Since they took away our furs, my father didn't have a winter coat, he only had a summer coat. As long as we were together, the whole family had some happiness but the feeling in the house was that we had to leave. We saw how the Germans where treating the Jewish people.

We celebrated the last Succoth together. My father was asking my mother what they were going to do without us. When the holiday was over, we had everything that our mother had packed. It was in two backpacks. On Tuesday of the same week, we decided to leave Krakow. The only thing we had to do was open the door and leave.

Leaving the City

It was the Tuesday after Succoth at nine o'clock in the morning. We had our backpacks on our shoulders. I did not sleep the night before. I was lying in bed thinking about leaving a blind man with a sick wife and two children. Even though Sara was twenty three and Chana was sixteen and a half, what was going to happen to them? What was going to happen to them in case we couldn't come back? It was wartime. How were they going to live, to have enough for food and expenses? How will they exist? I was lying in bed for hours and thinking about leaving with no one to take care of everyone. I fell asleep for only about three hours the whole night. In the morning I got up at six o'clock, put on my tefillim and started to pray. The whole family was on their feet. Mother prepared a cooked breakfast. We were sitting together at the kitchen table eating cooked cereal with bread, butter and coffee. It was very quiet. Nobody said anything. After we finished breakfast, we took our backpacks and my brother and I were standing at the door. My mother, father and four sisters were standing near us and waiting for us to say goodbye. All of us had tears in our eyes looking from one to the other. Their eyes were begging us not to go and leave them alone. In this moment I was thinking the same thoughts I had during the night when I couldn't sleep. What was going to happen to my family even though we had to go to save our lives? Who will help them? Who will give them money to live? How are they going to make a living? Who will give them food in time of war? My parents had enough money for about a month, but what about when that ran out?

I had prepared enough material for luggage in my small workshop. When I leave who will take care of the business? How do I know that I will be able to come back? Maybe they will close the borders and we won't be able to come back. That is what I explained to my brother in front of everyone. I took off my backpack and said, "I think it is better that Sara, our oldest sister take my place. She should go with Moshe." I cleaned out my rucksack and took out all my things. I told my mother to bring in Sara's things and put mine back in the drawers. When I looked at my mother, father and the children their faces changed. They looked at me with a smile. The atmosphere in the house changed. I saw that they were happy that I was going to remain with them. I said we were all in God's hands. Go together, God bless you and go in peace to Lvov on the Russian side. I will remain with my parents and the children. I said to my brother and sister Sara "as soon as you come there, first let us know that you are alive. Next, prepare a place for us and as soon as possible, one of you should come back. We will be prepared to go this time with you." They all came to me and kissed me.

After that, mother brought all of Sara's things and put them in the rucksack. They said goodbye to us. With tears in our eyes we kissed each other and again said goodbye. Our father said the blessing prayer to them and said God please give me the time that I should live to see them back alive. We were all crying. They both left the house. We stood at the window and watching my brother Moshe and my sister Sara marched through Miodowa Street where we lived to Starowishnia Street. I felt in my heart that I did the smartest thing. I saved my whole family from starvation.

They couldn't come back any more. All the ways were closed. A lot of people got killed coming back. The Germans didn't let you move from one place to the other. I felt that now I had accomplished one of the Ten Commandments, Honor Your Father and Mother. I sacrificed my life by remaining near the Germans, but I did not regret what I did. As long as I was with my family, they would have plenty of food on the table. I had peace of mind for what I did. I was proud of myself. I said to myself that it's destiny. If God will want to let me be alive, I will remain alive. God helped me to see the end of the war, but I lost my father, mother and sisters

Days and weeks and months passed by and there was no word or sign of my brother or sister. Nobody called us with any news. Our mother was very aggravated and talked to herself, "who knows what to do, what happened to them?" After ten weeks somebody knocked at the door and the postman came in. He brought a letter from Lvov, from the children. He put new life into my mother. You can't imagine the happiness in the house. I read the letter to everyone and their faces started to shine from happiness. It was like Simchat Torah in the house, from this first sign of life! I read and repeated it five times. The letter brought in new life to the whole family. Five days later a young girl came to the house. She had just come from Lvov. She was a friend of Sara, our sister, and she said she met them in Lvov at the Jewish Center (Kaltal). She saw them with our other cousins, Olshina's children from my father's sister Aunt Chava Olshina. Also Zacharieh Szumacher [later spelled Schumacher, he went to Israel, had two children, Bracha and Dudi], a cousin from my mother's side. She told us that they were preparing to come back to Krakow to take us Lvov. Then another letter came telling us that we should not worry. We should be prepared to take whatever we can and to bring precious things like gold or diamonds and money and to do it right away. They hoped that our dream will come true and that the whole family will be together again.

Life in Krakow in 1940 under the Germans

I was feeling very good about how I had acted that morning. I had had the guts to say "I am not going with you Moniek (Moshe). Take Sara with you". I felt proud of myself for what I did but now I knew I had the responsibility of taking care of my family. I started to look for how I was going to make a living. What could I do to bring home some money? Day by day everything such as bread and milk was going up unbelievably. So I went down to the streets to look around and see what was going on. I met with business people who had become matchmakers. Not "shidduchim", matchmakers for boys and girls but for merchandise. The German government was taking over all the Jewish stores, factories and offices. No Jew was allowed to open a store without the permission of the government. The Jewish stores had been closed and locked. The owners had taken the merchandise from their stores and put it in hiding places. They were selling merchandise in secret.

The businesses were done from mouth to mouth. They did not sell to strangers. They only sold to people they knew. Jews met on the streets looking to sell and also to buy. The matchmakers knew where to get merchandise; suits, pants, shirts, shoes. I got acquainted with the business people, a lot of them knew my father. He was well known in Krakow and so they trusted me. I became such a "matchmaker". If I had a customer who wanted a man's shirt, I knew where to go and could sell him a shirt. I was the Broker and I made a profit. You could get everything for money, but the prices went up everyday. I had six people to support who needed food and different things to stay alive but at the same time, I had to be very careful. Everyday the SS Commando sent out trucks to catch Jews to work—hard work, and some of them didn't come back.

The Germans found out what was now going on with the underground market so they hired Jewish agents to find out where the merchandise was coming from. It was very hard to know who was working as a German agent. Every day the Germans uncovered merchandise. they would come with big trucks and take the merchandise from the basements. They knew exactly where it was hidden. They used to check the pockets of Jewish people as they walked in the streets. When I took a piece of material that was 20 meters of cotton to make shirts or underwear, I had to carry it around my body. I had to be careful that they did not catch me because it was a big risk. When I was carrying it on my body and I saw a German truck, I started limping as I passed them and they didn't search me. They used to come to the Jewish section on Smoll Street on motorcycles. Sometimes I also sold luggage from my little factory, but most of the time I took it home with me.

In one way I was happy that I remained at home to help my whole family. What would they do without me? How would they make a living? But on the other hand, day-by-day there were new things from the German government. Every Jew had to carry a band on his arm with a Zion and on his chest a yellow star. All the Jewish stores had to hang a Star of David on the door. As you walked in the streets, you heard what the Germans were doing to the Jewish people. It was unbelievable. They grabbed a very religious man and dragged him to the old Shul (Synagogue). I myself saw how about twenty SS cut his beard and "payis" (earlocks) with a knife not with a scissor. He cried and they beat him until he fell down and they forced him to walk on his stomach. Then they took him to the hospital.

At one time, they wanted to show the world how liberal they were and they allowed us to pray in the old Shul for six months. The old Shul, located on the SzerokaUlica, was over six hundred years old. So the Jewish Center people did let the Jewish people know that every Jew could go to Friday night services at the Shul. Once it was a Friday night and we heard from the people on the street that the German authorities allowed us to pray in this old Shul because a commission from Switzerland was supposed to come to inspect. The Germans wanted to show them all the freedom they gave to the Jews. They called the Jewish Center president and he came to open the iron door to the Shul on Friday night. The Shul was surrounded by hundreds of SS and Gestapo. Hundreds of Jews started to come to the Shul. I was there with my father. The Germans brought cameras and movie cameras and they photographed the whole procession to show the world how good they were treating the Jews. They allowed them to come inside and photograph the Jews in Tallises and how we prayed.

They allowed us to pray the next day, Shabbat, but there were no more photographs. During the prayers, the Gestapo and SS surrounded us. They saw a Jewish man standing at the window, looking down from his house to see what was going on around the Shul. Two Gestapo went up to his house and brought him down near the Shul. It was a religious Jew with a beard. They started to make fun of him, asking him questions. They started to pick at his beard and beat him. They pushed him and he fell down. They forced him to walk on his stomach while they took pictures. He fainted from the beating. They told us to take him home. They did this daily and people were afraid to walk in the street.

I had luck. Once, when I was walking through the streets, I saw a German truck catching Jewish people for work. They went from stores and buildings and took the Jews to work. Who knows how many people didn't come back at all. I got very nervous because I had a roll of material on by body that I was going to sell to a customer. The German was almost near me. I was afraid that he would catch me and find the material on me. They would have finished me up in a moment. It came to my mind and I started to limp on one leg. He came to me and looked at me and he was hollering at me. "Hey, dog, you don't work?" I was walking like I didn't have anything and I walked and didn't look behind me. I was limping but my heart was beating. I knew they didn't like handicapped people.

I was happy to see my home! When I came into the building, my neighbor, Mr. Gziwach, met me. He said that he had heard from responsible people that the Germans were sending special SS to the region. They were going to go house to house and that we should be very careful. They were looking for radios and furs. Who knows what they wanted? Five weeks passed and every day we heard that worst things were happening to Jews. Jews were afraid to go out in the streets. It was very hard to make a living. When they saw a young man, they picked him up and took him to work. As I said many times, some of them didn't come back. I started to work at home making luggage. Every Tuesday my sister, Chana, would set up a market place on our street. She had blond hair and looked like a Christian. She was able to sell to them so it helped us to stay alive. When we sold five pieces of luggage, Chana worked with me to make another five. When I had time I went to the street. I was very careful that they didn't catch me. When I saw a German truck, I ran into a building and waited until they passed.

We rented one room to a religious man. We had two bedrooms and a big kitchen. This rented room helped us out. We had to wear armbands with a Zion and also a yellow star on our chest. But nobody believed their plan was to kill the Jews so we went on with life. We were waiting for Moshe and Sara to come back to take us to Lvov. We didn't hear from them again for five weeks.

My dear mother was worrying about it. At about 8:30 one morning on Sabbath, I was going to our neighbor's in the next building with my father to pray because all the Shuls and synagogues were closed. This was a private home. Every time we had to go to a different house because it was forbidden to pray together. About 15 to 20 families lived in this building and every building had a caretaker. He cleaned the house and kept it in order. At ten o'clock at night he locked the front door to the building. When somebody from the house came home after ten, he had to ring the bell. The caretaker would come out and open the door and he would get 30 or 50 grosz. If we came very late around two o'clock in the morning, we gave him one zloty. The caretaker from our building was Mr. Bomba. He was a Polish man. Everyone in our building knew that Mr. Bomba and his wife were anti Semitic so we couldn't pray on the Sabbath in our house.

This story is about my father and me when we were together with 20 people to pray. We closed the door to the room in the building where we were going to pray by putting a Cabinet in front of the door so that no one would know there was a room there. The room was in the back of the building, not the front. My father was the Cantor. He prayed very beautifully.

When we were in the middle of praying, it happened a second time. We heard knocking on the door. They took away the cabinet and they knocked in the door. Six German SS came in. We were sure the Polish caretaker had called the German commando about us. We sat down and didn't say anything. All of us were scared. I was standing next to my father. After their search they didn't find anything. They asked us to stand up and we did. We wondered what they were going to do with us in our Tallises. They asked us to go down to the trucks. They raised their voices "Heraus! Heraus!" (Out! Out!). I went to the guy who was hollering and told him that my father was completely blind. He listened to me and told me that I should step aside. So I did and they took the 18 people with the Tallises to the trucks to work but they left my father and me. They brought the 18 men back about six o'clock in the evening. We went home very nervous. My father said "when will my son come to take us?" Life must go on. It was no use to complain. Thank God they let us go free and we could go back to our home. This was the second time it happened. Every day we heard about many things that were happening to Jews. When I passed through the streets, I saw new placards hanging on the wall with troubles for the Jews.

When I came home I told my father we had made a mistake by not going together with Moshe and Sara. I heard in the streets that now it is impossible to make the journey. People were getting shot if they were caught. Also, we had not received any letters in almost two months. We had to do the best we could to stay alive. To make a little money from day to day was harder and harder. Food got more expensive. We had to stay in long lines to get only one loaf of bread at the nearest bakery. Life was getting worse and I started to worry.

Opening the Ghetto

In March1940 when I passed through the streets I saw notices on the wall written by the German government stating they were establishing a ghetto. The ghetto would be in Podgorze near Lwowska Krakusa. Every Jew who was to live in the ghetto must have a job and a legitimate place of work. Confirmation with a signature from the Company that he worked there was required. If he didn't have this he would have to leave the city with his family. When I went home and told my father, we had to decide what to do because my father could not get a job. I could get a job as a carpenter or as a luggage maker. I told my father that we had to look around and move to a small city near Krakow. My father and I didn't want to go to a ghetto because they are going to lock us up and surround the ghetto with German police. Life will be in more danger than in a small city. As we were thinking and talking, my father said that we had a nice neighbor on the same floor, Mr. Katz. We had lived together as friends with him and his wife and two children. They came here from Dzialoszyce. It was a nice little town with five thousand families. My father reminded himself that the president of the Jewish people there was Mojshe Josl Krug. My father knew him very well. He was at the wedding of his daughter.

Mr. Katz had a business selling shoes. He was still working so I went with my father to see Mr. Katz. We told him the whole story about what was going on no but he knew that before we told him. My father told him we wanted to get in touch with Mr. Krug, to ask him about an apartment for us because we wanted to move there. We knew that now would be a good time to arrange this. Later would be hard because we would not be the only people looking for an apartment. Mr. Katz said he had a wholesale business selling shoes. He went to Dzialoszyce twice a week. My father begged him to take the time to call Mr. Krug and tell him we wanted to move there and we needed an apartment.

The next time Mr. Katz went to Dzialoszyce, he called President Krug and made an appointment to see him. Mostly he wanted to see his parents who lived in Dzialoszyce. He looked around and decided to bring his family and also his business. He did not want to remain in the ghetto. He called Mr. Krug, the president of the Jewish Center, and talked to him about his family. Also he kept his promise to my father and talked to him about us and about coming with our family. He talked to him about us bringing our furniture to the new apartment. We had a beautiful bedroom set that was only two years old, a dining room set and a kitchen set. Mr. Katz came back from there very satisfied. He came to our house and explained the whole story to my father. He said he settled everything with Mr. Krug for both families. Mr. Katz explained that he also decided to move there because Hitler planned to keep all the Jews together so he could do whatever he wanted to them. He felt they wouldn't set up a ghetto in a small town.

We were very happy we were going there. After this promise, my father told me to write a letter to Mr. Krug upon the advice of Mr. Katz. Mr. Katz had given us his address. We wanted Mr. Krug's signature stating he would give us a nice place to live with our furniture. We told him we were six people and thank God, we had material and a shop to make luggage. We would not need his help because I was a professional luggage maker with equipment and merchandise. From that we could make a living. All this I wrote in a letter to him. I explained that he should only prepare the apartment for the six of us and our two year old furniture.

After two weeks time we got a letter from the president saying he was very happy we were coming to Dzialoszyce. He promised to prepare a nice place for us in a good neighborhood and that I shouldn't worry. He would do the best for us, but to come as soon as possible so that we would be the first ones with his signature, Mojse Josl Krug. We were very happy and decided to get ready. We did let him know and also told Mr. Katz that we were preparing to go very soon. We thanked him very much for what he had done for us. We hoped to live in Dzialoszyce through wartime and that peace would come soon and maybe the war would soon be over.

I was very careful not to write anything against the German government because we heard stories about people being stopped and searched. If they found a letter, it would be translated. If there was anything bad written against the government, that person and his whole family would not be seen again. I was careful to send the letter by mail since it was still okay to mail letters.

In Krakow the Jewish people started to look around for a job to work. They paid money to get a place and a "Bescheinigung" a certificate with a legitimate signature from your place of work (like a Green Card in the U.S.), only then could you and your family could go to the ghetto to live. Most Jews wanted to go to the ghetto because they had big families with children and grandchildren. Sometimes there were 30 or 40 people in a family. They wanted to be together. Nobody knew the plans, the purpose of keeping the Jewish people together. Most Jews went to the Jewish Center on the corner of Krakowska and Skawinska Streets and begged for a job, a steady job. They would register you and put you on a list you had to sign. They called some of the people to work because they established shops for tailors, shoemakers, carpenters and other different professions. If you had a profession you had a better chance to get a steady job.

Then there was a proclamation stating that until this specific date you had to get a job to stay in the ghetto. Meanwhile the Germans were catching religious Jews and cutting their beards not with a scissor but with a knife. It was terrible. The people were afraid to walk in the streets. The Germans came to the houses looking for radios and furs. The radios and furs had to be brought to the school by a certain date. If they found a radio or fur after that date, the person would be shot dead. The problems were growing day by day. Meanwhile we had to eat. We had to look for some way to bring food home for six persons so I had to think about what to do next. At the same time we were preparing to move.

We also needed money to live. Tuesday and Friday my sister Chana and I took five pieces of luggage to the market place on our street to get money not only to live but for our move. We sold all five but cheaper than the regular price. Two weeks later, we got a letter from Mr. Krug in Dzialoszyce that he was happy to hear we were moving there and he promised to prepare a nice apartment for us. He would do his best for us but we should get there as soon as possible because a lot of people were coming from all over and Krakow, too. Many people who moved from Dzialoszyce to Krakow were now moving back and we should hurry up. If we wait there could be a shortage of apartments. It would be better to take the furniture and come now.

We started to make a list of what we wanted to take with us. We only had a horse and wagon to move our belongings. We had to limit a lot of things. The main thing we wanted to take was the bedroom set, the pots and pans, clothing, underwear and also the most important thing was the raw material for the luggage because I had to make a living. We packed the luggage with our clothing, dishes, silverware and things for daily life.

All of us were working and preparing things for the move. We looked around to find a responsible driver with a horse and buggy. Our neighbor, Mr. Katz, gave us the name of a man he had used for many years in his business. A price was settled. This was August 1940. It was before the holidays. We told our Aunt Chava we were going to move. She was with her daughter Chane Feiga and her little son Jankus. Aunt Chava said she would like to move where we were going. She said she had a daughter with a baby in her house and also a daughter-in-law, Rusia, with two young kids. They all wanted to be together. My father told them to start preparing to move.

We started to pack the dishes in wooden boxes that I had prepared. We had to do everything alone. The driver said he would not be responsible for anything that broke on the way. We had some crystal and glass things that we put in strong wooden boxes. We took our clothing, underwear and shoes for all of us. We emptied out everything. We only took the new bedroom set. We left the living room set with the couches.

We left on a Tuesday a month before the High Holidays. The driver came at eight o'clock in the morning with another young man. He had a long wagon and two big, strong horses. They started loading the furniture first. We had gotten up a six o'clock in the morning and our mother made us breakfast. It was the last breakfast in our own home. The two Polish men carried the furniture and all the wooden boxes. They also carried my equipment for the luggage and the raw material that I needed for work. We left a beautiful dining room set and kitchen set. We thought we would come back to get the rest as soon as we got our apartment. We locked our apartment but my father and mother were very depressed about it. They were crying. I talked to them and told them that if God let us live until the end of the war we could start over again. We could get even nicer furniture. It had not been easy for us to buy the furniture that we had to leave.

We left the key from the house with the caretaker, Mr. Bomba. We had two other pairs of keys. We all went down together. In front of the house, I told my father and mother to sit near the driver. My sisters were sitting in the wagon. It was open and had no cover but we put something soft down so that we could sit comfortably. We said goodbye with tears in our eyes to the caretaker and said we hoped to come back soon with our whole family together again.

The two strong horses started running and we left Miodowa Street and came to Starowishnia Street. We passed the long bridge over the Wisla, water where we used to go swimming in the evenings. We were driving through little towns and villages and my father told us different stories to cheer us up and he told us not to worry only pray to God to help us.

He told us how he lived through the First World War from 1914 until 1918. During this time people were running from place to place and his family lived through a lot of trouble. The Russian Czar (Ruler) was anti Semitic and there were many pogroms. They made it very hard for the Jewish people. He told the story about how he became blind. He said he was born in the small city of Chmielnik near Kielce that belonged to Russia. When he got married to his first wife, Hinda, it was the time the Jewish people started to suffer from the Russian government. They spoke against the Jews in churches. The priests spoke against the Jews and started the pogroms. They attacked and killed Jews and the Russian government didn't take action against it. Day by day it was getting worst for Jews. They were hiding because young girls and women were being raped. He and his wife decided to leave for Austria.

They paid a smuggler lot of money to take them over to the other side. They went with the smuggler at night walking through hills and villages until they came to the Russian border. He took them directly to the Russian border police. He took the money and ran away. The border police put them in jail. One Russian officer took him to the basement and beat him up. He hit him in the head with his rifle so hard that he fainted. They took away everything they had and the next day they let him go.

When they came to the border, they met an Austrian and told him the whole story about the Russians and the pogroms and that the Jews were running away from there. Luckily it was a Jewish Austrian officer and he helped them to cross to the Austrian side. They came to Krakow but his head hurt him and his eyes started to give him trouble. My father told us how he then started to go blind. We children were listening and my mother fell asleep. She was sleeping all the time because she worked so very hard preparing everything.

She was a sick person, suffering from migraine headaches. She was living on pills. She also had a nervous heart. It had started years ago. At home I remember she used to get attacks and her whole body would shake. We had to call Dr. Fishel from the next street, Kupa Street. He would come right away, he knew her sickness for years. He gave her an injection. It took an hour before she opened her eyes. It scared us at first but we came to be familiar with the procedure and we got used to it. Every time she had an attack, the whole family would stand around her and wait until she opened her eyes. She had those attacks sometimes once or twice a month. We loved our mother. We believed in her like God. We respected and tried not to make her nervous. Mostly it happened when there was an argument with our oldest sister, Sara (Sala). She was a child from my father's first wife, Hinda, who had died in child birth.

After six and a half hours driving, we arrived in peace at Dzialoszyce. We went directly to the Jewish Center where President Krug had his office. It was 3:30 in the afternoon and I asked the driver to stop because the last letter he sent to us said to go to his office. I jumped down from the wagon. I had to stretch out first because of so many hours riding in the wagon. When I went up to the office, I asked for President Krug. They showed me to the second floor and I knocked on the door. A lady opened the door and she asked me what I wanted. I told her that we had just come from Krakow with my father, mother and three sisters and that they were sitting in the wagon. I said that we had our furniture and all our belonging. I showed her the letter with the President's signature stating that when we come here, he has prepared the key to an apartment for us, and we will be able to unload our belongings.

The lady was Mr. Krug's secretary. She was very pleasant and she told me that the president was not there now. He would be back in an hour or more and that I should come back then. She wrote down my father's name and what I had told her. I reminded her that my whole family was sitting in the wagon. I went to tell the driver and my family that we had to wait over an hour for the president to come back. Everyone climbed out of the wagon because we had no choice but to wait.

My sister, Chana, suggested that we take a walk around the city and she would stay with the wagon and watch our belongings. I took my father by the hand and my mother took the two children and we all walked to the city. One of the drivers went with us and said he was looking for a place to get a drink. We walked the streets together and after about six minutes we got to the market place. A guy came up to us. He recognized my father and asked if he was Simcha Frydman, der Badchen (the Entertainer). I told him yes. "I am very happy to see you!" he said. "You were at my sister's wedding. My name is Chaim Sternfield. My father has a restaurant near the Beth Hamidrash (Synagogue)" so we told our driver to go there to eat and drink.

Chaim was a very young man, about my age. We told him that we had just moved here. He was very happy and we talked together for about 20 minutes. We told him about how we were supposed to get an apartment here as promised by President Krug, that we had a letter signed by him and that we were supposed to see him soon. He told us that he hoped Mr. Krug would keep his promise. The people here didn't like him but they had no choice since the German command accepted him.

We went back to our wagon and the children played together on the street near the Kehillah (Jewish Center). Before you went into the Center there was a long bench. My mother and father sat there and my sister Chana came down from the wagon and sat together with them. It was already an hour and five minutes so I ran up to see if the president was there. When I knocked at the door the same lady came out. I asked her if the president was there. She said he was but I had to wait. I ran down and told my father that he was there and he should go back with me. I took him and slowly we went up and waited about ten minutes. Later the lady came to us and said that the president was very busy with other people who had also come from abroad. He could not talk to us today.

He does want to talk to us tomorrow. Meanwhile we were to take the furniture and all our belongings to the big Beth Hamidrash.

We were extremely disappointed and told her that we had a letter with the president's signature telling us he had an apartment ready for us, that was why we had come today. We asked her, please let us talk to him for just five minutes. She said she would talk to him again. She came out with a sour face and said he had people there and could not talk to us today. But he would send someone to help us unload our belongings. We had no choice. We were ashamed and nervous. We talked to mother and the children and discussed what to do. How can a Jew treat another Jew like this? There should be nothing but honesty at this time when all the Jews were in danger. Instead of helping us, what is he doing to us? How can we live in a Shul? The children were sitting and listening to us. He didn't even want to talk to us. He didn't even ask us if we were hungry. The president was a miserable man. President Mojshe Josl Krug was a very bad character. He was like someone from Sodom and Gemorra. He had no conscience.

My father was talking to us, "he signed the letter, but what are we going to do now?" My father told the Poles who came with us the whole story. They listened but they wanted to go back home. They wanted their money. It was getting late and night would fall in a couple of hours. What should we do? We heard that nobody is allowed to walk in the street at night because it was wartime.

We asked our mother what we should do. If we put all our belongings on the street near the Jewish Center, we might have had to sleep outside in the street with the children. We paid the two Poles so they could go home because they started to holler at my father. They wanted to be paid double for every hour they worked for us.

The first thing my mother said was to feed the children. It was almost nine hours since the children had eaten breakfast, she took the sandwiches she and Chana had prepared that morning from the cool box for everybody including the Poles. Some of the sandwiches had cheese and some had Kosher Salami. We were eating together and mother made some lemonade.

When we finished eating my mother said she wanted to go to the Shul to find out where they were going to put us. My father and mother and I went to see if we would be able to live there. We had been told us we would only need to stay one night, but now we didn't believe him, that president that didn't keep promises. When we went inside the Shul there were six families already living there. They said that each family has been promised an apartment. All four corners were taken up with families and furniture. They separated the families with blankets on the walls. Our hearts were heavy when we saw this, but we had no choice. We left the Shul and went back to the children. We still didn't know what to do. When we came back we saw our Aunt Chava's wagon with her daughter Chana Feiga and her six-year-old son, Jankus and her daughter-in-law and her two children.

We were very happy to see them. We told them our story and explained what was going on here. We told her what the president had done to us and where we had to go. When we were standing together and talking and discussing what we should do, a man came out of the building. He told us in soft words and talked in a fine voice. He said the president, Mr. Krug, sent him down to help us. We should now move in and he promised us that he would try as soon as possible to get us an apartment. He was going to send people to help us set up our furniture at the Shul.

The sun was going down and it was starting to get dark. The drivers were mad because they wanted to go home to their families. We saw that we had no choice. I told the man that I didn't trust the president. I felt that as soon as we moved in he would forget all about us. And why didn't he want to talk to us? He said he had an apartment and he took our money. When I finished talking my Aunt Chava said she understood me very well. Are we supposed to stay outside all night? As a matter of fact, there was a curfew and nobody was supposed to be outside. What about the small children? We'll have to start to unload our belongings. We told the man to send us help to unload.

About ten minutes later, two men came to help the drivers unload the furniture and boxes into the Shul. I wanted to take a corner but all the corners were occupied. I gave the first turn to our Aunt with her family to unload and we took the next place. Four people stated to load the area and set up the furniture. We took an available place. We tried to set it up like two rooms but there wasn't enough space to make two rooms. If we had a bigger family there wouldn't have been enough room.

The two people they sent to help us watched to see how much room every family took. When we finished the room with Aunt Chava, we started to set up our room. We started to bring in our furniture and the two drivers also helped with the furniture. Aunt Chava's driver also helped. They made a room similar to ours. With the four walls we had the same size as our Aunt Chava. They were six persons and we were six people. When they finished, we thanked the two persons for helping us. We sat down with the Polish drivers and we counted out the money for them. They wanted more money because they said they had spent more time there, so we did pay them more and they were happy.

My mother and sister, Chana, made the bed for the children and they went to sleep. It was ten o'clock at night when we all went to sleep. We were all very tired from such an exciting day but I was very hungry and couldn't sleep. I thought to myself, we are in a dump, so many other people in one place. God forbid someone had a contagious sickness. I thought about President Krug and how I didn't trust him, but I had to be an optimist especially since we didn't have a choice. I was afraid to sleep in a holy place with the Torahs, but I came to the conclusion that we had no choice in wartime. Who knows what Hitler was planning to do with the Jewish people? We have to be strong and to stay alive. We had to stay together. We didn't want to be sent away or be separated. God would give us health and luck to feed the family and to make a living.

Although I was in bed, I couldn't sleep. At the light of day, I got up, and got dressed. It was almost six o'clock in the morning. I wanted to wash up. After I found the washroom and toilet area, I washed myself. When I came from the washroom and walked to the place where I lived, I could hear breathing and snoring from the sleeping people. I tried to be very quiet as I came back so that I didn't wake anyone up. My parents and the children were so tired from such a terrible trip. Before I had gone to bed the night before I prepared the prayer book and Tefillin and I started to pray. Meanwhile I heard the noise of people getting dressed.

The first day and night we were all strangers. I didn't know anybody. Before my eyes I saw a different life ahead of us. I was thinking that I would have to get used to this life so different from our beautiful home with three wonderful rooms, with a kitchen, with a balcony. Now everybody was in one small place.

My parents got up and I took my father and showed my mother where the washroom and the toilets were located. I helped my father get washed. Going back to our "room" we met our neighbor near our place. They said good morning with a happy face and we answered them with a happy face as if we were happy to be there. It was like walking between Succoth (small huts). As we were walking, we came to a corner where my Aunt Chava was sitting. A shoemaker was sitting there fixing shoes. We stopped to see how he was fixing the shoes. We said good morning to him and he said good morning to us. We asked him his name. He said his name was Meir. He said that he had been there almost four months. He was very skinny, pale and looked very tired. He was living there with his wife, daughter and grandchildren. He didn't complain. He started at 7:30 in the morning and worked until seven o'clock in the evening six days a week. It was a hard living. He had come from Kielce and his son had left for Russia.

Life in the Shul (Beth Midrash)

When we got back to our room, my mother had prepared the Tallis and Tefillin on the kitchen table we had taken from our home. I took the Tefillin to pray. It took us a half hour or less and we prayed to God. When we finished, we ate the breakfast our mother had fixed for us. It was the sandwiches with cheese she had made at home before we left. This was our first breakfast in Dzialoszyce. The children were still sleeping and we did not want to wake them up. But when they smelled the food they jumped out of their bed and left for the washroom. They came back very fast. We all ate together and drank coffee without milk. After we finished, I asked my father to go back with me to the Jewish Center to talk to the president.

We went back to the Jewish Center and told them we had an appointment with the president that day. A lot of people were waiting and said they had come from Krakow looking for an apartment. The same secretary told everybody that the president had left for a week's vacation and that we should come back in a week. We both got hot and cold. I told my father that I knew that would happen and that we couldn't trust him. We left the Kehilla (community center) and walked to the market. We thought we might meet some people who knew us. We had the president's letter with us. We wanted to find Mr. Katz's parents. Nobody had a telephone so we asked for the street and the number of the house. They lived on the second floor. We went up and knocked at their door. The maid came out and we told her that we were neighbors of their daughter, Mrs. Katz. We told her that we had a letter for them. She went in to tell them and both the mother and father came out and asked us to come in. We went in to the dining room and they asked us to sit down. They were very friendly to us.

We gave them the letter which they started to read. They were very happy and they both thanked us. They said they knew my father from the weddings. They asked us where we were living. My father told them the whole story and we showed them the letter from the president and that he had promised us an apartment. Now he doesn't want to talk to us. They said not to worry that everything would be okay. They gave us a glass of tea with lemon and a piece of homemade cake. They again said not to worry that everything would be straightened out, but we had to have patience. They said that they had seen a lot of newcomers coming from abroad. They are very busy trying to get all of them settled. My father asked them to talk to him because they knew him very well. They didn't say anything.

We said goodbye to them in a friendly way. When I went back home with my father, I started to help unpack all the pots and pans and our belongings. All the children and my mother were working together to fill up the drawers with our clothing and underwear. When we finished I started to unpack all my equipment for the luggage so that I could start to work on it and to set up a place where I could work. I put most of the material under the bed.

I wanted to set up my little factory and a place to work because we had to eat every day and I didn't have anything to sell or exchange for food. I had enough of the raw material to start to produce, and I did. I started to work at 2:00 p.m. and my sister, Chana, helped me just like she did at home. We worked two and a half days. We made five pieces of luggage to sell. There was a market place on Tuesday and Friday. Poles from the villages came to town to sell their products; eggs and chickens, a little butter, fruit, vegetables and potatoes and to buy what they needed such as shoes, clothing, and underwear. They also needed luggage because they traveled all over.

That is how we started our life in Dzialoszyce. On Friday, my sister and I brought eight pieces of luggage from 30 centimeters to 80 centimeters long. We put cardboard on the ground and we set up the luggage waiting for customers. We were there from 10 o'clock in the morning until 4:00 o'clock in the afternoon. We sold two pieces of luggage. We exchanged them for potatoes, eggs and butter. We didn't see too many German soldiers as in Krakow. Polish police walked around and watched. It was a different life, much quieter. So we were able to get some food. Little by little we started to get to know the people. Next to us in the Shul lived a man with two daughters. He had lost his wife. They were very nice people and had lived there for five months. There was a woman with a son in his twenties. They were very nice people. Most of the time they read the Torah. There was a divorcee from Krakow. She was very fat. Her name was Mrs. Key. She was from a lower class of people. On the other side of the room lived an older "Cavalier" (ladies' man) named David Schwarzbaum. He was in his late thirties. We saw him at night when the neighbors would stand around the big coal heated oven, talking over their problems. It was already very cold outside and this was the only stove to warm the whole Shul.

My father began singing his new composition and the old "Cavalier", David Schwarzbaum helped with the singing. He didn't have a good voice but he knew how to sing. He fell in love with my father's songs. Every night we would do the same thing. Stand around the stove and sing.

From time to time we went up to the Jewish Center to see Mr. Krug. It was unbelievable; he never had time to see us. My father was very upset about it, so this man, David Schwarzbaum would come in to our room to talk to my father. I was afraid of him but my parents took pity on him. They invited him for dinner. When he was with us, he told us his story, that he was from Pietrykow, that he was a Communist before the war and the Polish government was looking for him. He was hiding from one place to another. He didn't write or sign anything. He was still afraid of them.

Next morning after breakfast, my sister, Chana, and I worked together and finished five pieces of luggage of different sizes. Again I stayed until I sold one. On Tuesday and Friday I took some luggage to sell at the market place. If I sold one or two for money or exchange for food products, I was happy. We had enough money for a week. Sometimes for a whole week we didn't sell one piece of luggage because Jewish people didn't buy anything only the Poles from the villages bought items. It wasn't easy to make a living. We had to take Moshe's and Sara's clothing and sell it for food. I went outside and tried to become a Broker as I did in Krakow. If somebody needed a pair of new shoes, I went to the guy who had hidden the shoes. He knew and trusted me. He told me the price and I brought him the money when I sold the shoes. It was not only shoes but also different kinds of material.

I was talking to my friend, Chaim Feldman. His father had a restaurant near us. He was a very nice boy about my age. He proposed that I join him and go to the village. I took a new medium size piece of luggage. My Aunt Chava gave me children's clothing to sell or exchange for food. Before the war she was in business selling children's clothing.

I went with Chaim to the village. He was used to dealing with those people all the time. We had to take off the Mogen David (Star of David) from our breast and arms. We went in as Poles, as non-Jews. I watched as he did business. He had experience since he went there many times with his father who did this business before he had the restaurant. He'd been going since he was eight years old so everybody knew him and trusted him. All the villagers loved him. They told me that he was their beloved Jew. He took their orders for what they needed, clothing and items for the house. He then brought everything they needed and they paid him weekly.

He was a peddler. Now in wartime he had to buy on the black market because there were no working factories. Everything produced went to the German Army. Clothing, shoes and leather had to be bought from private people on the black market. All the merchandise was hidden in their basements or in bunkers. I kept going with him and watched how he dealt with people.

On that first trip he also sold two pieces of my luggage and the used children's clothing that my aunt had given me to sell for her for food products. I took only the food that I could carry. I took a live chicken, eggs, fruit, flour, potatoes and some money. Everyday the food products went up in price so I would go back again to get the rest of the food that they owed me because I couldn't carry all of it. Sometimes when I had a full rucksack with food, I sold it for zlotys according to their prices. When we were ready to go home, we were loaded with a lot of food so I took some fruit like apples, pears and prunes. We only took as much as we could carry but I was also praying to God that I would get home in peace.

Chaim knew the ways through the woods so we took the short cuts through fields and woods. We didn't see anybody. We heard different kind of animal cries in the woods. My heart was beating very fast. I was scared to death of enemies, bandits and German soldiers. We didn't have a gun to protect ourselves, but we walked with God in our hearts. It reminded me of a time when I was in school. We were reading different stories about bandits in the woods. They were robbing people and sometimes killing them. I was really scared and started chanting Psalms from my prayer book. When we left one wooded place we went to another part of the woods. We heard the birds singing to us.

I was afraid of the Polish partisans. We had heard that they also killed Jews. The Polish A.K. (Armia Krajova-Polish Home Army) were the biggest anti Semites. This was on my mind when we walked and we walked and we walked with no end in sight. After three hours, we reached the Shtetl (village) Dzialoszyce. I was relieved but Chaim didn't seem scared at all. Why? Because he was used to it, this was his job even before the war. I raised my hand to God to thank him for my life.

After such a journey, I was going home and would see my whole family. When I went into the Shul that was my home, my mother fell on me and kissed me. She said a prayer thanking God. When I showed them all the packages, everyone looked at me like I had come from another world. My mother was crying with happiness, and she again thanked God for bringing me home. My father was sitting on the bed and I saw tears coming from his eyes. While he was crying, he said a prayer. I went to him and kissed him. I said, "Daddy, we have to trust in God so don't worry." I was crying, too. I was happy to see my sisters and my Aunt Chava.

My Aunt Chava, her family and my family had fun together. I started to unpack my rucksack with all the things I brought with me from the village. My mother was very happy with the food that I had brought with me. She put everything in its place. I gave my aunt some food for her children and the things that belonged to her. She took it home and was very happy, and she thanked me. It was getting dark, and I was very tired. I fell into bed and slept for maybe two hours. My mother woke me up to eat supper. My mother was holding a pot with water in her hand. I washed myself.

The water from the toilets was all we had. There was one toilet for men and one for women. There was a toilet outside for the public. After I washed myself, I sat down with the whole family to eat supper. They had waited more than an hour for me. I told them about my business with the village people and about my friend, Chaim. I told them that the people in the village liked him as if he was one of their families. The small children knew him and they touched him. It was unbelievable. Also, because Chaim told them I was his cousin and he would guarantee that I was a good boy, they treated me very well. I ate fresh baked bread with butter and farmer's cheese. It was very tasty. The farmers had a good life in wartime. The food went up in price everyday. I told my parents what we had done all day long and how I sold my luggage and the clothing and about the trip through the woods. I told them about how scared I was but that Chaim knew the way back, and thank God everything was all right. We had a lot of luck. We didn't see anybody and nobody saw us because he knew the short cut back. I told them the whole story. They listened enthusiastically. We sat and talked until 12 o'clock at night. Then we went to bed.

In the morning after breakfast, I told my father that we should go to the Jewish Center to try again to see the president, Mr. Krug, we should not let up. We asked the girl to tell him we were there but she knew the answer. She went in, he was there, but for no price and no reason would he talk to us. So we left again with nothing.

We went to see my father's friend, Chaim Plotkiewicz. Before the war, he was a very good friend of my father's. We found him at home with his wife. They were very happy to see us. They took us in to the dining room and had us sit down. They offered us coffee. We accepted and they brought us coffee and cake. Chaim and his wife were sitting with us and also had coffee. We talked together about what we were doing there, and they asked us whether we were able to make a living and if we had enough food. They wanted to know why we were living with so many people at the Shul. My father told them the whole story and about the unbelievable treatment we received from the president.

We showed them the signed letter from the president and that he had an apartment for us. Until now he didn't want to talk or see us. He was immoral. We now had to live with over a hundred people in one place, we have no choice. Some of the people were from medium class and some were very low class. My father said that we were going to the Center almost every day. Mr. Krug is there but for almost two months, his secretary told us he has no time to see us.

Chaim Plotkiewicz said that he knew the whole story and he was very interested. He had talked to the president about this because he knew him very well. He was a good friend of his and the only answer is to have patience and to wait out the situation here in Dzialoszyce. He said that everyday more people are emigrating here from Krakow, Tarnow and Rzeszow. All the apartments were taken. They were putting single people and families in apartments to live together. People were running away from the ghetto in Krakow because it was getting worse every day. He and his wife promised us that they would keep their eyes on things and they would remind the president about us. After about an hour and a half together, we thanked them for everything and we said goodbye to them. Going out Chaim said "please hold on. Don't lose patience and try to live a normal life. Soon God will give us our life back and the president will keep his promise to get you an apartment."

When we went home we told our dear mother where we were and what they had promised. Meanwhile we had to live a normal life. We had to get used to it. We should be happy that we were together with our children. We were healthy. God will give us what we need until the war comes to an end. We will be a whole family again together in peace. We will see our family back from Russia. I told them not to worry. Take life as it goes. Thank God we have enough food here in Dzialoszyce. We didn't see too many German soldiers. The SS commandos were stationed in Kacmierz not far away from us. It was good that the Gestapo or cement blocks did not surround us as they did the ghetto in Krakow.

I Work at My Profession

Everyday I got up early in the morning and prayed. At 8 o'clock I started to prepare a shop for myself in a small place where we lived. My sister got up in the morning and she helped me very well. She was trained and knew the job almost as well as I did. At 9 o'clock on Tuesday and Friday we took in both our hands 12 pieces of different sized luggage to sell or exchange for food because we had to eat everyday. We didn't sell too many pieces of luggage. When it was a Christian holiday, we did more business. It was not so easy. The Jews didn't need luggage. The farmers who came to town to buy products and to sell their potatoes, fruit, butter, eggs and live chickens sometimes would buy the luggage.

But still, it was better than the ghetto in Krakow which was locked. No one could get in or out to sell food, and it was also forbidden. The luggage sales were not enough to feed six people in our family. My father, little by little did understand that life must go on like it is. We were not starving. Sometimes we repaired luggage when people were passing from place to place.

My father again started to compose a song in Yiddish. Mostly it was about the war. He would wake me up during the night. He said, "Kalmen, be a good son and as long as it is in my mind and on my tongue, please write down the words from this song, *We are going to Dzialoszyce*" this is the title of the song. If you don't write it now I won't remember it tomorrow." I was half asleep but I jumped out of bed and took the book and wrote every word. He already had the melody and the music to it. I wrote the three verses of the song and I went back to sleep. It was 2:00 o'clock at night.

In the morning when we got up, my father said to me, "you see Kalmen, now I don't remember the words anymore." My brother Moshe used to write the notes in the middle of the night but now nobody else could do it. We found out that Mr. David Leszman, a musician who lived in our house until the war started, was back in Dzialoszyce. We went to him that same day and he wrote the music notes. He was very happy to see us.

The same night when all the people from the Shul were standing around, the stove was very hot but outside it was very cold. They were holding their hands over the hot stove. My father started to sing his newborn song. People sang along while outside the frost was burning. Everyone sang, "We are going to Dzialoszyce" helping out, creating harmonies. It came out so beautiful.

In this song he expressed why and how we came to Dzialoszyce and about our life here. When my father didn't remember all the words, I helped him out while we were singing together with the words I had written down during the night. When we finished, a young man in his thirties who had helped with the singing introduced himself as David Schwarzbaum. He was from Zowiece, Poland. My father thanked him for helping him with the singing. He didn't have a big voice but he had musical feeling. My father was singing other songs and the people gathered around the stove. They were all very happy and thanked us for the entertainment and the Yiddish songs.

Another young man introduced himself. He had come with his mother. His name was Hershel. He also helped with the singing. There were two sisters there with their old father, very nice people. One sister was in her twenties and introduced herself as Fela (Feigele) and the younger one was called Rachel. They had also helped with the singing. So from all of the people who lived there, this group would become a choir.

It was the beginning of October. Every Sabbath we went to pray at the small Shul of the Dzialoszyce Rebbe (Rabbi). It was about ten minutes walking distance. I remembered that the High Holidays were coming. At night it was very cold. In the daytime it was still warm. At night we covered ourselves with feather quilts. It was a very warm cover. During the Rosh Hashanah holiday, we prayed at the Rabbi's Shul. Also on Yom Kippur and Succoth. On the first day of Succoth, we received a package from Tadzikistan, Russia. It was from Moshe. I remember that the whole family was invited to the Succah by Mr. Feldman. This was the guy who had a restaurant near us. In the package from Moshe were pieces of soap, five packages of tea and some dried fruit. We were very happy. My mother and sisters were crying. I was happy that we had heard from Moshe but we had not heard from my sister.

Moshe wrote that he was in communication with Sara and that was a relief. We were enjoying the Succah together with the Feldman family. They gave us a very nice holiday food, like kreplach (dumplings), very good soup, a Carp dish, and meat. We all enjoyed a very good dinner. We hadn't had a meal like that in a long time. We thanked the Feldman family for inviting us to such a good meal.

Day by day it was getting colder and colder so every night we'd stand around the stove to keep our hands warm and we'd sing together. Little by little we got used to this life. The people liked us very much.

They had pleasure with us. We got to know everyone more and more. It was like one big family. If someone needed an onion, salt or flour, they would go and ask their neighbor. That was the life there. We sang together like one choir. Near us in the next section lived my father's sister, Aunt Chava with her daughter and her little son and her daughter-in-law with her three children. She had six people. The daughter's name was Ruria. Her husband, Abraham, had left for Lvov, Russia. My aunt was a very smart woman. She had brought five sacks of used clothing with her. Selling used clothing was her business. The Poles bought the clothing but they thought is was new and not used. New clothing was very expensive and was hard to get. The stores were closed because they had no merchandise. Twice a week she went to the market place and sold or exchanged the clothing for food. Thank God she made a nice living, because she had to support six people. She had to provide all the food and clothing they needed.

The Story About David Schwarzbaum and Us

David Schwarzbaum came from Zowiece, Poland. He was single and in his late thirties. He started to come to our home after the night near the stove when he sang with us. My father took pity on him and invited him for Kiddush on Saturday after the prayers in Shul. He started to come by during the week to talk to us, especially to my father. I didn't have time for him because I was busy with Chana making luggage. He would stand there looking at how we made our product. I wasn't happy about it and my sister was very mad, but we didn't say anything to him. When he left and we were sitting at the table, I told my father that we didn't like this stranger. We didn't know who he was or anything about his character. I didn't trust him. I felt we would have a lot of trouble with him. My father said that he was a poor man and we should help him. I agreed, but we had six people to support. He was a young man and should go to work in the city. It was the thing for him to do. But my father said he wanted to pay us back because we had invited him for lunch about five times. He wanted to help us take the luggage to the market place. I told him right away that we didn't need him that my sister and I could manage. We didn't need anyone, but my father said we would talk about it after Shabbat and give him an answer in five days. After five days he came back to my father and talked to him about the same thing. My father talked to me later and said, "My children, in wartime nobody knows what tomorrow will bring or what will be. We have to help a lonely man with what we can. He doesn't have anybody to help him." I told my father that we didn't need anyone else in our business. We sell three or four pieces of luggage a week. I had Chana to help me with the luggage. I felt he would be trouble for us once he learned how to make the luggage. I didn't want to look for trouble. We had enough problems of our own and we didn't need anyone else's problem. I didn't need a partner. I didn't want anybody on my back and my sister Chana was with me. I felt that no good would come of it. But this man, David Schwarzbaum, was such a nudnik that I told him openly that I didn't want his help carrying the luggage to the market place. My sister and me are enough. I didn't need any help. For five weeks he stopped coming. I was very happy.

Then it was Hanukah and my father and mother invited him for latkes. We were lighting the last Hanukah candles and it was my sister Chana's birthday. We also invited the next-door neighbors, the old man with his two daughters, our Aunt Chava and her family and children. They were all sitting around the long table and on our beds. There was not enough room at the table for everyone. We also invited the young woman and her son. They brought chairs with them. We started to light the Hanukah candles and my father said the Bracha (blessing). He was singing the Maoz Tsur Yeshu'ati (Rock of Ages) song and all of the people were singing with us. All the people who lived there came to our door and were listening to my father singing. I gave them something to drink in the glasses they had brought. It was an evening to remember. Afterwards, we were all standing at the big stove to keep warm. My father was singing songs of the eight candles of Hanukah. The people told my father that since he had come there was life in the Shul and we could for a time forget it was wartime.

The next day I started to work on the luggage. I was finishing up three pieces of luggage with my sister when David Schwarzbaum came in and started to talk to my father and started to help. It was Tuesday and the market place was opened. When we finished the three pieces of luggage, we started to pack. We had 11 pieces of luggage but only four showed since the others were packed inside. He grabbed one packed piece of luggage and ran, he didn't wait til we came out, he ran to the market place. I called him back and asked him where he was running. He remained standing at the door of the Shul. I didn't want to take the luggage from him. I didn't know what to do. My sister and I took the rest of the luggage to the market place together with him. My sister brought a stand. We took out another seven suitcases from the luggage, which were of all sizes. We stacked them so that it looked like there were a lot of suitcases. We waited for customers. David Schwarzbaum just stayed with us, not asking if it was alright for him to do it. I told him quietly he should go home that we didn't need three people to sell the luggage. He said that he didn't have anything else to do for the rest of the day and that he didn't want money from us. He said he liked my father and wanted to do it for him.

We had a good day. We sold five pieces of luggage because it was before Christmas. The Jews were not allowed to leave the city, but the Poles could travel with their families. They bought the luggage and we made some money. We also exchanged the luggage for food like butter, cheese, eggs and flour. After we finished selling, I went to Miller's bakery. I usually could only buy one loaf of bread but they knew my father so he sold me two loaves of bread. They were still warm. I bought different things. Some were legal some were not so legal. Otherwise we couldn't exist. It was a happy day in our house. I had a discussion with my father and mother about David Schwarzbaum. I told him that he came to our house and watched how we made the luggage and that I didn't need a partner. We were going to have lots of trouble with him, but my father, with his good nature, said that when we help someone charitably,God would help us, he would give us health and bread. I got quiet and did not answer. I said to myself that for today and in the coming year, we would see who was right, my father, or I.

When we were sitting together at the table for lunch I showed a newspaper to David Schwarzbaum. It was an interesting article about the things that were going on in wartime. The article was written in Polish. He told me he didn't know how to read or write in Polish or in Yiddish. I was astounded. I asked him if he were joking. He answered me "this is not a joke." When he was five years old, he lost his mother. His father had left his mother when he was a year old and he hadn't heard from him until now. An uncle on his mother's side raised him. At that time in Poland, they didn't force children to go to school or to the Hebrew School. I didn't believe it. He said that his uncle was very poor. He didn't have any money to send him to a private school. I told my parents that it was a funny story and not clear to me. I wasn't smart enough to know what he meant or about his motives.

Five days later, he told me another story, that he was a Communist and the Poles were looking for him. He had a different name and he couldn't sign his name because they were looking for his signature. Why did he tell me that? I really didn't know and I told him so. I told him he looked like a very able person and not an illiterate. He told me again that the Polish government was giving the German's the names of the high Communist people. He was now afraid of the government. My father told me not to talk to him about his past and that he believed what he had told me. He thought everything he told my father was true. I thought that he had put together a story so we would have pity on him. I didn't like his character.

From time to time we went to the Jewish Center to see the president. Maybe that particular day would be a lucky one for us, but so far he was a dead beat. He didn't want to see or talk to us. He always had an excuse, but we didn't get tired of going there. Maybe one day he would keep his word and give us an apartment as he had promised.

At night we would sit home because we were not allowed on the street late at night. Friday night we would pray at the Shul. We made a Minyan, with ten men. My father then prayed as the Cantor. The next morning we went to the home of the Zaloszycer Rabbi. He had a very big house.

He had a big family. A lot of people came to pray from all around. When I went there with my father they treated us very well. They had respect for my father because my father was at his son's wedding. He had four sons. I think two sons lived through the war. After they finished praying there was a Kiddush. Every man who came to pray had to give money for the Kiddush. If there was a wedding or Bar Mitzvah, they prepared a big Kiddush with cholent and kischka, "galler' (aspic), kugel, and other Jewish foods. We didn't know that there was a war because there was so much food. A lot of poor people came to the house. They found out that something was coming but it was very quiet. German soldiers came from Kazimierz to checkup and control the situation in Dzialoszyce. Kazimierz was the station for the Gestapo commandos.

There were a lot of affairs such as weddings, Bar Mitzvahs held there but with no music. My father sang at some weddings, and he was paid for it. He was singing for the Bride and Groom and all the people sang along. That was in a private home not in a big hall. On Saturday the people from the wedding came to the Dzialoszyce Rabbi because they had twoTorahs. That was the only place you could pray with Minyan. All the Shuls and Beth Hamedrish were closed. We were afraid of the German government. All over the country, it was forbidden to have religious activities. The Torahs were at the Rabbi's houses. In the small cities, they didn't care too much. They looked away. We had a much better life than in the ghetto.

There were some Jewish stores like tailor's, shoemakers and carpenters. There also was a Jewish restaurant. If you had money you could get anything, but the prices were very high. We could get some of those things because the storekeepers hid all the merchandise such as new shoes, clothing, underwear and suits. Their stores were closed but the merchandise was hidden in the basement or attic. They built cement walls around so the German's couldn't see the merchandise when they searched from house to house. It was Jewish matchmakers on the street who had connections with the merchants and the customers. You could get leather for shoes and material for shirts and dresses or suits. You could get everything if you had money.

Everyday it cost more money for food especially such imported items like sardines, tuna fish, and chocolate. These items were purchased through the matchmakers. There was a large bakery where we could get bread, challah and rolls under the table. The bread baked daily was rationed. Three brothers and a sister owned Miller's bakery. The oldest brother, I think, was Emil. All of them were single. Emil had a beautiful tenor voice. He would sing when we got together. Their sister married a man who worked for them. He worked there after the wedding and became a partner in the bakery. They had a very big wedding but privately in two apartments. There were about 300 people and my father was the Badchen. He sang without music for the bride and groom and all the people at the wedding. They were very rich people and paid him very well. Emil sang operatic songs all night and the Rabbi from Dzialoszyce married them (Chuppah V'Kaddishin). It was a wedding to remember forever with good food like we had before the war. My father was singing the new song he had composed. Everybody at the wedding sang together. All the richest and the nicest people from the city came to the wedding. We forgot about the war. The Jewish police were watching outside to make sure the German SS Gestapo was not around. The wedding started at 12 o'clock noon and ended at 9 o'clock at night. We couldn't go out in the streets after nine. The Chuppah was at three o'clock and some of the people went home.

Also, at the wedding they had a "Mitzvah Tenz", a special dance for the bride and groom. They were dancing with a handkerchief and the parents had to dance with the (Kalleh) bride through the handkerchief. There were no parents on the bride's side just the brothers, but the groom's parents were there. They were from Chelmno (Chmielnik). My father knew them from home before the war.

From time to time there were weddings in the city and many thought that we didn't feel the war so much in Dzialoszyce as in the other cities. Then a new law from the German commandos was instituted stating that Jewish men had to cut their beards by a certain time. They gave everyone a definite time for all to have their beards cut. If beards weren't cut by a certain date, they would punish people by taking their money or putting them in jail. There was a panic from the religious people. They said in the flyer that the Jewish police had the responsibility in this matter. If they found a Jew with a beard, they had to take him to the barber. After awhile if the Jewish police found somebody with a beard, they took him by force to the barber. I took my father to the barber to have his beard cut. Afterward he felt terrible. The same night he composed a song called "Berdle"(beard) and everybody was depressed. A lot of very religious Jews didn't leave their houses because they didn't want to cut their beards. The Jewish police hung up placards from the German commandos stating that if the Jews hid anyone with a beard and they were found out, they would be severely punished. They didn't specify how.

The German SS Commandos from all around Dzialoszyce were stationed in Kazimierz. They sent hundreds of their SS Army and Gestapo to control the Jewish people. They came with jeeps and they were driving around the streets in the city to find out about the situation in the area. We were afraid to go out in the streets. People stayed at home, even those who had cut their beards. Those who didn't cut their beard hid themselves in the house. They were stubborn and didn't want to cut their beard. There were a lot of religious people who were hiding in the bunkers that they had prepared.

    The German SS came to the houses checking. My father said that if they wanted us to cut our beards, we should do it because it was the law. It was not the worst thing. If God would let us outlive the war, the beards would grow back. A lot of religious people sacrificed their lives for this and didn't cut their beard. We saw them take a lot of men from their houses and send them to the barber.

Moshke the Bad Messenger

In Dzialoszyce there was a Jewish man named Moshke with a very athletic build. He was very strong and friendly to people. He was also very friendly with the Germans. He was working for the German SS Commandos and the Gestapo in Kazimierz. He also worked with a Jewish group to find out who the rich Jewish people were and where they were hiding their merchandise. He was looking for material, new shoes, and clothing. He wanted to find those people who were selling gold and dollars. He knew they were hiding the merchandise in the bunkers, basements and attics. Moshke knew everybody in the city. He gave the information to the Commandos. They found out where the merchandise was, where it was hidden, who sold and who bought.

The Jewish people in Dzialoszyce were very good business people. They had connections in Krakow before the war. They had everything hidden in bunkers such as leather, new shoes, dresses, sardines, tea and coffee that were imported before the war. They sold dollars, gold and diamonds. In the small cities everyone knew everybody else. Moschke got connected with the German SS and the Gestapo. He delivered the addresses of the rich Jews to the Gestapo. Before they came to him Moshke and his associates watched where they had hidden the merchandise so then they came with a big truck. They went straight to the hidden places and caught five Jews carrying out their merchandise. They took their merchandise and loaded it on the truck. If they didn't have enough room for all of it they would come back the next day. When they were finished they had taken everything. In every city small and large they found their collaborators who told them about everything that was going on.

The same thing happened in the Krakow ghetto. There was a man named Spic. I saw him in Krakow before I was deported from the ghetto. We called them the Jewish spies. They gave the Germans the names of the intelligent people who were doctors, lawyer, architects, and teachers. The Gestapo then kept an eye on them because they were afraid of an uprising or if they thought they had weapons. At night they would go to their houses checking for weapons. Moshke and his associates gave them all the information. We found out that there was a contract out for the Jews who were hiding outside the city with Aryan papers. They got paid for each Jew they found for them. The German Commandos promised them that they and their families would be safe and live out the war and also become rich.

The people in Dzialoszyce now were scared. Nobody knew when they would be coming. They were afraid to do any business because they didn't know who was an associate of Moshke. In July 1941, a lot of trucks came to the places where they had hidden new stuff. They grabbed people in the streets to help carry out the merchandise and load the trucks. I watched as they loaded hundreds of pairs of new shoes. Unbelievably, they filled up the truck with thousands of pairs of shoes worth millions of dollars. They had ten trucks for loading the merchandise. They broke down a cement wall and took out new dresses from the where the owner had hidden them.

It took all day. They started around eight o'clock in the morning and finished at five o'clock at night. I don't know how they were able to recognize the bunkers, but Moshke was able to find almost all of them. It was impossible to believe that there had been so many new shoes hidden. Moshke knew exactly where all the merchandise was hidden. They didn't take anybody with them, and that was a good thing. They only took the merchandise. I found out that a group of business owners had built the bunkers themselves.

This was just the start. Every day we heard and saw big trucks coming into the city. They had maps in their hands. They went into the building and after a half an hour, they came out and started to catch Jews who were walking in the streets to work. Some Jews were waiting to be caught to do this job. Usually after when they finished the job they gave them a pair of new shoes depending on what they had to carry out. Sometimes, when the Germans weren't looking, they threw to a side some clothing or shoes or leather and other people would pick them up. If they were caught them doing this, sometimes they got hit on the spot and some they took to Kazimierz and to the SS Commando. They didn't come back anymore.

When the Germans left after they finished the job, Moshke came with his associates. They were walking the street but nobody said a bad word to them. He would mix in with groups and listen to what they were saying. He wanted to know what happened today like he had no knowledge about anything. But people didn't say anything to him. They were afraid. That went on for a long time and business stopped.

One day about nine o'clock in the morning, a man came to us and said good morning to my father. He said his name was Mr. Dula and introduced himself as the father of Mrs. Katz, our neighbor in Krakow. Her husband's name was David Katz and thanks to him, we had come to Dzialoszyce. Mr. Dula was a very rich man. He was well known in the city. He had a wholesale business selling material like for men's shirts. He also had different material for dresses and suits. My father was very happy to talk with him. He was dressed elegantly. For more than a year he had never come to see us. We went to see him once when we first came to Dzialoszyce and brought him regards from his daughter and her family. Because of him, President Krug had promise us an apartment. He sat down with my father and talked to him about life in the Shul and what we were going through. We thought he had come to tell us that Mr. Krug had an apartment for us, but he didn't say anything about it. He invited my father and me to Kiddush Shabbat. My father promised him that we would be there. After the invitation to his house, he talked to us about our health and our family. He looked around and asked how a family of six persons could live in such a small space with only one toilet for 50 people to cook and wash the laundry. It was a very hard life. Before he left, he also looked around again and he said soon the war would end. Then everybody could go home. He said not to worry and he left.

We didn't understand why such a rich man had come to our house and talked to us to find out how we were doing. We wondered about the fact that he had invited only my father and me to come for Kiddush after Saturday prayers.

I told my father that I thought he needed us for something, I didn't know what. My father said that he was thinking the same thing. Until now he didn't intervene to talk to the president about our apartment. It was over a year since we went to his house and begged him to get us an interview with the president. The Sabbath arrived when we were supposed to go over there. We put on the best clothing that we possessed and we went to pray. The Rabbi and Mr. Dula were praying there and we concurred that from there we would go together to his home. As we walked, we talked about our troubles and what Hitler had done to the Jews. Who would believe that such an intelligent nation such as Germany would do such things to the Jews. They were known for their technology, their discoveries, and music. Many great Jewish people contributed their talents to Germany. Now look what they were doing to the Jewish people.

We hoped that the war would end soon and all the Jewish people under this occupation would be saved. We Jews had lived through many enemies and pogroms and we will also someday see the end of Hitler's regime. Then we came to Mr. Dula's house.

A Day With the Dula Family

They lived like rich people in a luxurious, beautiful apartment. They had very good taste and rich furniture. The floor was covered with carpets from Persia. There were crystal lamps and crystal glasses and real silver, gleaming silverware. His wife came in from the living room and gave us a big smile. She said to please feel as if we were in our own home. She started to show us the house. She took us from room to room including their bedroom. Each room was different and had new imported furniture. The dining room had furniture with a long table set for 12 people. It was prepared for Kiddush. There was also a small table with four chairs in the living room. In the dining room there were crystal, silver, antiques and figurines from all over the world. I couldn't take my eyes off the beautiful things in the room. I used to go with my father to visit very rich people in Krakow but I had never seen such riches as there were in Mr. Dula's house. It was like a king's palace.

They told us to sit at the table that was prepared to seat 12 people. On the table were two challahs. They were covered with a cloth that had Hebrew words that said, "Holy Sabbath" in different colors. Nearby there was a lilac colored crystal bottle with wine. A big silver cup was there with a picture of the Wailing Wall (Kotel Humoravi) and two salt and peppershakers. They also were real crystal. Next to each person there was a small crystal wine glass. All the invited guests took their places at the table. The children sat at the small table. Everyone was seated and talking to one another. They filled the silver cups and glasses with wine. They told us to stand up for the Kiddush. Then Mr. Dula made Kiddush. His wife was standing near him. He finished and everybody said, "Amen." They drank the wine and all the men went to wash their hands and say the prayer.

First Mr. Dula said a prayer for the Challah (Motze) and he cut the challah in pieces. They put it on a plate and everyone at the table received a piece. There were five servants who brought in the fish. They put a piece of carp and a piece of gefilte fish on everyone's plate. When we finished the fish they started to sing the prayers for Sabbath. The Miller brothers from the bakery were also there. Emil with his beautiful tenor voice was asked to conduct the singing and prayers. When we finished the first song (Zmirot) the servants brought in Galer (beef aspic). It was delicious. We hadn't had that for over two years.

We sang the second song and everybody in the room helped with the singing. It was beautiful. After we finished singing, they brought in Cholent and Kischka and kugel(more food). Just the smell from this was terrific. They gave each one of us a cup of chicken soup. It was very good and very tasty. When we finished the food, we started to sing the third song with the prayer. Then came the real thing, a piece of chicken and a piece of beef with horseradish and some cooked vegetables. It was just like a rich wedding. We were so hungry for this tasty food that we hadn't had in more than two years, but we couldn't finish all the food. At this time the war was forgotten. It was as if it didn't exist.

We were singing the fourth song and when we finished they brought in desert (tsimmes). It was big California prunes and all kinds of dried fruit cooked together. When we finished the desert, we started singing the fifth song. When we finished singing, Mr. Dula invited my father to say something from the Bible (Torah). I remember it today just as if it were yesterday. He said something about the Sabbath and how a Jew is supposed to act on the Sabbath and to keep the Sabbath holy. The people were astounded because sitting at the table were knowledgeable men who knew the Torah, the Rabbi from Dzialoszyce, and another man, a Chasid from the Yeshivah. They were teachers who taught the Torah all day long. They understood what my father had said from the Torah. He also sang a song for the Shabbat. I helped him with the singing and the whole room of people started singing along. It was beautiful. He also talked about it being Mr. Dula's 50th birthday and about his daughter and her family. He told how they were such good neighbors with a beautiful family, and that we were now living in Dzialoszyce thanks to them. He spoke about the good name and reputation of the Dula's and how they were well known for their gifts and charity.

My father was singing another song that he had composed. This song is comical and tragic and is about our moving from Krakow to Dzialoszyce. It relates how President Krug didn't keep his word even though we had his signature on a document. He treated us very badly and wouldn't even see us. What kind of a person was he? How could he be the president of all the Jewish people from Dzialoszyce? The people at the table didn't believe my father. They thought he was joking. They were laughing at us and it hurt our feelings.

The servants brought in tea with lemon. There were five plates of all different cakes. After that, we sang "Shir Hama'alot" which is a prayer before finishing the "Bentshen" (table prayers).

Mr. Dula chose a man very knowledgeable in the Talmud to say the last prayer. After finishing the last prayer, people went in to the living room to talk to each other about the war; about the children who ran away to Russia and that they probably did the smartest thing. All the Jews with their families should have done that also.

It was almost four o'clock in the evening and little by little, people started to say goodbye and left. Mr. Dula came to us and he asked us to stay until after Shalosh Seudot (the third meal), which comes after the evening prayer. We remained and prayed the evening prayer (Mincha) and some of the other families also remained because we had to have ten men for the prayers. After the prayer, they told us to sit down at the long table. The servants brought in plates with schmaltz herring and leftovers from the Kiddush, like cholent, kishka, and kugel, also bottled beer but nobody could eat a lot after that big party. After we said Maariv, the third prayer, of the day, Mr. Dula said Havdalah, the last prayer of the Shabbat. Then everybody left.

Mr. Dula asked us to remain because he wanted to talk to us about something very important. We remained and sat in the living room and he came and sat near us. We didn't say anything. We waited for him to talk. We talked together until he came to the point about the situation now in the city. Every day the Germans were searching and looking for hidden merchandise like material for leather shoes. They were coming to all the buildings and searching the basements and attics. He said to us that the place where we were now living, the Schul, he knew 100% that to us poor people the German's would not come. He said that Moshke, the Gestapo agent, wouldn't have them search us. He wanted to know if we would accept that he would bring some materials for making shirts to our room. He would then show us where to put them so that nobody would find them.

He told us that before the war, he had a business making clothes from this material, and wanted to save the material that he had in a bunker not far from his apartment. He paid monthly for a place that couldn't be recognized because of a cement wall. He said that he had 30 meters of fabrics packed in plastic bags or small packages. The shirts were called Checuvicks and Vidruwsky and also other names. He would bring it to us in luggage at different times during the week. The best place to hide it would be under the beds or under the mattresses. It could go in both beds so it wouldn't be too high and the mattresses would then be the same size. There wouldn't be an effect on the merchandise, the mattresses would be filled with straw and we would just sleep on them. Nobody would ever think that there was something under the mattresses, they would think it was just mattresses. We were told not to have the children there when we hid the material.

Mr. Dula said that some of his children would come as if they came to buy our luggage. They would take out two empty pieces of luggage and fill them up at their home. Afterward they would bring the two pieces of luggage back and leave them for about five days as if they wanted them repaired. They would leave with one piece of luggage with another smaller piece inside. We didn't want our neighbors to know anything about what was going on. They would only see new luggage going out and different luggage coming in. We sent our young children out to play in the streets while this was going on. My sister, Chana would stand at the entrance watching on the day we knew that they were coming to see us.

When they brought in the first transport, we told them to come next week for the same thing. My mother and I took off the mattresses from the beds. We straightened out the wood from behind the beds and we opened the luggage. We put the fabric over the wood evenly so that we could sleep well on it. Mr. Dula told us he would give us a nice payment. We didn't even ask how much. We knew that he was a nice man. My father said that to do a favor for a good man is also a big mitzvah. I was not happy about it. If, God forbid, the Germans found this material in our beds, they would finish us up. We would be responsible for anything that happened to all the people in the Shul. I told my parents how I felt, but my father said to do a mitzvah for somebody would please God and He would help us and everything would be okay. I always had respect for my father and mother and accepted their decision.

I put away the two pieces of luggage. When he came the next week, we gave him two pieces of empty luggage, one piece inside the other, but of a different color so it wasn't suspicious. On the Sabbath, my father and I went to the Rabbi from Dzialoszyce to pray. The Rabbi himself was the Chazan (Cantor) and his sons helped him. They all had good voices. When we came home, we made a Kiddush but I still had the taste from Mr. Dula's birthday party.

Every Saturday after lunch, the whole family got together. Aunt Chava and all her family came to our house, too. We all had questions and answers to discuss. We had a very good time when we were together for about five hours. After that we all went to sleep for a couple of hours. Sabbath night we got together again near the big stove to warm up. My father sang the new song he had just composed. "Where are my children? Where? They ran so far away. Blood and tears are running from my eyes. Who knows whether I will ever see them again?" Everyone around the stove was singing. It was like a real choir.

The next Tuesday at nine o'clock in the morning, someone from the Dula family came with two full pieces of luggage. They went out with one piece of luggage but there was another smaller one inside. He had a notebook and we wrote down how many packages he had brought.

For five weeks, every Tuesday we filled both beds. Each time a different person would come so it didn't look too suspicious.

We were going on with our lives. When the whole family got together for Sabbath, I told them about Mr. Dula's home and his birthday party. I told them about their home, the furniture, their crystal, their silver things, their antiques. I described the food that they gave us, unbelievable in wartime to get so much and such good food! They had different meats and fruits as if a war didn't exist. I told them about how elegant and rich they were, and that they had such good taste. They listened patiently.

The next day, my sister Chana and I started to make a new set of luggage. My sister knew the luggage profession as well as I did. She not only learned how to make the luggage but also to do repairs. We always prepared five to ten pieces of luggage. We didn't have any place to put the finished luggage so when we sold the ten pieces we started a new line of luggage. When the farmers came to town some of them bought the luggage. We were also selling things from our house like shirts, pants and other different things. We couldn't make a living from just selling the luggage. That's why we had to sell the goods from our home. We sold Moshe's and Sara's shirts, underwear, shoes and clothing. My mother used to say that if God helped us, we would live through the war. After the war, we would buy completely new clothing such as underwear and shoes for everybody.

A time came when Germany and Russia made an agreement and stopped fighting. At this time, we received a package and a letter from Stalingrad. It was from Moshe. The package contained soaps, tea, sugar, and sardines. Some things like the soap and tea we sold. This helped. It wasn't long before Germany attacked Russia. Then all the letters and packages from Moshe stopped.

Thank God we didn't take or borrow anything from anybody. Chana and I continued to work together. Also my father was invited to sing at weddings and they paid him. This helped us make a living, but not too many people got married. They were afraid or they had a quiet wedding.

Chaim Feldman, the one whose father had a restaurant hear the Shul, was a very good friend of mine. He gave me ideas on how to make money. He asked me many times if I needed money. We did need money but I didn't want to borrow from him. I told him we had to live with this. We couldn't borrow money because we couldn't pay it back. We would always owe money to people we had to live with.

He took me with him to the farmers' village and helped me to sell items that I brought with me. I sold some of my things for money. The people liked Chaim very much. They trusted him. They believed what he told them. He brought them new things like shoes, shirts, dresses and children's clothing. He had a big business with the people and he sometimes traded in gold. We bought a lot of food from them. When we left we had filled up our rucksacks and we were carrying items in both hands. We said goodbye and took the short cut home through the fields so we wouldn't have to go through the village. When we came home, he told me that anytime I needed food I could go back with him. He said he was happy to take me with him rather than go alone.

When I came into the Shul, everybody looked at me and saw that I was loaded with packages. When I came into our room, my father was sitting at the table composing a new song. He was very happy with me. My mother kissed me and she was crying with happiness. She thanked God that I was with them and she helped me unpack everything that I had brought back with me. My father begged me to sit down at the table and to take a pencil and the book so I could write down his new composition. If it wasn't written down right away, he couldn't hold on to it. He would forget everything. I wrote everything that he told me.

When I finished writing what he had composed, my mother made supper. We sat down at the table because I brought very good things like farmer's cheese, homemade sour cream, cucumbers, small radishes and fresh baked bread. She mixed the farmer's cheese with the sour cream, radishes, onions and salt and pepper. It was delicious.

The next morning my sister and I prepared our tools to start making luggage because we needed more sizes and we had the raw material. David Schwarzbaum came to our room early in the morning. He watched as we were making the luggage. I wanted to tell him that he had no right to watch us while we were working. I had told him that many times, but he wouldn't listen. I didn't say anything to him now because my father would be angry with me. I knew he wanted to learn the profession, but I didn't like his character or how he behaved. I was afraid that one-day he would do us harm. My mother used to invite him for dinner twice a week and sometimes on the Sabbath.

Once when we were standing at the market, he was standing near us when two German SS officers passed by. They stopped and looked at my luggage. When David saw them, he disappeared. I was scared myself, but I couldn't leave my luggage and go. They asked me in German if I had made the luggage myself. I told them that I did and that I did the job myself by hand. They told me they wanted to buy two big pieces of leather luggage. I told them I didn't have any leather that my luggage was made from semi-fiber material. One of them told me he would get me the leather and he wanted me to make two big pieces. I told them I would make the luggage for them. He asked me where I lived so I gave him my address. He wrote it down in a little book and left. After that I was shivering and worried because I didn't know for sure who they were or what they might do to us. But it was too late. I had done it already but I was mad at myself.

When I came home from the market place, I told my parents. My father was afraid but my mother was very smart; she told me that everything would be all right. They will bring you the leather and you will make good money. We believe in God and we will pray to Him that everything will be all right.

And that's what came to pass. The SS came to our address one morning around 9:30 and asked for me. The people were afraid when they saw them and everybody went to their own place in the Schul. When the SS men came I was prepared for them. They smiled when they saw me and said good morning. One of them was holding a package of soft leather in his hand. My sister and I were standing at our table working. I greeted them with a smile and said good morning to them.

I took the leather and looked it over. I told them the leather was a little too thick but I would do my best to make two big pieces of luggage. It had to be measured to see if it was large enough for two big pieces. He told me not to worry but to start working on it. If it weren't enough leather, then he would bring me more of the same quality and the black color. I told him if there were too much leather, I would give them back what was left over. I put the leather on the forms and measured it. I showed them that it might not be enough leather for two pieces of luggage. I gave them a price. They accepted and promised that the following week they would bring me the additional leather to complete the job. I told them I didn't know how long it would take because I couldn't work fast at my place at the Shul, and I didn't have any machines. I had to do all the work by hand and they would have to have patience, but I told them to come back in two weeks to check on the progress because we didn't have a telephone. They accepted everything I told them but they didn't give me a deposit. I was afraid to ask because they gave me the leather as a deposit. They left their names and addresses and said they were from Kazimierz not far from Dzialoszyce.

This was where the German SS Commands and the Gestapo for all the little cities around there was located and Moshke, the spy worked for them. He was the one who found out the places where merchandise was hidden and gave them the addresses. When they came with trucks, they knew where everything was because of him. When they told me that they lived with the Commandos and the SS, I was afraid because we had hidden merchandise from Mr. Dula in our room. My parents were very afraid but my mother was very smart. She said to us, "the robber doesn't steal where he lives". She didn't want us to be afraid and she also didn't want our unrest to unsettle the neighbors so we didn't talk about it any more and we just hoped to God that it would finish in a nice and profitable way.

I put aside all my other work and my sister and I started working on just the two leather luggages. I had told them I would try to finish them in two weeks but it's not for sure. I took my forms from the big luggage, but I had to make a new form to make the size luggage they wanted. When I finished the form, I took it and put on the leather. I cut out the main portion for two pieces, but I couldn't make two luggages from this leather. I made one piece and I took cardboard and put glue on the cardboard with the leather together because the leather was very soft. This would make it stiffer. I stretched them and put them on the floor of our room. I put very heavy things on them to press them down. After two days I took out the ready leather and it was dry. I was trying hard to finish because my family was living with worry. They were afraid. I didn't have locks for very big luggage that I needed for that size. I only had the other smaller luggage locks. I had to put the smaller locks on.

Everyday we only worked on those two pieces of luggage. I wanted to finish them as fast as I could because we were all afraid. It took me almost eight days to finish up. When we finished, we checked again to make sure everything was done okay. We had to wait another eight days and every day seemed like a year. Everyday we put on some crème to make them shine.

We went back to our luggage work and that guy, David Schwarzbaum came every day to stand and watch us working. He talked to my father about helping us. I refused him and told him that I didn't have enough work for three people. I didn't even have enough work for my sister and she was an expert. It didn't help. He was a pest. I didn't throw him out because I respected my father. But later my father and I paid a big price for that and my father saw that I was 100% right about him. My father believed in everyone, but I didn't. I recognized him for what he was as if I were a prophet. I knew that he would do harm to my family and me. My father did not believe it. He used to tell me "don't worry my son, nobody will be able to do harm to us." I reminded my father that he had trusted the president, Mr. Krug. He promised us with a signed letter that he had an apartment ready for us as soon as we came here. Where is the apartment? He didn't even want to see or talk with us for more than a year and we are still sitting in this garbage. Also you had so many friends here. People here had you at their children's weddings. Has anyone come to you with help? Now they don't want to know you at all. Do they ask about your children and how you support them or how you make a living for them?

Everyday the prices for food are higher and higher. It's not so easy to make a living. We had to sell our clothing like suits, shirts, shoes and blankets. The luggage sales were not enough. We had to sell dresses and different things from the house. Everyday was worst than the last. We also sold Sara's and Moshe's things. It wasn't enough but it saved us from going hungry.

The people from Dzialoszyce were very rich. The German's had confiscated items worth millions of dollars from the bunkers that they found but there was still good merchandise worth, believe me, millions of dollars but they didn't give anything to the people who were going hungry. They didn't care. They could have made it a lot easier for us.

The two SS came back to the Schul at exactly the time they had promised. The luggage was ready. They both looked over the work we had done. They opened the pieces and looked inside and at the outside. One said okay,it looked like they would be very happy. Their faces were smiling but the other German was mumbling under his breath like he was talking to himself. I didn't wait. I told him "my dear man, you have to understand that my work and the finishing are the very best, you can see it yourself. The luggage are made very strong and will last for years." I reminded them that the luggage was made of leather and that it was especially large and should have had large handles and a special finish. They had been told that before I started work and had said "ok, make it". I had finished the pieces with what I had in stock. It didn't make any difference because the luggage was strong and beautiful. The one said that he was very satisfied and gave me a hundred zloty.

The other German again started to look it over inside and out until the first one said it was getting late and he should pay me that they didn't have time to play around. Then the other man gave me a hundred zloty. I wanted to give them the excess leather but they told me to keep it and make something for mychildren. They said goodbye and left. It was as if someone had taken a stone from my heart and also from my parents' hearts. We were all glad that the job was finished.

Typhus Fever in the Shul

About five weeks later, a sickness broke out in the Shul. Five people in one day got sick with very high temperatures. The doctor's found out it was an outbreak of Typhus. No one could go out and no one could come in. The Jewish police surrounded the Shul (Beth Hamedrish) so that we couldn't have any contact with the people outside. The Shul was closed and the healthy people inside were nervous. People started screaming at one another until the Jewish police intervened. The commandant from the police was the son of the guy from the restaurant and the brother of my friend Chaim. I cannot remember his name. The commandant told me that Chaim asked him to ask me if I would become the commandant of the Shul to keep order there. I would be a member of the police. I would get paid, have a police uniform and they will give me orders how to take care of the people in the Shul. I didn't even talk this proposition over with my parents. I told the commandant that I couldn't undertake the position of policeman in the Shul because I was too weak for this job. I felt you had to be a strong man to tell people to do this or that. I was not the person for the job so I refused the offer.

As soon as David Schwarzbaum found out about this job, he let the commandant know he wanted to become the policeman of the Shul. He was accepted for the job and became the commandant. The next day he started to make trouble for people. Five days later he came to mean said "I worked for you for a long time and you didn't pay me for my work". He didn't come around to talk to my father anymore, he didn't even sing with him because now he felt he was a big man. He wanted a big sum of money from me, which we didn't even possess. I told him to come in to us, to talk to my father about the work he thought he had done. He didn't want to come in to talk about it, he must have the full amount of the money, if not, he would see what he could do to us.

He started to make trouble for us. Meantime we were locked up. I couldn't talk to anybody, but we talked to my friend Chaim, and told him we needed to talk to his brother, the commandant of the police. As long as we were locked up we couldn't do anything. David Schwartzbaum wouldn't let me do my work because he said it disturbed people who were trying to sleep. He wouldn't let my father sing around the stove any longer. I didn't listen to him. I did my thing and I worked to show him that I wasn't afraid of him. My parents were aggravated because they saw that I was right not to start anything with him because he was dangerous, especially my father. I told them not to worry about it, that I was not afraid of him, only the Germans. I told them we would go to the police to report what he was doing. He was a Mafia man and was making noise to press out from us more money.

As soon as they opened the door of the Shul and we could mix with the people outside, we went to the Jewish police and told them we wanted to talk to the commandant of the Jewish Police. He called us into his office because he knew my father. He asked us to sit down. We sat down and told him the whole story about David Schwarzbaum, how he started to come by to talk with my father, how he stood watching how my sister and I made the luggage and how I told him we didn't need any help. We didn't have enough work for us, who is buying luggage now? When we make five pieces it takes a long time to sell them. The sale of our luggage was not enough to make a living for the family. We had six people to feed and we had to sell our clothing to have enough money for food We sold my sister's and brother's clothing who left for Russia, their suits, underwear, shoes. I went to the farmers with your brother, Chaim, to sell the clothing in exchange for food so that, God forbid, we didn't have to take anything from anybody. I had told Mr. Schwarzbaum that I didn't need anybody, but my father had pity on him. My father often invited him to our Sabbath dinner and also sometimes during the week. I had warned my parents not to invite him, that he was going to make trouble for us. Also that we ourselves didn't have enough, but my father said he was a lonely person, he didn't have anybody, so we didn't say anything. He came in to see what we were doing. Now he has become commandant of the Shul.

He said he did work for us, but I never let him do anything for us. He grabbed the luggage to go to the Market place. I told him to talk to my father about what work he had done for us and why he wanted so much money. He didn't want to talk about it. He said he would turn it over to the Jewish police. That's why we came to talk to you. I asked the Commanadant what we should do. The Commandant said if he did anything bad to us that we should come to him right away, but he would set a time for a Jewish Court (Din-Torah) because he himself couldn't do anything. Both sides had to be heard. There would be two Lawyers, they will sit there like in a court. We left his office.

About three days later, a Jewish policeman came to let us know that in a week on a Tuesday at three o'clock in the afternoon my father and I should go to the Jewish police. One lawyer would be on our side, the other on the police side. They will hear both stories.

A week later, we went to the police and David Schwarzbaum was sitting there already. Two Advocates came in with the commandant and two other policemen. After ten minutes we were all ready and the judge entered. Everybody stood up and then they told us to sit down. They first asked David Schwarzbaum what he wanted and we both had to swear on the bible that we would tell the truth. He lied and said that I had hired him eight months ago and that he worked for me since then. He said that we had not paid him even a penny, that he had no money and why didn't I want to pay him. He wanted 4,000 zloty, the equivalent of around two thousand dollars.

After him they asked me why I hadn't paid him. I told them my story about how we were a family of six people and we couldn't make a living. We never hired him because there was not even enough work for myself and my sister. I said that my mother and father had pity on him and had invited him for dinner every Sabbath and lunch during the week. He started to come at the times when we were working. I told him that I don't wish him coming when we were working but he came by force. He never touched a hammer. But when he knew we had to go to the market, with force, he grabbed two pieces of luggage from us and went to the market, but he didn't make the luggage. We didn't have enough work for us. We could not make a living on the one or two pieces of luggage we sold each week. We had to sell our own clothing to get bread and milk for the children. I had warned my father that he was a bad character and would make trouble for our family. My father didn't listen to me. We are still selling our own shirts, dresses, suits and shoes.

He had come to us from time to time and wanted to help, but I didn't let him. He never helped me with my work. How can he now ask for money from me when he never did anything? He had said that he didn't want any money from me. It was good enough just to spend time with my father. We have been at the Shul for a year and a half and no one ever complained that my work was a disturbance. We have a shoemaker at the Shul. He starts working at seven o'clock in the morning and no one complained because he has to make a living.

After listening to me, the Advocates asked him what he had to say about my testimony. He told them I lied. He said that he only ate with us twice on the Sabbath. After that they gave my father the oath and asked him to give his testimony. With tears in his eyes, he told them how I had warned him about David Schwarzbaum. That he would give us trouble because of his bad character, he wanted by force to learn how to make luggage. He said to me "Reb Simcha, I don't want money from you. I like your singing and you are inviting me almost every Shabbat and also during the week for a meal, why shouldn't I do something for you?" I told my son Kalmen that he was a lonely man and for a mitzvah we should help him and to please do it for me. Let him carry out the luggage because it makes him feel better. Now my dear people, what is he doing to us in the Shul? The Torah says that you will get paid back for the good things you do. I do not even possess what he has asked for. I don't owe him anything. He didn't do anything but take out the luggage to the market on Tuesday and Friday and then not every week. We were so good to him. How can he do this? My son was smart. He warned us. He said he is a snake and he would come back one day and be at our throats. We are a family of six people. We have to live.

The Advocates were listening to my father speak. They asked David Schwarzbaum what he had to say about my father's testimony. He told them everything was a lie. They asked me what I had to say. I said I can bring a witness as to how many times he saw him coming to our place to eat. It took three hours. They told us to go home that they would let us know the verdict.

It seems that, because he was employed by the police, the lawyer from the police worked in his favor so the verdict was that he had worked for us eight months even though he just helped take the luggage to the market for us. We had to pay him within a week. The verdict said that instead of eight months they cut it in half to four months and we owed him 500 zloty per month or 2,000 zloty. This was a terrible verdict. It was a shame that the Jewish police in Dzialoszyce could do that to us because of the connections he had. We didn't possess any money. We lived from day to day. It was like Sodom and Gomorrah. No justice in Dzialoszyce. If I didn't have any money I would have to pay him in luggage worth 2,000 zloty. We protested against it. There was no righteousness in this city. We proposed to go to the official Polish government court, but it didn't help. My father asked them how they could do such a thing and that we had six people to support. We had to sell our dresses, suits, shoes, underwear and shoes to stay alive. Do you want to kill us just like the Germans? You are the murderer. We don't have enough pieces of luggage to give him. How are we going to live? My father was crying. He said that we would have to work three months for nothing. We didn't have the raw material and could not comply with the verdict. "You can put me and my whole family in jail," he said," I will not pay him a nickel. He didn't do anything for us, but he ate with us for eight months free. We gave him meals. I took from my children and gave to him.

I do not recognize this verdict. God will pay you for what you have done to us. It is wartime and we are all in God's hands. We are all Jews under the German occupation and no one knows which of us will come out after the war ends. If I live, I will all my life remember this verdict, what one Jew did to another in time of war. I say here right now that we have no money and no luggage to give away. You want six people to die of hunger. Not by my life! We will not observe the verdict. We will not pay one cent!" and my father started to cry.

My son told me from the first day to send him away, but I let him stay because he was a lonely man. Many times my son sent him away but with force he always came back to watch the work and how we made the luggage. I told my son to let him stay and observe, but my son told me he would make trouble.

The police did send someone in and told me to give him the luggage. If not, I would be put in jail. I wanted to go to jail rather than pay, but my father said "what will happen to us if you go to jail. You see my son, they have no pity for us. They didn't care if we starve", so we gave him one piece of luggage. Until now I can't look at the City of Dzialoszyce. It reminds me of Sodom and Gomorrah. Not one policeman from Dzialoszyce is alive now. The Germans took all the policemen along with the commandant and lawyers and sent them to Beldzyce(Belzec) where my mother and sisters were sent.

I haven't forgotten President Mojshe Josl Krug. He was a crook. He had promised us an apartment. If he had kept his promise we wouldn't have had all those problems. We found out that the apartment he promised us was given to somebody who had paid him more money. He was a corrupted man. If he had asked us for more money we would have given it to him.

After the verdict and giving him one piece of luggage, Schwarzbaum still didn't stop making trouble for us, every day something else. We went to the Jewish Center and told them that we couldn't take any more problems from David Schwarzbaum. If they don't give us a place, we would come there with our children and sleep there for as long as it took. We told them the whole story about the verdict. My father told them it would be on their conscience. I went in with my father to the president. I didn't ask anybody, we just walked into his office. We told him that if he didn't help us now I would write about him and what he did to us. My father had tears in his eyes. He told us to go home. He said he would give us a place to live within a week. We went home.

After three days, he called us back to the Community Center and a Jewish policeman went with us to look at an apartment. It was an empty ruin that was used for selling small magazines during wartime. Nobody wanted to go in. Inside and outside there were only bricks with no walls. We would have to put up cement walls inside and outside. We would have to hire a contractor to do the job. There were no windows. They were all broken. There were three small rooms, a very small kitchen and no doors. We looked at it, and we didn't like it, but we had no choice. They said they would put in doors and windows. I told my mother and father that it was better than staying at the Shul. It would take six months to fix it up, but it would be our own place. It was after Pesach and not too cold. We could not stay there in the cold weather because we had no stove, but we were happy and accepted. We went home and started to prepare to move.

We went to Mr. Dula so he could take back his merchandise. We told him to do it very cautiously because if the commandant of the Shul saw them, it would be a big problem for us. He came the next morning with some of his family. I gave him the new luggage. We filled them up with the merchandise, so that it looked as if they had bought it from us. The next day he did the same thing. We told him to leave the luggage at home that we would give him two new pieces of luggage. When he came back the next morning, Mr. Schwarzbaum looked at him but since we had one luggage inside the other he thought it was just a sale. It took three days for us to clear out the merchandise from the bed. He didn't give us anything for keeping the merchandise in our beds.

President Krug sent a man to put in the doors and windows and to clean up the debris because the place smelled. They cleared all the cats and mice from the place and then they cleaned everything. We had the windows and the doors, but there were no walls and no real ceiling. We hired two men with a horse and carriage to move our furniture. The people at the Kehillah told us not to say anything to anyone that we were moving. It was better to surprise them. They were afraid that everyone from the Shul would then ask them for an apartment. We didn't tell Aunt Chava and the children, they told us not to say anything. Only when we came to take out the furniture, then we told Aunt Chava that we couldn't tell anyone. Thank God we got rid of that scoundrel Mr. Schwarzbaum and even though the new place was a piece of garbage, not painted, we were very happy. They loaded up our furniture and took it to our own place. You can't imagine how happy my parents were.

We thought that little by little we could fix the place up. We wouldn't have to answer to anybody because it was our own place. I told my sister Chana that we shouldn't wait too long, we both would paint the house inside and outside. From outside the house looked worse than inside. The next day we both started to work on the house. We made it nicer and nicer. My parents were dancing with happiness. They said that this should have happened a year and a half ago and we wouldn't have had so many problems. I told my parents to please thank God.

Then I heard that the Germans had shot Moshke, the guy who worked for the Germans. They buried him on one side of the city. When we passed by we saw that one foot was left outside with his shoes. Everybody was happy that he was dead. He had made so many Jewish people unhappy and he made them poor. He took away everything from them.

That was the start. We heard that the Germans had broken into a businessman's house. They called him der geller (yellow) Spokoyne. They killed him in his apartment in front of his family. Everybody in the city got scared. That was the start of the real criminal days. Everyday we heard something else. We started to live with panic.

We heard that in the cities they took people from their houses. The richest people and the professionals were targeted. They would beat up the doctors and lawyers and take them from their homes. They didn't come back. We heard in the city that they are going to send all of the people in Dzialoszyce to concentration camps to work except for children and old people. Everybody must work. All the families would be together but the young men and women would work in factories for the Army. That is what the Jewish Police told us, that it had been going on for months but we shouldn't worry and not be scared. It would be a long time before they built up those camps so that everybody had a place to work. The elders and children would have special people to take care of them. No one thought that Hitler was ready to destroy the whole Jewish population when he occupied Poland. If we would have had a suspicion of the things going on or that they were going to send us to the death camps or the crematoriums, we wouldn't have gone freely. We would have been prepared. We might even have had weapons. We would have fought house to house. Even the women would have fought. Germans wouldn't have felt that they had it so easy and could walk over everyone. We would never have let them kill us, but the Jewish Police told us not to worry that they needed us to work and weren't going to kill us. They didn't have enough workers. The Jewish Police did fool us. They didn't know anything themselves. They believed the German Commandos.

The problem was, no one knew what plans they had for us, the "Jewish solution." We heard that they took the Jewish people from Kielce, Rakov and Chmielnik (Chelmno) to camps and all of them are working there. That was our problem. Every Jew had to have a place to work for the Germans. If a Jew had a place to work, nothing would happen to them. The Jewish Police prepared us months ahead that everyone had to have a place to work. We understood what they wanted, that the Jewish people had to work for them. Nobody knew that they were preparing crematoriums in order to gas and burn the people. It looks as if the Jewish Police helped the Germans a lot to finish up the Jewish people. When they finished with the whole city of Jews, they killed the police with their commandant. Some of them were sent to Treblinka and Auschwitz.

The "Aussiedlung"— Finishing the Jews in Dzialoszyce

It was Wednesday, September 1942 at exactly six o'clock in the morning. We heard a rush of people running and talking loudly. I jumped from my bed and went to the window to look out. I saw German soldiers marching in the street. I heard the marching feet as daylight came. My heart was pounding. I did see that something was going on and it was going to happen to us. We had been in the house for three months. It was not finished. We had done some work painting and cleaning. We were happy on this small narrow street not far from the market place. The apartment was painted and cleaned up but it was not finished. I got dressed fast, washed myself while everyone in the house was still sleeping. On a normal day we usually got up about 7:30 a.m.

After about a half hour looking out the window, I saw the Jewish Police going from house to house. They talked through a microphone and said that all Jewish people including men, women and children would have to go to the market place by 8:00 a.m. We must stand in line because we were being sent to work. I woke up my parents and the children. They jumped up scared. They got dressed very fast. It was six thirty in the morning. I told them what I had seen and heard. They were sending us to camps to work. The first thing is to start packing. My mother prepared a package for us to take with us. Everybody was helping with the packing. My mother put a shirt and underwear in the package. My father was very worried. He said, "What are they going to do with me? I am a blind man. I am not able to work. Are they going to take me away from my wife and children?" I told him that we were in God's hands and He would help us. We weren't going to be separated. We were a family. My mother, with tears in her eyes, made us our last breakfast. We had bread with butter. She said "my dear children, eat fast and a lot because we didn't know when the next meal will be. Eat my dear children . . ." She started to cry. My father, also, started to cry. I told my mother and father that crying would not help. We all have to be strong. I believed they were taking us to a camp for work. There they will give the young people hard work, and for the elders and children they would give light work. That was what the Jewish Police had told everyone almost three months before. We probably will live together in barracks with other people like we did at the Shul for almost two years. I wanted to change the mood and the hope. I told them again that a person shouldn't loose his hope.

It was already 7:30 a.m. My mother made sandwiches for each of us. She came to me and said I should change my pants, she gave me warmer pants so I wouldn't be cold. She told me she had hidden her diamond ring in the belt of the pants in case I encountered danger, she hoped the ring might help. She whispered it in my ear so no one else heard her. I looked at my mother and started to cry. I didn't want to show everybody that I, too, was worried. My mother made two sandwiches for each of us. She put them on top of the package she had made for us. My mother said quietly, to me, "my son,who knows what Hitler is going to do with us? I only hope that we will see each other again. My father started to cry and said, "What is going to happen to me? I am a blind man. What kind of work will they give me?" I then said to my mother and father "we are religious people and we are in God's hand. He will take care of us. No bad things will happen to us. A Jew should always think about good things". In my heart I wondered what they were going to do to the older people and children. My mother gave us a glass of milk. I said again "do you believe in miracles? We have to be optimistic.

Before we left my mother gave us another piece of bread and butter and she told us to eat now because who knows whether we are going to eat anymore today. We were prepared to go. The Jewish Police came to our house and told us that in 15 minutes we all had to be at the market place. The German Commandant said that if they found any person in his home or hiding after that would be shot dead. We all fell on each other and kissed each other with tears in our eyes. My father said "I pray to God that we would see each other again." We kissed the Mezuzah, the prayer that hangs on the door. My father and I packed the Tefillin and my father took the Tallis. As my father went out the door, he said the prayer, "Shema Yisrael", and I took my father and I held his hand. My sisters, Chana, Ryvka and Mira were holding my mother's hand. That was the last time we walked together.

We all marched together to the market place with our packages in our hands. We saw from far away thousands and thousands of whole families standing in line and more coming. I saw hundreds of Germans and Ukrainians surrounding the market. We heard crying. Then we saw our Aunt Chava, her daughter Chana Feige and her daughter's son Yankele. We went to their place to be together. The market filled up with the Jewish people from the city. I saw how the Gestapo along with the

Jewish Police went from house to house looking for hiding Jews. They looked all through the houses from the basements up.

We were all standing together and kissed each other. When we were walking my sister, Chana disappeared and we didn't see her anymore. My mother asked where Chana had gone. We saw that the Jewish Police brought in more people who were hiding in the bunkers. We saw a lot of our friends. We saw Mr. Dula with his family. We saw the Rabbi from Dzialoszyce with his sons and family.

We all had to stand in line. We also saw the Polish farmers coming with horses and carriages by the hundreds. We saw about five hundred Ukrainians in black suits. They surrounded us with rifles in their hands ready to shoot to kill. Also in all the streets the Gestapo SS stood together with the Jewish Police. They spoke through a microphone that all Jewish people should leave their houses. If they caught any Jew at home or in the bunkers they would be shot. They were running wild from house to house looking for Jews. Some Jews came out from the bunkers and went with their families in line. They killed sick and old people on the spot. It looked like a slaughterhouse. We heard hollering from the Gestapo and saw dead people lying in the middle of the market place.

People were standing ten to a line. We saw a lot of other people coming by truck. I couldn't count them all because they were standing on the other side. The German soldiers jumped from the trucks making a line and they marched together to the city with the Ukrainian battalion. They surrounded the market place. According to my knowledge it must have been about ten thousand Jewish men, women and children. We were waiting to find out what they were going to do with us.

When they finished running from house to house, when all the Jews were on the spot, then the microphone was calling to make a line of ten people in a line. We tried to make a line. I was the first one and was holding my father's hand. Next to my father was my mother. She held my father's other hand. With the other hand she was holding my youngest sister's hand. Mira was nine years old. My sister, Ryvka, was holding Mira's hand. Ryvka was 11 and one half years old. At this time I was 22 years old. My father was 45 years old and my mother was 44 years old.

That was the last time in our life we stood together. There were lines and lines behind us. Our Aunt Chava was behind us, her daughter Chane Feige and her grandson, Yankele. He was six years old. We were standing just so and they were bringing more and more Jews from the bunkers and basements

I was standing and holding my father. A Ukrainian soldier with his gun on his arm was standing near me. He looked at my father. He came even closer. He looked straight at my father. My father had a very short beard. He had it cut after it became law that all Jews had to cut their beards, but it had grown since then. He said something to my father in the Ukrainian language that we didn't understand. He put his two hands on my father's collar, this image stays always in front of my eyes, I will never forget it, and caught him on the front of his jacket and pulled him out to him. He was pulling him and I was pulling my father back to me. I was holding my father very hard. This took about five minutes. I didn't give in. I was still holding my father with both hands when the bandit let go of my father. He picked up his gun and hit me in the chest. I fell down and thought for sure he was going to shoot me.

I was lying on the ground I saw that he again had grabbed my father by the front collar and pulled him out of line. I got up and told the Ukrainian in Polish that he was my father. I asked him why he had pulled him away from me. I said that my father was a completely blind man. I tried about five times to pull my father back into line. He got mad and pointed his gun at me and said that he would kill me if I tried to pull my father back again.

I had to let him take my father from me. He took him by the hand and brought him to a separate area where he remained standing alone. He didn't beat him up. He heard the cries from my mother and two sisters. Also my Aunt Chava and I turned to my mother and held her hand. My father was still standing alone, and with tears in his eyes tried to talk to us. He said, "Who knows whether I will see you again. Where are they going to take my wife and children? What do they want from me? Who knows what they are going to do to me?" He tried again to talk to us and said, "I will never see you again." He was shivering and he cried, "God have pity on my wife and children." I told my father not to worry that we would be together again. The same Ukrainian took the old people with beards and women out of line. He took them to where my father was standing.

I saw farmers coming with horses and wagons. They put all the men and women on the wagon. I begged the Ukrainian soldier to help my father, and he did. They filled the wagons and took them away. That was the last time I ever saw my father. We found out later that they took sixteen hundred people to the Jewish cemetery where they had prepared a large hole. They threw the people in the hole. They didn't even shoot them. They just covered them with soil and buried them alive. We were still standing and waiting to find out what they were going to do with us. We heard them over the microphone saying that we should stay in line. Anyone who tried to escape would be shot.

The last march with my mother and sisters started. We were walking to the railroad station. We passed the cemetery. From a distance we heard shots and crying. We walked about a half hour. When we came to the railroad, we saw wagons. They started to segregate the older people and the children. They started to beat the mothers, and even the young mothers and children. They hollered at them and wanted them to run to the wagons. The Gestapo and Ukrainians surrounded them. They could not run away. They pushed the old people and mothers with children toward one of the wagons. They filled the wagons with a hundred people. They couldn't even sit down. They were packed so tightly that they could hardly breath, they were packed like herring in a jar.

And the younger people, also young women, also with hollering and beating. We also had to run to the wagons. They did the same thing but not like the older people and children. We at least could stand easily. When I got in the wagon I immediately went to a window so I would be able to look for the wagon holding my mother and the children. I saw the German murderers. They opened up sacks of chlorine powder and threw it into the wagon with the women and children. They locked the door and one SS man was on the wagon outside watching to make sure no one jumped out. The chlorine was so strong that we could smell it in our wagon. I could hear the crying and coughing. They couldn't breathe. They died a terrible death in the wagon. When they came on the place, they were all dead. It was unbelievable that a German human being could do something like that to anyone. When I saw what they did to my mother and sisters, I started to cry. I expected that they were going to do the same thing to us but their train left and our train was still standing.

They brought in young Jews which were hidden. We stood for more than an hour in the wagon. Some people were very tired and couldn't stand any longer so they sat down on the floor. They did not use the chlorine powder on us. One SS man was standing on a step outside guarding us so we could not jump off. They closed our door and the train started to move slowly. Nobody knew where we were going. Also there were Jewish Police watching us. They didn't know where we were going either. I was standing all the time thinking about what they were going to do with us, seeing what they did to my father and now to my mother and sisters and to all the Jewish people. I thought about jumping out the window. I knew they were taking us to die. I saw before my eyes the picture when the Ukrainian soldier grabbed my father and pulled him out, and how he put him on the carriage and horse. I felt guilty that I let him pull my father away. I should have grabbed his gun from him and killed him.

After two hours driving, we came to a station. One guy told me that we were in Miechov. The train was stopped and the Germans opened the doors of the wagons. Over a microphone they yelled for us to jump out of the wagons. Again we had to stand in line. No one from the family was with me. I was alone.

We marched to a big place that looked like a market square that was not far from the railroad. SS Gestapo and Ukrainians surrounded us. The Jewish Police came with us. The sun was burning like a fire. It was very hot and probably over ninety degrees. We were all very thirsty. We needed some water. There were about five or six thousand people in one place. The heat was terrible for us. We needed a drink of water. I started going around between people to try to find my sister, Chana. She had disappeared when police surrounded us, we couldn't run away. I did believe that I had already lost my whole family. I was looking for a friend or someone I might know. I didn't find anybody.

Somebody told me that the Jewish Police said the women and children were sent to Theresienstadt. There was going to be a Jewish city set up and we would find them there. I didn't believe it but I was always an optimist. I believed in God. I thought that through God anything was possible. It was a miracle for Jews when they were liberated from Egypt and all the Jewish people went into the deep sea and nothing happened to them. Why, dear God, don't you give us a miracle now when we need it? We are going to a death camp. Help us now. We were sitting on the ground. The heat was getting stronger and stronger. It was as if we were in a fire. We were very thirsty. We asked for water but we didn't get any. A lot of people were fainting. Over the microphones, the Germans were asking for doctors and that they were to go to the Jewish Police. The Jewish doctors then started taking care of the sick people.

It seems that they called for Jewish Kehilla (community) elders in Miechov and they sent people with water and lemon juice. This saved us from fainting. Everyone could have as much water or lemon juice as they needed. We were sitting on the ground waiting all this time. Jewish women and men were going around with barrels of water and lemon juice. We saw them and talked with them and they said to us, we do expect the same thing here in Miechov. Who will give us help, water and juices?

We saw the worried faces, seeing what they did to us. We sat more than four hours on the ground waiting for the next verdict. Where and what were they going to do with us? Then another message from the Germans came over the microphone. They told us to get up and stand in line. They counted us and we started to march to the railroad station. It didn't take us long to see again the wagons waiting for us, not knowing where they were going to take us. Again, they segregated the young men and women to a different wagon and the remaining older people were put in a different wagon. The Germans hollered for us to run to the wagons. They started to beat and push us. We jumped in the wagons until they were full. We couldn't sit down. We stood all the time like herring. A German soldier guarded us so we wouldn't jump from the wagon or out the window.

We drove for three or four hours. It was nighttime and very dark. They stopped and opened the wagon and they let us out. They were hollering at us as if we were animals until no one was left in the wagon. And again the microphone was calling us to stay in the line. After a half hour we started to march again to a place where we saw electric wiring all around. We didn't know which camp this was or where we were. We saw barracks, all empty. We were the first group. They counted us again before we entered the barracks. They put seventy persons in one barrack.

The First Night in a Concentration Camp

After they had counted us they sent me to Barrack 26, coming in with 69 more people. They gave us a place to sleep. From one corner to the other of the barracks, I saw that the beds were made like bunk beds down the middle of the room lengthwise and on both sides of the room. I decided to sleep near a window on the top bed. I figured that when they came to get people for the dirty work, they would usually take the people on the bottom bed. Also the window provided more air. They had given me another place but I myself changed it for a top bunk.

This started a new life for me without my parents or anyone from my family. When I took the top place, I saw that it was a sack made up of straw instead of a mattress. We called it a *Shenick*. There was a pillow filled with straw and a blanket. We had no sheets. They gave us a piece of bread, 250 grams, a piece of margarine and two cigarettes. I was very hungry and tired from the terrible day we had. I lost my parents, my home. Now I am a slave, a prisoner in a camp. What I saw all day long, how they beat us when we entered the wagon. I ate the bread with the margarine. I exchanged the two cigarettes for a half portion of bread. I didn't smoke and that helped me a lot to live through the war.

I was very tired and I went to my Koike (bed). I fell asleep but all night I had dreams. I will never forget that, my father came to me with tears in his eyes and he said, "Kalmen, my son, I want you to know that the Germans shot me. I am in the Jewish cemetery at Dzialoszyce. The bullet went in my right eye, but I am alive, I am between sixteen hundred Jews in one grave. If you could come and take me out of there, from the deep grave, you could save my life". I got up, it was the middle of the night, it was very dark. I could not see what time it was. I was lying and thinking and I asked myself, is it was possible that I can save my father's life? . . . . and I said to myself, it is only a dream. Even if I wanted to help I couldn't. I myself am now in prison surrounded. Don't think about it. And so thinking, I fell asleep again.

At six o'clock in the morning, a bell was ringing. I jumped down from my bed and ran fast to the washroom and got dressed very fast. I was standing in line together with everybody else. That was the first night,

I said to myself. Now I am lonely like a stone, but, I said to myself that I am not the only one. I am together with all the Jews. I have to fight to stay alive. As we were standing in line the German commandant, "Miller" they called him, came in and he himself counted us. Everybody got an aluminum pot called a *menoshke* and everybody, one after the other, went to get very hot black coffee. When we finished they divided the people into groups for different jobs. Each group had a HJ (Kapo) a Jewish, not German, guard watching him and I asked where are we now? What is the name of this place? They called it Plaszow Gulag. It was a small city near Krakow. It was a concentration camp, a work camp. The commandant of the Gulag was Obersturmfuhrer Miller.

The First Day in a Concentration Camp

When the "Kapo" (Jewish guard) took the group of people outside the camp to the work place, he did not tell us where we were going or what we would have to do. As we were waiting at the main door, I looked around trying to find out where we were. I saw a big place where a lot of barracks had been built. There was a wooden house where a German SS was standing and watching us to make sure no one ran away. The little house was higher than the barracks. When he looked down he could see the whole camp and what was going on. There were two SS watchmen all the time. The camp had electric wiring. If anyone tried to escape and touched the wire, he would be electrocuted to death.

For the first time in my life I came to the conclusion that I was no longer free. It was more than a jail. At least when you went to jail you had a certain sentence of maybe two to five years. Then when you served your sentence, you were a free man again. I didn't know if I would ever get out of here alive. I had one hope. I knew that the Jewish ghetto was not far from here, and maybe I would be able to get in touch with my Uncle David, my mother's brother, and his family.

We were still standing in a group of about 30 people waiting to go to work. It was 7:30 a.m. and I saw a man coming toward us. He said in German that he was our manager (Kapo). He said he was going with us to show us where we were going and what we had to do. He told us to stay together and do the job given us. He said that nothing was going to happen to us. He warned us not to run away because if we were caught running away, we would be shot.

We started to march with him for about 30 minutes until we came to a place where a German SS with his machine gun started walking with us. It was very hot. When we marched through the streets, the Poles looked at us. We came to a place with a small storage area built of wood for all the equipment we needed. The Kapo had the key and opened up the storage shed. He gave everyone a shovel. We had to dig a big hole. He told each of us the length and depth of the hole. It had to be a certain size and it was like doing piecework because each of us had to do a certain amount of work. After they made the calculations, they brought in big pipes made of cement and measured it with a string. The Kapo explained how many meters had to be finished. The engineer of the building would be coming to inspect and we all had to do our piecework. Because we came to the workplace a little late and we didn't know exactly what to do we were told to do as much as we could. We helped him with the measurements and put in pieces of wood.

At lunchtime they brought in a big canister with hot soup. Everybody was very hungry. It was the first day for all of us to be doing such hard work. The soup was made of carrot tops, beets and cucumbers with some potatoes. We were standing in line for the soup and they gave us a menoshke from the soup and for the morning coffee. The soup was very hot. They gave us some leftovers from the soup. We were so hungry that we didn't care what it was, for us was the best soup ever. It was our first soup at the concentration camp. I didn't expect that they would give us chicken soup with a piece of chicken, but we were so hungry that we thought this soup tasted better. Our good years ended now.

I thought to myself that I was in a camp or a jail. Why? I hadn't killed anyone. My only sin was that I was born a Jew. The German SS surrounded me. Everything here was strange to me. This was the first time I was a slave. I was very hungry. Until now I was never hungry.

I heard a whistle from the Kapo and we went to get in line. We were about 30 people altogether, all men. We still had our own clothing. It was very hot and about six o'clock in the evening when we finished working. The Kapo told us to bring all the equipment, clean it and bring it back where it belonged. The Kapo was a Polish guy. He wasn't too bad. He was understanding and patient. He gave us time to learn the hard work because we were not used to it.

At 6:00 we left the place. We marched to the barracks through the streets. The Poles looked at us. It took about a half hour. When we came to the main door, they counted us and the SS man walked with us and watched us. We got lost. Everyone was in a different barrack. When I came to my barrack, I was very tired. This was my first day, I had worked very hard and I wasn't used to it. I got into my bunk bed and fell asleep right away. I begged my neighbor who was next to me to wake me up when they came in with the bread and margarine. When he got his portion of bread he came and woke me up. I went there and I was the last one. The *Stueben Alteste* (manager) of our barrack was a German Jew. When I got my portion, he said that the next time I should come earlier because if I didn't come on time he would have to send my portion back to the kitchen. I thanked him and told him my name.

I went back to my bed and ate my bread and margarine. I was still hungry. I exchanged my cigarettes for more soup tomorrow. On these first days in the concentration camp I missed my parents very much. I was physically and mentally broken. I looked around the barracks to see if I saw a friend or somebody from the family. I went to the next barrack to see what was going on there. I was looking for people from Krakow or Dzialoszyce. I found a neighbor of mine. He lived in our building in Krakow. His name was Abraham Klachersky. He was in his forties and had been a very rich man. I was very happy to see him. He also hadn't wanted to remain the Krakow ghetto so he had gone to Schiowitz (Studgowiec?). He lived there with his family until the *Aussiedlung* (expulsion) took them away from their home. He had a wife and four children, two girls and two boys. He had lost his whole family because his children were still young. I then met a lot of people from Dzialoszyce. The son of the Dzialoszyce Rabbi was there. My father and I used to visit them in their home.

It was nine o'clock at night and we heard a whistle, which meant we had to go to bed. I left their barrack and went back to my barrack. I got undressed and went to the washroom to wash myself. I went back to my bunk and they turned off the lights.

In the middle of the night I got up because I couldn't sleep. I couldn't stop thinking about my parents and family. I was always very close to them especially to my dear father. I was his right hand. I always took him where he wanted to go. I was always ready for him even though I was very buy with my job. I would drop everything and go with my father. I couldn't believe that I would never see them again and I fell asleep.

The whistle blew at exactly six o'clock in the morning. I jumped from the bed and went to the washroom and got dressed. I was standing waiting for them to count us. I stayed in line for the hot, black coffee. I finished the coffee and I went to my group. I was standing and waiting for the Kapo to arrive. We were waiting for the German Commando to take us to work. About five minutes later the Kapo came with a paper in his hand. The SS soldier had his gun on his arm and he told us to stay in a line of four. We marched from the main door the same way we had done the day before, through the streets. We came to the same place were we had worked yesterday.

The second day was already much easier for me. It looked as though I would work like this for the rest of my life. I had to get used to it. There was a German engineer there. They called him *"Meister" [Master, equivalent to Dr.]* He was busy preparing the equipment for everybody for work. The bin was already opened. We all said "Guten Morgen" good morning to him and he answered with a smile back, good morning. The Kapo called us to come and get the equipment we needed for our job. Everyone should continue the work they had started yesterday, the same length and width and depth. Everyone took their equipment and started working at their place.

It wasn't such an easy job. The soil was hard and the sun was burning. The soil was very dry and hard. We had to first work the dry dirt and then throw it from the hole. We were not used to doing this job. I had to rest after a half hour of work. After five minutes I started to work again. My hands and legs started to hurt me. I did understand that each beginning is hard, but as you get used to it, it becomes easier. I thought to myself, after five weeks I will be an expert. In the situation that I'm in now I have to be an optimist in to stay alive. No matter how bad it will be in the war time, I must think about overcoming it to stay alive to tell the world about what the Germans did to the World and especially to the Jews.

I worked until lunchtime. At 12 o'clock we stopped working and stood in line for the soup. I was very hungry. Some people had complained about the soup they had given us yesterday because it had no taste, was very watery and only had tops from vegetables. We told him that the work was very hard and the soup was not enough. Today they brought us a much better soup with potatoes and carrots, a thicker soup. and after lunch we rested for about an hour.

We heard a whistle and we again started working. It was very hot and the soil was very dry. It wasn't easy to chop the soil, but we did what we could. We threw out the soil with the shovel. I made it deeper and deeper until it was four meters deep. It was very hard to throw out the soil from the hole. One of the workers couldn't do the norm. He said it was impossible. The German Master did understand that it takes time to get used to this work. The Kapo, the Polish guy started to get a little rough with us. He said we should work faster, but one of the workers was a doctor and he told us to stop working. He went to him and told him in excellent Polish that if he worked us too hard we would become slower and do much less work because it was a very hard job and we had only started. He said it would probably be five weeks for us to get accustomed to the job. He also talked to the German Master and explained to him that we are only human beings and not machines. We hoped to do better later. When we finished working, I had trouble straightening myself out because the work involved bending down for hours.

After we returned our equipment, we stood in line four abreast and started to march through the street of Plaszow. We came to the Gulag and Commandant Miller was in Barrack 18. As soon as I went in I went to the line for my 250 grams of bread, margarine and two cigarettes. This is what we had to live on for a whole day. We had a cup of black coffee in the morning and soup for lunch. I exchanged the cigarettes for a half portion of bread. It was a big help to me. I ate my portion and went to my bunk. I was very tired from the hard work on the job. For me it was like a bad dream. I couldn't believe that I could do such hard work.

I couldn't even fall asleep so I rested. After half an hour I got down from the bed and looked around the barrack. I went to the other barracks looking for friends or family. Maybe I would find somebody from my family or a friends. I met a young man from Krakow whose name was Chilek Winer. He was two years older than me. He knew my father very well because my father was at his sister's wedding. We started a friendship. He told me that he had been going to the Jagelonsky University where they only accepted Jewish people with special abilities. He had a scholarship from his high school years. He was a special person with a lot of knowledge. It was almost nine o'clock and I had to depart. I ran to my barrack straight to my *Koike* (bed) and fell asleep.

The next morning was Saturday, the Sabbath. After we were counted, and had gotten our black coffee, the Kapo told us that they were going to take us to be deloused, and that we would be able to take showers and get clean. There didn't have showers here yet because this camp was only two weeks old. They were going to take us to the Krakow ghetto for showering. Everyone was going to have a shower or bath and a haircut. They would cut off our hair completely as if we were in jail and they would disinfect our clothing and gave us fresh underwear. When I heard that we were going to the Krakow ghetto, I was very happy. I knew that my Uncle David and his family lived there. Because he was a professional, a shoemaker, he worked for the Germans and could remain in the ghetto. If he was still in the ghetto, maybe I could find them and get together with them. I hoped that my Aunt Zelda and the children were there.

The whole camp marched in line. There were more than a thousand people. We marched through the streets of Podgorze-Krakow to Kalvanska Street where the ghetto was located. This was the first time I had been back to Krakow since I moved to Dzialoszyce in 1940 with my whole family. The Poles were looking at us and how the German SS were guarding us with the rifles and ammunition. In my heart I was thinking, the Poles are free people, they live a normal life. We Jews had done no harm to anyone, but look at what they were doing to us now. Why? I had lost my whole family and they have made us slaves. Who knows what they are going to do to us? I said, dear God, why are we getting such a horrible life? And I said to myself that I have to try to hold on to faith to be alive. The war would not be forever, it will come to an end, and to Hitler and his helpers will also come to an end. His regime will fall and he will be killed, but when, how long? We young people hoped for a life so that we could tell the world what they did to us.

And so, thinking and marching, we came to the ghetto, which was located in Plac Zgodi and Lwowska (Zgodi Place and Lvovska Street?) by the main door entrance were the SS police. They started counting us then they let us in. When I came into the ghetto, I felt like at home. I knew I would find a lot of school friends and my father's friends. From far away I saw some people I knew but SS soldiers surrounded and watched us. We could not take one step. We came to the delousing place. It was a Mikva, a ritual bath. Jewish people went there all day Fridays to cleanse themselves before the Sabbath. It was located on Josefinska Street. There were a lot of showers. It could accommodate about three hundred people. We were standing in line in the street. They let us in about three hundred at a time. The rest were waiting outside. It took a whole day. When I came inside I was sent to have a hair cut. They took off all our hair and we now looked like slaves or inmates of a jail. I went to the shower. They gave us clean underwear and they took our clothing and disinfected it. When we finished, they put the whole group together and sent us outside.

We were waiting on the street and I saw signs written in Yiddish. Some stores were open, like shoemakers, carpenters or tailors, their signs were written in Yiddish. I was filled with wonder at the sight of this Yiddish ghetto. I saw many faces as they passed by and looked at us. It was forbidden to come to us because the SS guards were watching us. We couldn't move. While we were standing there they brought big cauldrons with soups. It was very hot and everybody had his pot. I got in line and the guy who was serving the soup gave me a full pot. The soup was very thick with tasty potatoes and pieces of meat. The Jewish Federation (Kehillah) had sent it to us from the ghetto. Since we left home I hadn't had such a good and tasty soup. I thought about being able to come here and remain in the ghetto. I would, at least, be like a Mensch, a person, not like a criminal with such a hard job every day with Miller at the Gulag camp. I was born here in Krakow and I saw my school friends walking free and living in a home. I thought, if I will be able to run away in the ghetto when they take us here to shower, I could help myself much better here between friends.

While I continued to stand there I looked for somebody I knew from my family or my mother's family like her older brother, Uncle David and Aunt Zelda and their children. We knew they had remained in the ghetto when we left Krakow. Their oldest son Zacharieh ran away to Lvov in Russia. Before we left in 1940, their younger son, sixteen-year-old Hershel contracted pneumonia and died because they didn't have enough medication. I went to the funeral with my father where I took my Tsitsi's (a fringed garment) that I was wearing and gave it to the Chevrah Kedusha (the burial officials) to put on him according to Jewish law. I will always remember that. My mother had a younger brother also named Hershel. His wife's name was Helen and they had two sons. One was called Moniek. I stood in the street for so many hours and looked and looked for someone I knew. I didn't see one person from my family.

I decided that at the first opportunity, I wanted to escape. I wanted to do it, but on this day it was impossible. There were too many police and many SS men guarding us. I thought about how I had to prepare myself to escape.

We were waiting till 4:00 in the evening till everyone was ready. Then the Kapo blew his whistle and we started to march to the front and main gate. We were to file in a line at the gate and they counted us again. We marched through the street from Podgorze and the Poles were looking at us until we came to our camp. They called this work camp "Miller Camp Gulag." At the gate they let us in. They didn't count us this time and each of us went to his barrack. I went to bed because I was very tired from staying outside so many hours. The sun was very strong. I was thinking about what was happening to the Jewish people. We had become real slaves as in Egypt but much worst. They wanted us to work hard with the cement and blocks to build them houses but they killed whole families. Now I was an orphan. I lost my father, my mother and sisters. They all died such a horrible death. I had seen with my own eyes what bad things they had done. They had killed great rabbis who had knowledge of the Torah, young people in the Yeshivot (schools of Jewish Studies) learning the Torah. The Bobower Rabbi, the Belzer Rabbi, the Radomsker Rabbi, day and night they were learning the Torah. In Krakow, doctors, lawyers, intelligent people. These people hadn't harmed anyone. Why did we Jews have to suffer so much? I said to myself, dear God why did you make me an orphan so young. I pray every day to you, even in the camp. I still used my Tefillin but I made sure no one saw me. I was suffering only because I was Jewish. I couldn't fall asleep. It was a question without an answer. At seven o'clock I jumped from the bed and went to the line for my portion of bread with margarine and two cigarettes.

I started to get used to this life. What else could I do? I tried to stay strong. I didn't lose hope. I was an optimist. I believed in God and in destiny. I had to fight for life everyday and every minute during this time of war. The war couldn't last forever. I had to believe in three things, first is hope, second to believe in God and third not to lose patience. How bad could it get for me? I ate the bread and margarine and drank cold water. I also exchanged the two cigarettes for a half portion of bread for breakfast with the black coffee.

I went out to another barrack to look for somebody who I might know. I talked to different people. It was almost nine o'clock when the man in charge of my barrack blew the whistle. I went to wash up and I went to sleep. My top bunk was near the window where I could get more air. I slept well, but I was dreaming about the Krakow ghetto. Escaping was on my mind and I had to prepare myself to run away when they took us to the delousing on Saturday, if I would have the chance.

At six o'clock in the morning I heard the whistle. I got up, washed and was in line for the counting and to get black coffee. After I finished the coffee, I went to my group. The Kapo told us to get in line. He had five SS men with him waiting for us to march out. After ten minutes, we marched from the camp through the streets. It was the same place where we had worked the day before. The German Master was there already. We all said good morning and he answered with a friendly good morning. They gave everybody their piecework for the day. The Kapo showed everybody the work they had to do that day. No one believed they could do the piecework because it was too much, an impossibility for one person.

All of us started working. I started shoveling the soil from the hole. The work was a little easier because we knew what they wanted from us. I worked with the shovel and the spade. I threw out the soil and made the hole deeper and deeper. I did learn the profession. We worked until lunchtime. The Kapo came to inspect our work. He went from one to the other checking if it was alright. At lunchtime they brought the soup. We stood in line and they gave us hot soup, kohlrabi with the tops from carrots. We got used to this food. For the whole week, we worked very hard digging out the soil.

On Saturday, they woke us up at six o'clock in the morning. The same thing happened. We stood in line, were counted and we got the hot black coffee. They told us that they were taking us to the Krakow ghetto for the delousing, taking showers, hair cut and to disinfect our clothes. They were going to build shower in our barracks where we could also be disinfected, but it was not finished yet. They took half of the people from the last time. We didn't know why they were only taking half, but I was one of those going.

We marched, about 800 people, to the ghetto through the streets. We had less than half the German police guarding us as last time. We came through Kalvanska's main street to the gate. They didn't count us. We didn't know why. We marched through the streets to the ghetto. and we came to Josefinska Street where they had the Mikveh, where every

Friday the religious people came to clean up before Shabbat. They let small groups of us in and the rest were waiting outside. When one group came out the second group went in. I was with the second group. We took showers, they gave us underwear and checked to see that everyone had their hair cut.

When I came out, I remained standing in line, looking around. I saw my cousin, Mirele, the daughter of my Uncle David, who was my mother's brother, across from me. When I saw her she looked at me and I looked at her but the German police were also standing and watching us. But today were less police than last time. I was thinking, what should I do? If I would be able to get out or away from here, I would have a place where to hide, but do you do it? One thing that was good was that I wasn't wearing the striped clothing from the camp, I was wearing my own clothes still from home. Even though they were watching us, I might be able to mix in with the people walking around. Before we left the camp they had warned us that if they caught anyone running away from the group, they would be shot. That was ringing in my ears. I was shivering. My body was like a machine going. I didn't know what to do. I had the opportunity but I was afraid and I came to the conclusion that it was not the right day, maybe next time.

By the next time I would have a plan. I had to prepare for my escape when we marched to the ghetto between the people on the street. I will get out, but I would have to be in the middle of the line to be the first on the left side. I would have to see the opportunity to mix in with the ghetto people. I would have to do it as soon as possible because I couldn't take the hard work at Miller's Gulag any longer. How much longer could I live on the soup made with carrots tops, beet tops and grass? How can anyone live on that? I would have to take chances. When we finished the shower at four o'clock in the evening, we marched out of the ghetto through the streets of Podgurze with the Poles looking at us again until we came to Miller's camp.

When we came in, the same things started again. I knew that this was the way of life here. I had to try to do a good job because when you do a good job they wanted you and they needed you. Then you had a chance at life. It was six o'clock in the evening and everybody went to his bunk because we were tired from standing so many hours outside in the sun, and it was so hot. I didn't want to fall asleep.

At seven o'clock a whistle blew. We had to stand in line for our 250 grams of bread, margarine and two cigarettes. I had a steady customer for the two cigarettes who gave me his half portion of bread. Sometimes the Kapo and the head of the barrack were together standing there. Some people were coming to them and whispering in their ear that they had gold or dollars to exchange for bread or soup. They made deals with them quietly so no one could hear them. We knew what was going on. I didn't have anything because I had to give up my belongings on the first night. When we came in they said if they found any money or gold, that person would be shot so I gave away everything. Some people had hidden money in different ways and they exchanged it for bread and soup.

When I ate my portion and the half, I went from our barrack to one of the others. I was still hoping I would find somebody I knew from Krakow because they were building new barracks and everyday new people were coming here. As I went from barrack to barrack, I found some people from Krakow. I found someone who went to the Talmud Torah School. We talked about our problems and he told me he had lost his whole family the day they took us away from our homes. He had lost everything, his home and all his belongings, but the main thing was the loss of his family. At nine o'clock I ran back to my barrack exactly as the whistle was blowing. I went to my bunk and fell asleep. I was so tired that I slept all night.

At six o'clock in the morning the whistle blew again. I jumped from by bunk, washed up and got dressed very fast. They counted us as we stood in line and then we got our black coffee. It was very hot. Meanwhile I was looking for my group. Now we were forty people. The SS soldier marched us from the camp through the same streets just like every other day.

We came to our job and said good morning to the Master. He also said a very friendly good morning. Everyone received equipment, and we started working. We made a wide and deep hole. They brought a tractor and then big trucks with large pipes size 100/100 made of cement. They also had a forklift. They unloaded the pipes from the trucks into the deep holes one by one. They fitted them one inside the next the entire length. This was for canalization. When one truck finished unloading it's pipes, another was waiting to be unloaded and the first truck went to bring more pipes. They unloaded and fit together six trucks of pipes into the hole and then it was 12 o' clock.

We had our lunch. This time it was a little better soup with some potatoes and kohlorabi. We had an hour for lunch. We rested and I now was starting to get used to the job and the hard work. After lunch they finished loading the big pipes. Then we had to cover them with the soil we had removed. The Master and the engineer looked at our work and we knew they were satisfied with the job. We worked until five o'clock but we couldn't finish, it was a long line of pipes. The Kapo and the Master were running around and checking that everything was done right. They were happy. At 5:00 we carried the equipment back to it place. We were standing in line and marched back to the camp though the streets like everyday. Today they were good to us. They were not hollering at us.

This camp was only two months old and we didn't see any shootings or killings. There were no beatings but we were very hungry all the time. The work was very hard and I made up my mind that the next time we went to the ghetto for the delousing, I was going to try to escape from the group. I knew that my Uncle David lived in the ghetto with his family because I had seen my thirteen-year-old cousin, Mirele, passing by. She saw me and recognized me. I knew she must have been with her parents. At that time I couldn't do anything because they were guarding us and she could not come and talk to me either. So the first step that I would have I would be on the street. This is very important. So I prepared myself for this act. I didn't say anything to anyone about what I was intending to do, but in my heart, I was very afraid that they shouldn't catch me. I knew I would be risking my life. We worked all week at the same place and I waited for the Saturday to go to the ghetto.

And I decided to wait the third time. When we went back to the ghetto Saturday, they took us to the delousing. They only brought half the people that day because they were building new barracks and they had to work on Saturday. It was a rest day for us. We finished in the ghetto around two o'clock. They took us and marched us through the street with the Poles watching us and waving their hands as if they felt sorry for us.

When we came back to the camp, they took us to the kitchen and we got our soup. After an hour it was our rest time. They took us to work inside the camp because it was getting bigger. They had us building more barracks that they were preparing for more people. On Sunday we rested. I started walking around through the barracks to try to find somebody from my family or a friend from school.

Monday morning was like every other Monday. We waited for our work group. The Kapo and the two SS men walked with us to work. It was the same place and the same work. We started again a new job, the same work. We had to dig again, shovel the soil the same length, take out the dirt and put it aside. We now knew the job much better and we prepared canalization 500 meters in length and three meters deep. It was very hard to dig out and to throw the dirt out of the hole but they didn't bother us because they knew we were doing a good job.

The doctor who was working with us begged the Kapo to allow us to go to the grocery store to buy bread and some food. The Kapo went to the German Engineer for permission to allow us to go. He agreed to let us go because the government had not yet decreed that we couldn't. Two of the people in our group went to the grocery store. They bought two breads and asked to have each cut into ten pieces so twenty people got a piece of bread and I was among those people. I had another piece of bread with the lunch soup and it was very good. The next day another two people went to the grocery story to buy two loaves of bread. Again they cut it into ten pieces. They also bought a small salami and cut it into 20 pieces.

I didn't have any money but my neighbor offered to lend it to me so I happily borrowed money from him. I didn't know when I would be able to pay him back. When it was my turn to go to the grocery store I did the same thing but I bought a small salami and hid it. I carried it on me and nobody knew, not even my co-workers I brought it back with me to the camp and sold it for double the price. I already had a little money because there were a lot of people with money but they couldn't go outside so I started a little business in the camp. The Kapo profited from it as soon as it started to grow. Every day when we shopped at the store we brought something for the Kapo so he wouldn't say anything. We started to bring in different groceries to the camp and we made some money. We started to eat better.

I did this all week until Saturday. In the morning after the roll call and the coffee the Kapo and only four SS men took us to Krakow. Usually there were ten or twelve German police. It now looked as though they trusted us a little more. There were only nine hundred people. Before there were four times as many. They had started to build delousing facilities at the camp with showers and toilets. They wouldn't be bringing us to the ghetto for delousing anymore. The Kapo took 250 people to take showers and changed thier underwear. It only took 50 minutes for them to finish. They didn't cut our hair because they had done it two weeks ago.

I was in the second group out of four for the shower. I took a shower and they gave me new underwear. They deloused my clothing. I joined my group in the street. I was standing in the middle of the line. I thought I would have a chance to just slip away from the group. My heart was beating very fast because I had decided to run away. I was afraid that when they finished building the showers at camp I wouldn't have any other opportunity to run away.

I looked around, then I saw that the people on the street started to run. I saw a lot of people coming from all over. I saw the Jewish police dressed in their police suits, marching in the street. I recognized the commandant of the Jewish police marching in front. His name was Shapiro and he was a religious Jew. They remained standing not far from where we were standing. More and more people were coming because they couldn't pass on the street. Everyone was standing around to find out what the police were doing. A big crowd surrounded us. Our group were mixed up with the people. There was more coming because they couldn't go further. I was standing, like I said, the first one next to the people. I decided to run away now because this was my best chance. I told the fellow standing next to me that I had seen my cousin in the crowd and I wanted to talk to him and he should take my place in line so they wouldn't notice that I was missing. He said OK and my heart was beating hard. I got away from my line as far as I could mix in with the crowd. It only took a half hour and the whole thing was finished. The commandant and the police marched away from the place and I was a free man in the ghetto.

Where do I go now? How can I find out where my Uncle David lives? They used to live on 3 Lwowska Street on the second floor. I knew where it was and I went there to try to find him. I walked through the streets of the ghetto and I was scared to death. I told myself not to worry. Here you are among Jews. It is much better than in the camp where I had to work so hard with no food. I found Lwowska Street 3 where I thought it should be located. I found the building and went in. Their apartment still had their name on the door, David Schumacher. I knocked on the door and my Aunt Zelda opened the door. When she saw me she started to kiss me. We both started to cry. Her daughter, Mirele, the little boy ? and the youngest son, Moishele were very happy to see me.

It was exactly dinnertime. My Uncle David was at work and my aunt invited me to dinner. My uncle worked at a German factory making new shoes for the Army. Their oldest son, Zacharieh was in Russia and their younger son, Hershel, had died of pneumonia about two years ago. My family and I were at his funeral. I ate dinner as if I were at home. I enjoyed it very much. I was very happy to be there. Since I had left home three months ago, I hadn't had a meal like this. When I finished dinner, my aunt asked me about my father, mother, the children, Aunt Chava and her family. Then I told her the whole story about what happened in Dzialoszyce, and our life in the synagogue and how Aunt Chava lived there with us with her family. I explained how they had taken us from our house. I told her how they had taken my father from the lineup and they shot him with 1600 people. They sent the rest of the family away in railroad wagons and who know where? I told her I was alone and they had taken me to Camp Miller where it is impossible to live because of the hard work and the lack of food. I said I had to live on 250 grams of bread with margarine and soup made of carrot and beet tops and that I was constantly hungry. It was very hard to stay alive. Every Saturday they brought us to Krakow for showering and delousing. When I knew they were almost finished with building the showers in camp and they would no longer bring us to Krakow, I knew I wouldn't have any chance to get out of there, so I decided to run away. I knew that my Uncle David had a working card that allowed him to remain in the Ghetto. About a month ago when they brought us here for delousing, I was standing in line and I saw Mirele passing by, but I couldn't do anything. I did understand that, thank God, you were still living here.

I told them I wanted to live in the ghetto. I would try to find a job, because without a job I could not stay in the ghetto. I started to cry and my aunt started to cry about the loss of my whole family. I didn't have anybody. My aunt said she didn't know what they were going to do to the people in the ghetto. Sometimes they would go from street to street cleaning out the people. They had put about five thousand people in trucks and no one ever knew where they had been taken. They never came back. Most of them were people without identity cards.

I asked about my aunt's brother, Refuel. He was a custom lady's tailor. He was very rich before the war. She told me that he and his family lived in the ghetto not far away from here. He worked for the tailor's union. I asked my aunt to allow me to lay down on the sofa because I was very tired and nervous. When I heard they picked up people in the streets who didn't have identity cards, I was afraid. I fell asleep on the sofa until my Uncle David came from his job. When I opened my eyes, I felt so good, like a free man. I had forgotten that I was in the ghetto. When my uncle saw me he started to cry and we kissed each other. He asked about my parents and Aunt Chava. I told him the whole story about my father being killed in Dzialoszyce with 1600 people. I told him I didn't know what had happened to the people they had put on wagons in the railroad. I told him how they had separated the young people from the old and the women and children. They listened to my story and everyone was crying.

Meanwhile I found out that I can't stay with them permanently in the apartment where they lived, they had put in two other families totaling eleven people. It was a two-bedroom apartment with a big kitchen. Everyone used the kitchen and my uncle told me that living in the ghetto for two and one half years was difficult. The Germans instituted new laws every few months. They would go from house to house and those people without identity cards were taken away in trucks. They were young and old and they never came back. Mostly, they took the intellectuals such as doctors, lawyers and architects. They just disappeared. There was always hunger in the ghetto. Many people were dying from hunger. Some Jewish men worked with the Gestapo.

They gave them the addresses of the illegal people in the ghetto. They came in the middle of the night and picked them up.

While I was there the five days I saw the tightness of three families living together in one apartment.

I decided I would go to the Jewish Center about myself to try to find a place to sleep, get something to eat and find work. I told my uncle what I was planning. He told me I could stay with them until I found a job and he would try to help me. This was my first day in the ghetto and I had supper with them. It was bread, butter, a piece of cheese and a glass of tea. Everybody was eating the same thing for supper. It was almost like being at home. About 10 o'clock in the evening my aunt made a bed for me on the floor. I slept very well because I was very tired from such a hectic day. I wasn't hungry for the first time in three months.

At six o'clock in the morning I got up and it was still dark outside. I waited until my Uncle David got up because he had to be at work at eight o'clock. My aunt was up but the children were still sleeping. Aunt Zelda prepared breakfast of fresh bread, butter and farmer cheese. We also had coffee with milk and sugar. I was thrilled. After breakfast, I thanked my aunt and uncle for the beautiful day they had given me. I said goodbye to them and left. Before I left I asked for directions to the Jewish Center.

I went to the Center that was in the ghetto. I couldn't be without an identity card with a signature from an employer. There were a lot of other people there. I saw some people I knew, and they also were waiting for a job. I sat for a while waiting to be called. When I was called into the office a Jewish woman asked me about my situation and what kind of work I could do. I told her I was born in Krakow on Krakowska 28 and that I didn't have a family any longer and that they had taken my whole family from Dzialoszyce three and a half months ago. I told her I was looking for a job and a place to sleep and food. I didn't say anything about my family here in the ghetto. She gave me a card and that I should go to that address. I was told to come back the next morning at exactly eight o'clock to the same place and she would have a job for me. I told her I had been a carpenter before the war, but she told me the job was not permanent. The German military wanted people to do different kinds of work. Everyday they came with jeeps to get the people who were waiting outside the Jewish Center for different kinds of work. I asked her where I should go to sleep and eat.

She sent me to a big building with very sad looking people inside. It was for poor single people. The second floor was for women. I went to the building's office and gave a lady my card. She gave me my bed number. It was a big room with bunk beds on both sides and also in the middle like in Camp Gulag where I had come from. I wanted a top bed but they were taken so I was in the middle. There were about 60 people in the room. They gave me a small drawer for my belongings, but I didn't have anything. The number on the drawer was the same as on my bed. The mattress was a long sack filled with thin straw. I had a pillow made of the same straw and a blanket. People were coming and going. They had given me a slip of paper to get soup and 300 grams of bread with margarine and two cigarettes.

The First Day in a Place for Poor Guests

First I went to get the soup. I had my dish and it was much better soup then we got in camp. I found a potato. It was a thick soup. I ate my soup with the bread and margarine. It was delicious. I was happy. I told myself that I had made a good decision. So far I was a free man. There was no one standing over my head with a gun. The two cigarettes I put away. I knew I would find somebody to exchange my cigarettes for more food. I started to look around maybe to find somebody I knew. There were people my age there, but most people were at work. I went out to the street because I had the card from the Jewish Center that said that I worked for the German authorities on a day by day basis.

I walked to different places because I wasn't afraid. I walked from one street to the other looking for someone I might know. And so the day past and it was already five o'clock and people started coming back from work. I looked at everybody in the face, maybe I'll find friends, or also family. As night fell I went back for my portion of bread, margarine and the two cigarettes. Also, there was black coffee. I ate it because I was always hungry. I went to sleep very early.

I got up at six o'clock and went to the washroom. I got my black coffee with saccharine and at eight o'clock I was at the Jewish Center. I waited in line until a German came and took us to work, but it wasn't always the same job. This first day they took me and three more people in a big truck to the woods to help cut trees. It was very hard work and another truck arrived to the same place with more Jewish people. We were altogether ten men. We had to remove the trees. They had a forklift to load trees onto the trucks, but we had to do all the hard work. The whole time we were working, hard, they were hollering at us and hitting us. Not every day was the same. Some days they took me to clean the streets in the city outside the ghetto. That was a light job. Everyday while I was waiting to be taken for work I saw new faces.

When I finished working at five o'clock they would sign my identity card stating I had worked that day and that I was legal to live in the ghetto. After work they brought me back to the place where I was living. They gave me good soup with potatoes and vegetables. It tasted much better than the soup in the Gulag. They gave me more bread, but I was always hungry. There was not enough food. Sometimes I went to my Aunt Zelda and Uncle David's house. It was like my home, but at nine o'clock at night I had to go back home.

In the ghetto all the food was rationed. They only allowed one person so much food. If a person had money he could buy food on the black market. After nine in the evening anybody who was on the streets of the ghetto was put in jail. There where I lived, I met David Schwarzbaum who had remained in the ghetto. He was the guy who lived with us in the Shul in Dzialoszyce and had made so much trouble for my family and me. I tried not to have any business with him. He slept far away from me.

One night the Gestapo and the Jewish police came in and woke us up. It was one o'clock in the morning and everyone had to jump out of his bed. We had to stay in line while they searched our bed and under the bed for weapons. They made a mess of the room. Everybody had to show his identity card that we were legal and working. They picked up five people and took them out but they didn't find anything. We were scared but they left. The next day we heard that the underground in the ghetto and the partisans outside and also the Polish underground had been preparing an uprising. One guy from the group was a spy for the Germans. They caught the whole group and their leaders. They found weapons that were connected to the Polish underground. They had sold the weapons to the Jewish people in the ghetto. That was the biggest pulldown to the uprising against the Germans in the ghetto Krakow. The Gestapo, the SS and the Jewish police had a list of the top men and the members of the group and their addresses. On this night, when the Gestapo and SS were also in our place, they took five hundred people to Monte Lupi in the middle of the night to the woods and killed all of them. The intelligentsia, doctors, lawyers, teachers, fathers, mothers of small children were included. They confiscated the weapons. This happened because of a Jew named Spic. He worked with the Gestapo. Someone from the group worked with Mr. Spic and that's how they learned about the uprising. This happened between Rosh Hashanah and Yom Kippur.

When I went to work the next day I saw people running and crying. I understood what had happened in the ghetto. When I came back from work I found out what really had happened. Those people they had picked up never came back. When I came back from work, I saw unhappy faces in the big hallway. They said there was supposed to have been an uprising, nobody knew from that group, even their wives didn't know what was going on. Nobody expected that someone from the group worked with Mr. Spic. It was supposed to be a big uprising together with the Polish underground outside of the ghetto who had been ready to help us. They had prepared a lot of weapons. The day before the uprising, the Germans went to their houses and confiscated all the weapons, they killed the whole group along with the Polish underground. Some were sent to Auschwitz and Treblinka.

So everyday I went to work in a different place. I prayed to God that I would be able to come back alive. Everyday I had to have a signature from work so I could stay in the ghetto. I went to the Jewish Center to ask what I should do about Rosh Hashanah. While I was waiting for them to call me, I saw a young man about my age. I started to talk to him. I asked him different questions and he told me he was from Krakow. He was also doing day labor. I asked him what I should do about Rosh Hashanah. He told me to tell them the day before the holiday that I didn't feel good and wanted to see a doctor. He said to say that my chest hurt or that I had a sore throat. When they called me into the office, I told them the story about not feeling well. The Jewish woman just looked at me and smiled. She understood that Rosh Hashanah was in two days. She gave me a slip to see the doctor.

The Jewish hospital had moved from Skawinska Street to the ghetto. So that day I didn't go to work. I went straight to the hospital. When I got there, I showed them my slip from the Jewish Center. They sent me to Doctor Schwartzman and Doctor Imerglick. They asked me where I lived and worked and what was wrong with me. They took my temperature, but I didn't have a temperature. I told the doctor that my chest hurt when I coughed and my head hurt me. Also, I had a sore throat and felt weak. He lifted my shirt and told me to breath. He looked at my eyes and ears. After he had checked me, he didn't say anything. He told me to stay home for three days and stay in bed. I was to drink a lot of tea with lemon and honey. He gave me aspirin to take three times a day. He said to drink a lot of water and as much soup as I could get. I asked him for a slip in order to get the soup. He gave me the slip and told me to come back in four days. He also wrote the work exemption for three sick days on my identity card. I left the doctor very satisfied. They were Jewish doctors and I remembered them from before the war because we had lived on the same street as the hospital. I was so happy I didn't have to work on Rosh Hashanah. Maybe I would be able to go to the Shul.

I went back to my place, went to the office and gave them the slip from the doctor. I told them I was sick and needed more soup. I showed it to the manager of the place. I went to my bunk. I took the aspirin and fell asleep. I didn't take anymore because I didn't need them. At lunchtime I went down and got my hot soup. When I went back for more soup because I had a doctor's order for more, they gave it to me. After I rested a few hours and with no one watching me, I went outside to look for a synagogue to pray. When I found out where the synagogue was located, I returned to bed so the manager would see that I wasn't faking.

The next day I stayed in bed but I went to the man who was taking care of us and showed him the slip from the doctor that said I needed more water, more tea, more soup. I got coffee instead of the tea and more water. At lunchtime he gave me a double portion of soup but no more bread, just my usual portion. I stayed in bed almost all day long. This was Erev Rosh Hashana and I was planning to go to the synagogue in the evening. I took a shower but I didn't change my clothing. I didn't have anything else to wear.

I went to the synagogue alone. When I went into the Shul, the Cantor was in his white shirt and white *Kitel* (robes). He was standing on the stage and the Choir surrounded him. They were dressed for the holiday. They had just started to pray. The German police, Jewish police and the Gestapo were standing at the entrance. I had to show them my identity card and they let me go into the synagogue. I was amazed, the synagogue was full, packed with Jews wearing Telleisim (Tallises) and dressed in the holiday garb. It was a conservative Temple because both men and women were praying together. It was very strange for me, but I was very happy. The Cantor was dressed in a long sleeve white *Kitel* and the choir were young people. I could hear everyone's voice.

I was sitting in the back not far from the door. I looked around and saw people still coming into the synagogue. I saw so many people I knew. I recognized them from before the war. Some were my father's good friends. I had come to Shul in my everyday clothes, that was all I had, but everybody came in beautiful suits and had nice dresses. Nobody criticized me.

I really wanted to see my aunt and uncle Shumacher but it was too late to wish them the greeting, L'Shana Tova after the prayers so, I promised myself that I go there tomorrow. The service was very beautiful and I enjoyed it very much. I approached some friends of my father. They were looking at my work clothing. I saw the pity in their eyes, but they were very friendly.

I went back home. There they gave me a small Challah and a little honey and my portion of bread with margarine. I said the Kiddush prayer near my bed, and I started to cry. I saw before my eyes my father, my mother, my sisters. Just a year ago we were all together. Now I was alone, had lost everybody, everything; my home, my freedom. In the wartime, there were days when we didn't have enough food, but we were together. My father was still singing and he composed new songs. He made people happy. Now I didn't know what was going to happen to me or to the people in the ghetto. I went to sleep. I knew that tomorrow I didn't have to go to work. I am sick. It is Rosh Hashanah. I will go to the synagogue. After Shul I will go to my uncle's and his family to wish that we should have a Healthy and Happy New Year and an end to this terrible war. I wanted to be with my only family all day and to feel the holiday taste of our home. I wanted to taste good food and not be hungry.

When I got up in the morning, I drank my black coffee and I went to the synagogue. It was packed with Jewish people. I believe the Cantor's name was Mr. Griner. He also worked for the Jewish police and was a captain. I had seen him marching. He was praying and singing beautifully. He had a fine tenor voice and he sang with great feeling. It was a pleasure to listen to him. The German and Jewish police were at the door. They checked everyone's identity card. I was sitting in almost the same place as the day before. All of a sudden everyone stood up and remained standing. I didn't know what had happened. Then I saw Commandant Shapiro with his son-in-law, his wife and his daughter and two small children coming inside at nine o'clock. They had started services at eight o'clock. It was a big synagogue that had an 800-seat capacity. It was packed full of people. A lot of Jewish police came together and sat with the commandant. When they sat down, everybody else sat down, too. It looked very dramatic.

I counted six Sefer-Torah scrolls when they opened the Ark. We prayed without any disturbances. Everybody understood every word the Cantor said. When the prayers were finished the Jewish police made a line on both sides so the commandant and his family could walk out through the middle aisle. Everybody in the synagogue stood up until he and his family went outside. Then everybody went home.

Instead of going back to my place, I went to my uncle's on Lvov Street to wish them a Happy New Year. I knocked on the door. When they opened the door I went in and kissed my Aunt Zelda and the children. My Uncle David was not home from the Shul. He had been praying someplace else. I talked to the children while my aunt prepared lunch. After awhile my uncle came home. We greeted each other with kisses and wished each other a Happy New Year. He was very happy to see me and invited me for lunch. Now I was even happier. I knew I was going to eat a home-made lunch today. The table was prepared with wine and cholent and one big beautiful challah. Uncle David made the Kiddush and we drank the wine. He and I then went to wash our hands. He made a Motzi on the challah that Aunt Zelda had baked herself. He sliced the challah and everyone had a piece. It was so fresh and good. I could have eaten the whole thing. She had gefilte fish that she had made herself. We then had noodles with chicken soup, beans and a small piece of beef. I didn't expect that it would be such a good lunch. We had an apple compote (stew) for dessert. Everything was delicious. We ended with a glass of tea. I hadn't had such a good home cooked meal in so long. Afterwards we sang zmirot (songs) from the holiday very quietly. We finished with a blessing, that God had given us food to eat.

My uncle and his wife were not very religious but they kept a Kosher home. They always kept the Jewish traditions. He didn't wear a beard and she didn't wear a wig. I came from a religious home where my father at one time was studying to become a rabbi. When he was blind he became a *Badchen,* an Emcee. On the Shabbat he wore special clothing and a large hat that the Hassidim wore called a *Sztraml*. He had a long brown beard.

While I was talking to my uncle he asked me about my life up until then and what had happened to my family. I told him that my brother and sister went to Russia and we had packages from my brother when we lived in Dzialoszyce but we hadn't heard from my sister. He asked what our life was like in Dzialoszyce. I told him the whole story about how we lived at the Shul, and Aunt Chava was there with her daughter and her five-year-old grandson. Also, her daughter in law and her three children were there. After five month's, her daughter in law and her three children disappeared. We don't know what happened to them. I also told him about all our other problems. I told him the story about my father and mother and the children and how they had taken all the Jewish people from their houses to the market place. My whole family was there except my sister Chana. She disappeared before we even got to the market place on the first day. First they took my father and put him on a wagon with many other people to the Jewish cemetery and shot them. Then they took us to the railroad and divided us into groups. They separated the men from the woman and children. The young people were also separated and that is when I lost all my family.

So there we were, sitting and telling the horrible stories and crying. My Uncle David said, "what is going to be with us here? Hitler made his plans to kill all the Jews. Do you think he will let us live?" I said, "We are all in God's hands." My uncle started to question God. I told my uncle that I didn't have the answers to these questions that we should ask the remaining rabbis but I did not want to question against God. We shouldn't fight. The main thing was that we were all together for the evening.

I went with my uncle to the large synagogue he went to for the Minchah service. The Cantor and a choir were there and the synagogue was packed with people. The Cantor prayed the Maariv (evening) service. It was really very beautiful so much so that I forgot I was in the ghetto. After the prayers, I wanted to go back to my place but my uncle invited me for Kiddush and supper so I went back to his house. We had wine, fish and challah. Afterwards we had coffee and cake. I enjoyed myself as if I were at home. I couldn't sleep there because there were three families in this one apartment and I had to be back in my own place. I said goodbye to everybody and thanked my Aunt Zelda and Uncle David for inviting me to have such a nice holiday. I then went home.

When I got home, I got my portion of challah with margarine and honey and put it away for the next day. I wasn't hungry and went right to sleep. The next day I took a shower and went to the synagogue. They started the prayers at exactly eight o'clock in the morning. At nine o'clock the commandant and his family came in and again everybody in the Shul stood up. Five policemen came in with him. They went up to the first row. He had all his medals on his police uniform and he was praying in a Tallis. When they read the Torah, he was given an "Aliya", the honor of coming up on the Bima to say the prayer over the Torah. He had a very nice voice and said the prayers very loudly. They also gave his son in law the same honor. Outside there were five Jewish policemen who were standing at the entrance. They checked everyone's identity card to make sure everyone had a signature stating that they had a job. This was the second day of Rosh Hashanah and when I came into the synagogue, my Uncle David was already seated. I took a seat next to him. He liked to pray here.

When we finished praying, he again invited me to his home for lunch and Kiddush. I was very happy. When we got there, there was a beautiful tablecloth on the table. Everything was prepared with the challah and wine. It was so beautiful. Aunt Zelda's brother, his wife and children were there. I greeted them with a Happy New Year, L'Shana Tova. I had known them before and they were very happy to see me. He was one of the best tailors of better women's clothing. He had a workshop with ten workers. He was tall and handsome and his wife was beautiful. We all sat at the table. Uncle David made Kiddush over the wine that they had made themselves. There were two large challahs that my aunt had baked herself. We washed our hands and say the Motzi (blessing over bread). The food was delicious. My aunt had made the delicious noodles for the soup that had beef. Also the desert was tasty. I was very satisfied. It was just like home. I had been going around hungry for four months. Now I was in paradise.

We all sang the prayers that I remember my father sang. We finished with the Benchen (after meal prayers.) I said the Brachat questions and they answered. We finished the prayers and afterwards we had tea and a piece of cake. The apartment had two bedrooms and a large kitchen. The one family living there had one child. The other family also had one child. They were from Germany and sitting in the kitchen with us. There were two single beds and another long bed. We were sitting on the beds around the table and we started talking politics.

Rafuel was a very intelligent man. He used to come to our house before the war. He would come over on the Sabbath and talk politics with my father. He was very pessimistic. He saw everything black. He thought that the biggest mistake the rich Jewish people made was that they could have saved their lives by leaving the country and did not. They even could have gone to Russia. But the rich Jews were too busy with their businesses. They could have gone to America or South America. The poor people could have gone to Russia. But no one believed that the world would let Hitler kill all the Jews when he came to power. The young people should run to the woods. But if you had a family with small children it was a different story. He told us that when he first went to Lemberg, in Russia he had an apartment for his family. When he came back to get them it was too late. He couldn't return because of the war with Russia. He told me I should try to run away from the ghetto to the woods. Perhaps I could get Aryan identity papers as a Pole because in the end all the people in the ghetto would die.

I told him about how I had lost my whole family and that they had shot my father and I didn't know about the rest. I didn't know whether they were alive or dead. I told him how I had come to the ghetto. I thought to myself that Rafuel was one hundred percent right. It had been a pleasure talking with him because he was such a smart man. But now what should I do? Where could I go without any money? He and his family then said goodbye and they left. After I finished talking to my uncle, he fell asleep on the sofa. I thanked my aunt for the beautiful time she had given me with such good food.

It was time for evening prayers and I went from their home to the synagogue. I walked to the Shul and on the way I was thinking about what Rafuel had advised me to do. When I came to the synagogue, it was only half full. There were German and Jewish policemen at the entrance. We prayed the evening prayers and I went back to where I was living.

When I got back I went for my bread and margarine and I kept it until morning because I was not hungry. I went to bed but I couldn't sleep. I was still thinking about Rafuel's plan. I was very excited about the holiday and being with my family and being able to eat such good food. I enjoyed it very much. I had heard a good Cantor with his choir. I was lying there for hours before I finally fell asleep.

I got up at six o'clock in the morning, got my coffee and bread with margarine and ate the bread from yesterday. I went to work because my vacation had come to an end. I didn't have a steady job so everyday they took me to a different place. I was waiting for work when a truck with two SS men came along and took me and another four Jews to a warehouse with groceries and canned goods. There were imported goods like sardines, tuna, salmon and other items. They lifted the goods with a forklift on to trucks. Five us straightened out the boxes. We filled the trucks and they took them to the railroad. We loaded them onto wagons. They were very heavy. It was very hard work. They were hollering at us to work faster. All day long we lifted the wooden boxes onto railroad cars. We finished at five o'clock and we didn't even have lunch. I came home very tired and hungry.

    When I got back to my place, I heard that there might be another uprising being planned. So in the middle of the night the German Gestapo came in looking for people without jobs. They were also looking for weapons. They were afraid of an uprising. I had made friends with a young guy. He had just come in and was around my age. He told me his name was Henek Korngold and he was born in Krakow. Every night we would get together after work. Sometimes it would be at my bunk and sometimes at his place. We became good friends. We would talk about our problems. He had gone to the Jewish Center as I had done to get work.

    In the morning we would stand together and sometimes we worked together in the same place. He told me how he had lost his family. His parents had also left Krakow for a small town near Kielce, I think Stasnow, because they didn't want to live in the ghetto. They had lived there for two years until the "Aussiedlung" the expulsion. He told me that his parents had been very wealthy and had a factory producing soft leather in a small town near Krakow. They had 18 Polish workers. During wartime they were in contact with their manager, a Polish man. His father had left the whole factory with merchandise and lots of money even gold and diamonds with him. They had made a contract with a lawyer that during the war; he was to send them money to live on. If they were in danger, he was to help the parents and the family. He was to take them to a farm and hide them until the end of the war and all the money and half of the factory would belong to him. They were partners. They signed the contract with a lawyer. I noticed that he always had money. They sent him more through a Polish man. He was an engineer who worked for the electric company, that's what he told me. He said that if the engineer will see that something was going to happen in the ghetto, he would get him out and take him to the man's house. He then would hide him. It was an interesting story and everyday we became friendlier. We would talk together about everything, and I saw that he was very honest and fine boy. I hoped everything he had told me was true.

In the morning we went together and waited for work. He told me his parents were not Chasidim but very religious in a traditional way. He had a religious upbringing similar to mine. He was learning at the same Talmud Torah School as I attended. He was one class ahead of me because he was a year older.

Every night after work, we met together at one of our bunks. We had so much in common. I told him my story and who my father was. He said he remembered him well. My father sang at his sister's wedding. We discussed our situation and I told him that I had an uncle and his family in the ghetto and that I was at their house for Rosh Hashanah on both days. I told them that while I was there I had forgotten I was in a ghetto. I had so much food like my mother used to make. It was delicious and the second day of Rosh Hashanah they had invited me. My aunt's brother, Rafuel was there with his wife and children. He had been a very rich man and we discussed politics. I told him that the main thing that came out was our situation in the Krakow ghetto, Hitler's plan is to kill all the Jews, we don't know when they will come here, but they had taken away all the Jews from all over Poland, except for the ghetto.

Our situation here is in danger. We don't know which day they will come and take us to Auschwitz or Treblinka. It will be too late to save our lives. He told me that there was nothing he could do. He had a wife and three children. He had plenty of money but where could he go to save his life and the lives of his wife and children. He told me that I was a young single man with no responsibilities. He said to run away from the ghetto to the woods or to the partisans. He thought maybe I could get papers but to get them as soon a possible. Why wait in the ghetto for death?

I didn't propose running away from the ghetto together because I had just started to get to know him, but it was on my mind since I had talked with Rafuel. I felt he was right. Perhaps Henek would talk to the Polish man about me. It was about a week since we had started to talk about our past and how we had lost everything. I knew that in five days it would be Yom Kippur and I didn't want to go to work on that day. I thought about what I should do now. I figured that on the day before Yom Kippur maybe something would happen.

We went together again to work and they took us into the woods to cut trees. We were standing and holding the trees while they were cutting them. When the tree fell we moved away and it fell near us. I said, "Oi!

The tree hit me!" I sat down and complained that my leg hurt. Henek complained about the same thing. They moved us to the side and I was very scared if they would take us back to the ghetto or if they would shoot us. Who knew what was on their minds? We were taking chances by not being able to work. I told the SS man that I thought I would be ready to work again in one or two days, that it was a small hit. I got up and started walking slowly. They then gave us easier work to do. They were good to us and I went back to work and finished the job. They were also cooperating with us.

When we went home I told the SS man that my foot hurt me and I wanted to go see the doctor. Henek told the SS man the same thing. The SS man gave us a piece of paper saying we had been hurt at work and it was okay to see the doctor. Henek and I went immediately to the emergency room at the hospital. Two doctors came in and we gave them the slip of paper. They asked us what had happened. The doctor looked at my foot and I said, "Oi, it hurts me here." He told me to go home and put some ice on it. He told me to stay home for at least four or five days. He gave me aspirin to take three times a day. The doctor told Henek that he didn't see any swelling and he gave him the same thing he had given me. It was late. The next day was Erev Yom Kippur and I was home in bed. I asked for ice and they gave me some. We didn't have to go to work. It was a pleasure.

After coffee, I dressed and told Henek that today is the day before Yom Kippur. At night was Kol-Nidre. I wanted to go to my family and wish them a "gmar chatima Tovah" a good verdict. I went to my aunt and uncle's and when I went in my Uncle David was at work. I took 18 zloty and I made *Kapureh Shlagen,* a religious thing that means "Chai", to life. My aunt invited me for lunch. I had a very nice lunch and thanked her. I also kissed the children. I went back to my home and prepared myself for synagogue, for the Kol Nidre prayer. I shaved and showered and went with my friend, Henek Korngold, to synagogue.

When we came to the synagogue, there were bright lights hitting the building. At the door there were SS soldiers, Gestapo and the Jewish police. They checked everyone's identity cards to make sure they were still working. It was six thirty in the evening and the Jews were wearing white shirts (Kitel) and Tallaisim (Tallises) with their Machzorim (prayer books) in their hands. The Shammes (custodian) from the synagogue announced when Commandant Shapiro came in with his family surrounded by Jewish police. Everybody stood up and they again went to their seats in the front. They put on their Talleisim and prayed together with everyone. I missed my father, mother, sisters and brother. I was still by myself. It was only a year ago that I was with my family for Yom Kippur praying at the Rabbi's house in Dzialoszyce. Tears were running down my face. I asked Henek, who was sitting next to me, "Why aren't our parents here with us?" He gave a hard breath and said the same thing. The Cantor began to sing with his quiet, sweet tenor voice. He said the Kol-Nidre, the most important prayer on Yom Kippur. The choir sang with him so beautifully. It hurt my heart. He finished Musaf, the second prayer. We were then supposed to come back in two hours. On the way home, Henek and I talked about the next day. Thank God we had a doctor's signature saying we could stay home in bed for a few days.

On Yom Kippur we both fasted. We went back to the synagogue for the Mincha prayer. There was a break in the service. Commandant Shapiro and his family were sitting at their places. I thought that I would like to talk to him because he was a friend of my father's before the war. I went to the policeman who was guarding him and I asked him if I could have a few words with the commandant that he was a good friend of my father's. He told me to go up to him but to make it fast. There were still about fifteen minutes left in the break. I told my friend, Henek, I was going to wish the commandant a Happy Holiday (Ketivah vi-Chatima Tova), which means a very good verdict and a Happy New Year. I went up to the commandant and wished him a Happy New Year. I told him my name was Kalmen Frydman and my father's name was Symcha Frydman, the Badchen, from Krakow. He didn't let me finish and asked whether I was the blind Badchen's son. I answered him and he asked me what had happened to my family. I told him that we had lived in Dzialoszyce for two years but now I was alone. I had nobody. He looked at me with a somber face. He told me that my father was a genius, a tremendous head. He said that he was in love with my father's songs and that they were beautiful. He remembered how he had known the whole Torah by heart. He told me they had been very good friends. I was astounded and started to cry. He said, "come to see me after the holiday anytime. Just tell them you want to see me and I will try to help you as much as I can". I thanked him very much and told him I would see him shortly. I wished him and his family all the best and a Happy New Year and went back to my place. I told Henek that my father and Commandant Shapiro were very good friends before the war and he wanted me to come to this office after the holiday. He wanted to talk to me.

Henek and I were sitting together when the synagogue started to fill up. The second Cantor, Mr Griner, started to pray the Mincha. Hundreds of people came in for the last prayer, *Neeleh*. There were no seats for them so they were standing inside and outside the Shul. Then the

Cantor prayed the last prayer. Everyone was praying and crying from their hearts. Believe me, we had something to pray to God about. We all knew where we were and what was expected of us. We didn't know if any of us would still be there next year. Everyone was very emotional and prayed to God that the war would end soon and that they would find their families. A lot of people were standing near me and crying. The Cantor and his choir were praying with such feeling. It was enough to break your heart. They said with a loud voice, "Please God, enough killing, hanging and beatings. Why, because we are Jews? Where is the real truth? Why aren't they punished?"

Ninety percent of the Jews in Poland were very religious. There were many Rabbis, rich people, Chasidim. There were hundreds of thousands with young men studying the Torah, small children. They had never sinned. Why did it happen to us? Were the Christian, Islamic or Buddhist people better than us? That was what the people in the synagogue were thinking and asking. Maybe now the door to heaven would open and the war would come to an end. I heard the Shofar signal the Tekiah! Tekiah! (the shofar blasts that end the service). When the prayers were finished, they announced that we should wait for the commandant and the police to leave. Everybody stood up and waited while Commandant Shapiro and his family left the synagogue. After they left everybody started to walk out. The men went upstairs to pray. When we were finished my friend, Henek and I went home. We were very emotional and had wet eyes.

On the way home we talked about our life in the ghetto. Henek told me that he had received a letter from the Polish man who was managing his father's leather factory. He was preparing a place for him to hide and he should see to it as soon as possible because they were going to take the Jews from the ghetto in Krakow. No one would remain in the ghetto. They were going to send them to Auschwitz, Treblinka or some other extermination camp. The man said that he wanted to do what he has promised Henek's father. He wanted to keep his word. He said that his neighbor worked for Governor Hans Frank's office and he told him about the ghetto, but he didn't know the exact date.

I listened to what Henek told me. He asked me if I wanted to go with him. He would write a letter and ask about me. He would tell them that I am a good family friend and that we were like brothers, that we both had lost our whole families. He wanted to ask him if he would allow me to go with him so we could be together. But first he wanted to know if I was willing to go into hiding with him with this Polack. In my heart, I was very happy that he had asked me to go with him but I didn't want to show him that I was **very** anxious to go with him. I told him that he should give me a few days to think it over and I will give him my answer then.

We went back to our place and they gave us our portion of bread and margarine. I was very hungry because I had been fasting all day. Henek also had fasted all day. I had my portion of bread from the day before. I ate both of them and then went to bed.

The next day I still had off from work. I went to see my Aunt Zelda and stayed there all day long until my Uncle David came home from work. I had lunch with them and they invited me for supper. We had bread, butter, white cheese and coffee. I talked to my aunt and uncle about talking to Commandant Shapiro. I told them about Henek's proposal for me to go into hiding with him. I would have a chance to run away from the ghetto and hide on a farm. I didn't know whether the Polish manager of Henek's father's factory would accept me. My uncle told me that I couldn't trust the Poles. He had heard that the Poles took in Jews for the money and once they had the money they would turn them over to the Gestapo. But not all the Poles were like that but you had to have lots of luck to find and an honest Polish man. My aunt said that I should take a chance because here in the ghetto, good things will not come for the Jews. It started to get dark, and I said goodbye to my aunt and uncle and went back to my place.

I was not hungry. I had a wonderful day with my family and their children. When I arrived home my friend, Henek, was eating his bread and margarine. I took my portion for the next day. He told me he had worked today. It was a bad day, working in a ditch for a Polish man. He had given him a lot of trouble. He beat him up and Henek was crying from the bitter day. He said to me "you see what kind of a life we have when you work every day at different jobs with different people. We don't have a steady job in one place. As long as I have money I can buy food," he told me, "but everyday we were playing with our lives. We didn't know who is going to be our boss. We've heard about the many Jews, went to work and never came back. No one knows what happened to them and nobody cares. Even if the family wanted to find out, they couldn't get an answer from anyone, not even the Jewish Center knew.

If we don't have a job with the proper signature, they could come at night and take us away to the death camps." Henek told me the Polish man was very good to him and was still sending him as much money as he wanted. He had sent a letter to him telling him that the Germans wanted to get rid of the ghetto. They were picking up young people for work but the rest would be sent to Auschwitz or Treblinka. They wanted to liquidate the ghetto and that I should come to them. That meant that he wanted to help me and hide me and keep the promise the man had made to this father. Henek thought it was safe for me to go with him. He told me he liked me very much. He said that the war wouldn't last forever, it had to come to an end some day. The problem was that no one knew when. At least we would have a chance to be hidden and a chance to be alive after the war. He told me that his father had left a big fortune that was to be used to hide the whole family and now he wanted me to go with him.

Because he had heard that this would be the last *Aussiedlung* (expulsion) of the Jews in the ghetto, he wanted to leave Krakow. He knew that no one would remain and I was the only one left from my whole family. I knew he meant business. He said that he had no choice but to look for a man to take us from the ghetto. He had the address and would take off his armband and go there. We talked about our situation, what we should do. I asked him, "how do you know that he will take me in, that we will be together?" So my friend said," I will be open and clearly ask him. I will tell him the whole story, that we are holding on to each other like true brothers., and I wish that you should allow him to be with me. He will tell me yes or no. I will tell him how old you are and that you also lost your whole family. Then later we will know what we have to do." We then went to sleep.

In the morning, we were both standing near the Jewish Center and we saw the Germans coming with autos and trucks. They took people to work. We went together as well as two other Jews. They took us to a military place. It was a shop with wooden boxes, large and small. A man with a forklift loaded the boxes full of accessories [spare parts?] and we had to straighten the boxes so that they could fit more boxes in. They were very heavy. They took us to the railroad station and a man with a forklift unloaded the trucks into the wagons [railroad cars?] there. We had to work very hard in both places. There were only four people and when we finished we again went back and brought more boxes to the railroad station. At lunchtime we rested for an hour. They gave us half a bread and margarine. At five o'clock, they took us back to the ghetto.

When we went home they gave us soup and our portion of bread with margarine. After we finished eating, I was very tired from the hard work. I turned to my friend and said, "where you will go, I will go, I want to be together with you". He was very happy to hear that from me, that I accepted to go with him. He went out and came back half an hour later and told me that he had sent off a letter to the Polish man that he had written five days ago. Maybe by tomorrow or the day after tomorrow we would have an answer. He told me he had a Polish man here, an engineer architect who worked nights here and lived near the

Polish factory manager. He was the guy who brought him the money and who took the letter. He was getting paid very well, but he is a very nice man and very reliable. He had been working with him since they had left Krakow. Henek told me that the Polish manager was very good to them during the war. His father received money and letters from his manager when they lived in the small city.

Every morning we waited at the Jewish Center and waited to be picked up for work. The German SS came and took six Jews plus us. We jumped on the truck and they took us to a factory that manufactured pipes from cement. They made different sizes small and large. Other things made at the factory with cement used for insulation. We loaded trucks with this material until it was full. There were three big trucks and on each truck they put two Jews. My friend and I were on the middle truck. We had moved together to fill up the truck with merchandise with a forklift operator helping us. It was hard work. At 12 o'clock we had an hour for lunch. We rested. I ate my portion of bread that I had saved from the day before. We didn't get anything to eat this day.

My friend and I started to discuss what we were going to do now. He told me that you could get anything in the ghetto if you had money and connections. There were some Jews still "doing business". They had an "arrangement" with some of the German police at the gate to the ghetto. For money one or two of the SS men could be bribed to let you get out of the ghetto as if you were going to work. My friend had a connection with the Broker. I him that I didn't have any money. When I had been taken to the Miller work camp in July I had to give up everything I possessed. They had told everyone they would be shot if money, gold or diamonds were found. He told me not to worry, that he had enough money for both of us. We should just live through the war and be free, then we would talk about money and how much we spent. After lunchtime, we went back on the truck to finish up the loading. They took us to a military place and we unloaded all three trucks. The eight of us had to help put together the goods on the floor. They worked with a forklift. It was a very hard day's work. When we went home I was tired. I got my daily soup with the bread and margarine.

It was the day before the holiday of Sukkot but we didn't see any Sukkahs. In the evening we went to the synagogue to pray, and in the synagogue, the lights were very bright. We were sitting in the Shul when the Cantor started the service. Outside at the gate there were Gestapo checking everyone. It was a pleasure to hear the Cantor praying. It awakened my heart. When the service was finished, we went home.

It was Sunday morning and we didn't have to work on Sunday. We went to the Shul at nine thirty. Commandant Shapiro and his family came to the Shul and sat at their places up front. As usual, the Jewish police surrounded him. The prayers were so beautiful and the Cantor made Kiddish over wine. Prayers were finished at 12:30 p.m. and we went home.

I told Henek that I was going to my aunt and uncle's to wish them a Happy Holiday. I thought I should take my friend with me but I was a guest myself and they lived in a small apartment with three families. Also food was very scarce so I didn't say anything and left.

When my Uncle David saw me he was very happy and smiling. There were silver candleholders on the table with a beautiful tablecloth. The challah was covered with a Sabbath holiday cover. There was a bottle of wine on a tray. Everything was so holy. The home cooking smelled so good. I greeted my aunt and the children with kisses and they invited me to lunch. The first serving was carp. It was so good with the fresh challah. We had chicken noodle soup and beans. There was beef just like we used to have at home. We had a small portion of apples for desert. It was delicious.

My uncle was not very religious. He was very traditional. But on the Sabbath and the holidays, he was very holy and they kept Kosher. It was almost the same as before the war. After we finished the meal, we sat and talked about what had happened to my whole family and about my brother and sister who left for Russia. I still didn't know what had happened to them. We also talked about Ruria, Aunt Chava's daughter-in-law who had disappeared with her three children. Her husband, Abraham, was in Russia. We discussed my life in the ghetto, when Rafuel and his family came to visit. He discussed the situation today and what might happen tomorrow. He was a very intelligent man and he again said that anyone who could should leave the ghetto and as soon as possible. He had heard that the Germans were preparing another ouszidlung at the Krakow ghetto. Our days were numbered.

Rafuel had done work for an SS general. He had made costumes for his wife and they told him he should prepare to either hide or run away. They were going to send some of the young people to labor camps to do hard labor. Most of the professionals would be sent to Plaszow and the rest would be sent to either Auschwitz or Treblinka. He had a shop with twelve people working for him and he worked for the officers making clothes for their wives. The dresses he made were beautiful. They told him to beware. I told him my story about how my friend wanted to take me with him and escape. Rafuel told me that I had nothing to lose. He said that he only hoped that the Polish manager was a responsible man. He said that if he were in my place he would do it. I said goodbye to him and the family and thanked them for the good meal and the good time they had given me. That was the first day of Sukkoth (Tabernael), and I went back to my place.

I told my friend, Henek, what my family had advised me about the coming ouszidlung from the Krakow ghetto, but they didn't have a date. It could take a week or six months. They didn't know. We both then went to the synagogue for the Mincha prayers. The Cantor finished the prayers beautifully and we walked back to our place. I saved my portion of bread and margarine for the next day so that I could take it with me to work in the morning.

We got up at six thirty and had our hot black coffee. We went to wait for them to pick us up for work. They took eight of us to the woods to cut trees. We worked very hard cutting the trees into different sizes. Some were short, long or medium size. It was a very hard day. When we finished the job, the German officer arranged for us to work there again the next day.

When we returned to the same workplace the next day, we had to help load the cut trees on to trucks. They had a forklift, but we had to straighten out the trees on the truck by hand. They were very heavy. They took us to the military carpentry shop where they cut them to make furniture or boxes. It was the eighth day of Sukkoth holiday and we finished the job at five o'clock. Then they took us home.

When we came home Henek went to look for his mail. He came back with a letter from his father's factory manager. His name was Maciek Jaroslowsky. Henek read the letter to me. It said that I could go with him but I would have to bring money. My heart was pounding inside me. In the letter he didn't ask Henek for money because his father had settled this with him a long time ago. The letter asked for the date that we would be leaving the ghetto because he wanted to prepare to have us taken to the farm of his parents.

Henek started to work on preparing for us to leave the ghetto. He had connections and I didn't ask too many questions. Henek's father had taken care of giving the Polish manager money and was sure of him. In the meantime Henek and I had to go to work everyday. We went to the synagogue again and the prayers from the Cantor led me to believe in God and that He wanted us to live. Rafuel's words were on my mind. I remembered that he said I should run away and hide if I wanted to live. But I wondered if I could trust the Polish manager. I asked Henek about the manager's character and whether he could be trusted. He said that before the war he was very trust worthy and we shouldn't be scared. We didn't have anything to lose. If we remained in the ghetto, would we be safer? He said we had to take a chance. I told Henek that I wanted to change the subject. It reminded me of the time I went with my father to prayers and I held his hand because of his blindness, I was his right hand. Remembering this, I started to cry. I was an orphan with no mother or father and tomorrow is a holiday, but I had to go to work. They had us cleaning the streets in the main city. The job wasn't too hard.

When we went back to our place, we ate out soup and bread. We went to the synagogue for the Kafot dancing with the Torah. When the Cantor started the prayer, Commandant Shapiro and his son-in-law came in and everyone stood up. When they finished the prayer, they started the Kafot, dancing with the Torah. They removed all the Torahs from the Aron Shrank and the Gaba. The board of directors was in charge of it and they gave it to the old member of the synagogue who went there all year round. The Cantor was singing and the people were dancing with the Torah. Mr. Shapiro and his son-in-law were given a Kufa. It reminded me of home, and how happy I had been. They finished the prayers and we went home happy but sorrowful that our parents weren't with us.

As Henek and I walked home, I mentioned the letter from the Polish manager and that he had accepted me to go along. The only problem was that I didn't have any money. They had taken everything from me so where was I going to get any money? Henek told me not to worry about the money. He said that he would tell the Polish man that I had money and that I was trust worthy. I will write him another letter letting him know that he is responsible for my money and that he will give it to him. I hoped that the manager would keep his word and his promise to Henek's father.

I hoped that he would treat us well and give us a nice hiding place and that we wouldn't be hungry. Henek again told me not to worry about money. He said he was going to look around for the right connections and find out how to get out of the ghetto in a legal way. We needed papers saying we were both going to work outside the ghetto. After a week Henek paid the German guard. We could only go when this particular guard was on duty at the main entrance. A Yiddish Mekler and a Jewish policeman settled it. They were all in on our plan. We only had to pick the right day and the right hour.

While we waited, we went to work everyday so no one would get suspicious. Henek let the Polish manager know that we were ready. It depended on the day the German guard who he had paid was on duty at the gate. It would be on a Tuesday at eight o'clock. Henek wrote the Polish manager and told him the day and hour we were leaving the ghetto. Henek knew where he lived because many times he went there with his father. I didn't even ask for the name of the street or the number of the house. When all the arrangements were finished, the next letter that came from the Polish manager wrote that he was ready for us. He said he and his wife were preparing a nice welcome with good food and in friendship. We were happy and we started to prepare for our voyage.

It was after Sukkoth and it was getting cold but not freezing. After work the next day, I went to my Uncle David's to say goodbye to them. I told him the name of the Polish man was Maciek Jaroslowsky but I didn't know the address and I didn't want to ask Henek. Aunt Zelda made a package for me with underwear, a sweater, a warm hat and two shirts with long sleeves. My uncle gave me 500 zloty and I said goodbye to them. We kissed and we all cried. They wished me good luck. My aunt said that she would pray to God that the Pole would keep his word, and I left.

Meantime, every morning Henek and I went to work as usual. We were impatient and a little nervous while we waited for the day that we would get away from the ghetto. It was a lucky hour when the day came. It was a Tuesday at eight o'clock in the morning after Sukkoth. Hench and I went to the main gate and we both had our identity cards. We had two written papers to show to the guard. When he gave the papers back to us we walked out of the ghetto. We removed the Zion patches and the armband from our clothes.

We walked to the streetcar and bought two tickets from the conductor. We showed him the address. My heart was beating. I was very scared, but I thought to myself that I shouldn't be scared anymore. We were free men and I started to smile a little. I thought that everybody was looking at me. We changed streetcars and I didn't know where I was because it was deep inside the city. Before the war, I had never been to this section. We took our places in the streetcar and then came to our stop. Henek started to walk down a street named Flonenska. I was very nervous and took a deep breath. I told Henek that we shouldn't stay too long on the street that we should find our building as quickly as possible.

When we found the building my heart was beating. I tried to be quiet and strong. We walked up the steps to the apartment where the manager lived. It was a big building where many families lived. It was after nine o'clock and had taken us more than an hour to get there. We looked around but didn't see anyone and no one saw us. Henek knocked on one of the doors. A man answered and greeted us with a smile and told us to come inside. He introduced himself as Maciek Jaroslowsky. He was tall and handsome. He locked the door behind us and held his finger to his mouth and told us to be quiet. He asked us if anyone had seen us walking to his building. His wife, Marysia, was tall and beautiful. She greeted us with a smile and said good morning. She told us they had two children who were in school.

Maciek talked in a low voice and he begged us to talk very quietly because he said that the walls had ears. We had to understand that.

Marysia told us we could take a shower. I felt better after their warm greeting and relaxed. Henek and I took a hot shower. It was a pleasure. We got dressed and Marysia invited us into the dining room for breakfast. We sat at the table. On the plate was fresh bread from a bakery. On the other plate were butter and farmer cheese and a dish with sour cream from the farm. They already had breakfast because it was now after ten in the morning. We were always so hungry we ate all the bread and food on the plate. She brought in more fresh bread and two cups of coffee with sugar.

After breakfast we went into a room with a sofa where two people could sleep. There was a place to hang clothes and a table with four chairs. Maciek came in and sat down to talk with us. He asked Henek what had happen to his parents, and how it had happened. He wanted to know all about the ouszidlung. He asked where they had been taken and what had happened to them. Henek told him he didn't know where they had taken his parents. Henek reminded him about the contract he had made with his father that was signed by a lawyer. He was supposed to undertake finding the whole family and hiding them so they would have a chance at life. After the war, the factory would belong to him. He showed the contract to Henek and they both looked it over.

After that he started to ask me questions in a friendly manner. He asked me my name, where I was from and my age. He wanted to know about my parents, too. I answered his every question. He asked about life in the ghetto. He told us very quietly that there were five German families living in his building. The husbands were in the army and two worked for the Gestapo. The others were in the SS Waffen. They wore uniforms. My heart started to jump.

Maciek said we could stay at his house that night. In the morning he would take us to his parent's farm. They lived near Krakow not too far from where we were. They had a big house with a garden and his father had prepared a hiding place for us. It was going to be comfortable and no one would know we were living there. We would have enough food from the farm and never go hungry. He said there was plenty milk, butter, chickens and all kind of fruit. He said very seriously that he would be in a lot of trouble if the people in the building found out what he was planning. We were both very happy when he told us he was going to take us to the farm.

Henek took out a stack of dollars and told Maciek that his friend Kalman Schulmacher said to give it to him. The money was for food for as long as we stayed at the farm. Maciek took the money and smiled. He looked very happy. He put the money in his pocket and thanked Henek. He told us not to worry that he was going to take us to his father's farm.

His mother and father were two old people with no children living with them. They would provide food and had five workers with them who were very nice people. They had already prepared a warm bed for us both. You can sleep and live there and no one will see you. He also said they had cows that gave milk and not to worry about food. He said that he would come from time to time to make sure we were treated well. He told us we would have everything we needed until the war ended. He said we would then be free men again and we would all be happy together. We sat and talked together. We were very happy with all these friendly promised we had just received. His wife came in with a plate of fruit containing apples, pears and large plums. She said the fruit was from the farm. The atmosphere was terrific. It was friendly and warm.

There was a knock on the door. I started to shiver. His wife went to the door. It was the next-door neighbor asking if she wanted to go shopping. She told the neighbor that she didn't want to go because she was waiting for her children to come home from school and she was preparing food for them.

They both left Henek and I alone so we could rest. Henek said that he had told me not to worry that the people were honest and nice. I told him I was very happy and I hoped it would be like this all the time and that they would keep their promise. We fell asleep.

At two o'clock we heard knocking on our door. When we opened the door Marysia invited us to lunch. The table was covered with a beautiful tablecloth and had fresh bread that she had baked herself. She then came in with a large dish with hot soup. She filled our dishes with the soup. The soup was very thick with meat. Everybody was sitting at the table, they said, "smacznego", which means good appetite, and we said, "dziekuje", which means thank you very much.

We all started to eat. We knew that the food was not kosher but we had to get used to it. If we waited for kosher food in the ghetto, we would have starved to death. Most of the time in the ghetto I was hungry. I started to eat the soup and bread. The food was very good. Henek and I were very happy. I thought, "Thank God. We are in good hands. They are treating us very well. They looked as though they were very nice and elegant people and meant what they said."

When we finished eating the soup, Marysia brought in a plate with meat. I took a piece and looked at Henek and smiled. I took another piece of meat. It was the most meat I had eaten since I left home. It tasted so good. She then brought in a plate with homemade cake with chocolate. We had tea and lemon with the cake. After the meal we thanked her and told her what a good cook she was and that everything tasted delicious. Afterward I sat and read the Polish newspaper while Marysia and Maciek cleaned the dishes from the table. Maciek asked us if we were still hungry. We smiled and said that after such a good meal with so much food, we couldn't possibly be hungry. We told him his friendliness couldn't be better and thanked him again for everything. He thanked us for the good feelings toward his wife and him.

Maciek told us he and his wife were going shopping. He asked us not to discuss anything in front of his children when they came home from school. We were to tell the children that we were good friends who had come for a visit. He left and soon after the children came home. They opened the door with their own key. They came into our room without knocking because they didn't know we were there. They were surprised to see us and asked us in Polish who we were and what we were doing there. We told them we were good friend of their parents and we had just come for a visit and their parents had gone shopping.

The boy looked about 12 years old and the girl was about ten years old. She again asked why we had come for a visit. Henek told her that he had business with her father and that they had been good friends for a long time. They left and closed the door. When the parents came back from shopping, Marysia prepared lunch for the children. We didn't know what they told the children about us. We felt like lucky people to be there and we thought it would be wonderful if they treated us this way all the time.

We didn't see a telephone. We thought perhaps it was in the bedroom and could look for it in the morning. Henek didn't want to look through the house because they might find us in the bedroom since we wouldn't be able to hear the front door opening. We sat talking quietly because we knew that the walls had ears. Henek asked me what I thought about the treatment we had received. He was surprised at how much food they had during this time of war. I told him we should thank God for the treatment we had received and hoped that it would continue until the end of the war.

I felt that Maciek should take us to the farm at night. Why did he want to wait until morning? Henek said that first he had to let his parents know we were coming. We could hide here for now and anyway no one was supposed to be on the street after nine o'clock. It would cause too much suspicion. We talked about being out of the ghetto and not in German hands. I thanked Henek for his good heart in helping me even though I didn't have any money. I was enjoying my freedom. It was now seven o'clock at night. All the rooms had Venetian blinds on the windows. The blinds were closed so none of the neighbors could see that there were strange people in the apartment. Then they called us into the dining room for supper.

On the table was fresh white bread cut in slices with butter and farmer cheese with fresh sour cream. The whole family was sitting with us at the table when Marysia brought in a platter of fresh small red radishes and green onions. I was shivering and scared that one of the neighbors would knock on the door while we were sitting at the table. Maciek told his children that if anyone knocked on the door, they should not answer because he didn't want to be disturbed while eating. We ate a good supper. It was very quiet in the room. We only heard the sounds coming from our mouths. Maciek told us to eat as much as we wanted because of our miserable existence in the ghetto. Then someone knocked on the door and no one answered. They just went away. Maciek had his finger on his mouth. We then had coffee with fresh baked cake. It was very tasty. When we finished we thanked them very quietly for the food and for being so friendly toward us. We thanked everyone for the wonderful treatment all day long. We then said good night, "dobranoc."

When Henek and I went back to our room we smiled at each other and said that these people were nice and honest. We both hoped that when we went to the farm, the people there were going to be as friendly as here and we would be treated the same. It would be wonderful if they only gave us half as much as we had just received until the end of the war. While sitting and talking Hench told me that the beginning of 1940 he and his father came to Maciek's apartment. That is when his father discussed his plans for his family with Maciek and his wife in case the Jews from Krakow were ever sent to a concentration camp. Maciek was to find a hiding place for his whole family. In return, Hench's father would turn over the business and the merchandise would belong to Maciek. They had gone to a lawyer and both signed a contract

Marysia knocked on the door and came in to make the bed. It was a couch that opened up into a bed for two people. It was very clean and she gave us two pillows and a cover. It was very cold outside and cold in the apartment. When we turned off the light Henek and I still talked for a while I said a night prayer and then went to sleep

In the middle of the night at about one or two in the morning I heard noises coming from the other room and noticed that the light was on. I woke Henek and told him that there were people talking outside. We didn't know what was going on. We thought they might be preparing to take us to the farm, but we knew there was a nine o'clock curfew. We pretended not to hear anything then there was a knock on our door. Three Gestapo in uniforms came in shouting in loud voices, "Stehe sofort auz, right away." We still pretended to be asleep. They again told us to get up and fast. We opened our eyes and both jumped out of bed. They told us, "Faster, faster." We got dressed very fast. They didn't ask us question or allow us to wash our faces or anything. We noticed Maciek and Marysia standing in the kitchen watching them take us. They didn't say a word. Until now I don't know if it was them or their neighbors who told the Gestapo. I know that no one saw us coming in. They didn't say a word to the Gestapo or us.

We took our baggage with us and left the house with the three Gestapo behind us. They pushed us into a car that was parked near the entrance to the building. They didn't say a word. I was shivering and nervous. I knew that they were going to finish us up. Now I thought that Maciek and Marysia were finished with us and wouldn't have any more problems. After about twelve minutes, they came to a place with a sign that said, "Monte Lupi Criminal." They put us in separate rooms for the rest of the night. I couldn't sleep. I was lying on the floor and wondering what was going to happen to me.

At eight o'clock in the morning they took us to an office and asked for our credentials. They called me in first and I showed them my identity card saying that I went to work every day while in the ghetto. They wanted to know how I had gotten from the ghetto to Maciek Jaroslowsky's? I told them my story and how I had just met them and they were going to give me a steady job. I said that I had met the other man at their house. They brought me back to my cell and I went to sleep. In about an hour they called me back to the office where there were five Gestapo sitting around me. They wanted to know my whole biography and how I had gotten to this place. I told them that I wanted a steady job and was taken here thinking they had a job for me.

They took me and another guy I had met there to a tender. There I met Henek and three other men. There was also one woman. It was nine o'clock in the morning and one Gestapo was sitting with us. The journey took three quarters of an hour. Soon they stopped the car and opened the door. They took us to a big hill. I saw below hundred of men, women and children. Uniformed SS, Gestapo and Ukrainians surrounded the people. There was a big hole, and I heard yelling, "Ziehdich aus, ziehdich aus, get undressed, get undressed, aber schnell, aber schnell, but fast, but fast." The Ukrainians were wearing uniforms but they were different. They were getting their guns set up to fire. The people got undressed. We heard yelling and crying from the women and children. What I saw there was unbelievable. These people were all Jews that the Poles had found for the Germans who had been hiding. They had called the Gestapo and for each Jews they had received one kilo of sugar. Also there were some Jewish people who worked for them. The people got undressed and the guards made them run into the deep hole. When they were shot they into the deep hole.

It was very cold outside and there was a cold wind blowing. The SS were watching and giving orders. The Ukrainians did the shooting and the bodies fell into the big hole. The hole was very deep and I saw this with my own eyes. I said my last prayer, "Vide." Then Henek and I started to get undressed. When we were undressed we started to move backward because they were bringing more and more Jews so we decided that we wanted to be the last ones. We knew we weren't going to get out of this alive. I thought maybe I would have a chance to run away and hide or maybe they would stop, because I wanted to live.

Henek and I were naked and it was very cold. We were so nervous and shivering from the cold. I saw with my own eyes a slaughterhouse with men, women and children standing by the hundreds waiting to be shot. I hear the children crying. I saw a mother holding her eight-month old baby. They shot the mother but not the child. She fell into the hole but her baby was still alive. I didn't have any more tears to shed. I prayed to God to please help us and to punish the murderers.

The Gestapo brought more and more Jews and Henek and I continued to move backwards so we would be the last ones shot. We wanted to stay alive. We didn't want to die. We wanted to have a life. I cannot forget this picture. It stays with me always. The Ukrainians were wild. They were hollering and did the shooting. We heard voice telling the people to get undressed faster and faster. They wanted the people to stand at the corner of the deep hole so that when they were shot they would fall and slide down into the hole. Some bodies didn't fall down so the Ukrainians took their Uzis and pushed them down. This was going on for more than two hours. I think it was almost 12 o'clock and the killing continued.

They brought in more Jews. Suddenly, we saw horses coming from far away. On one of the horses there was an SS officer. He jumped from his horse and told the Ukrainians to stop. Everything stopped and he looked at the naked people. There were about five hundred people. Over his microphone he asked for ten young men to come to where he was standing. Henek and I and another eight Jews, still naked, went up to him. He looked at us and sent two older men back. He told us to get dressed fast.

He picked out two young Jews and brought them to us. We were looking for clothes to fit us since we couldn't find our own clothing. Henek and I were the first to get dressed. The clothes didn't fit, but I didn't care. I wondered why the officer had asked us to get dressed. What was the point? I found a pair of shoes but they didn't fit. I wore them anyway. When all the ten young Jews were dressed, he told us to wait. We found out later that he was the commandant from Plaszow.

He told the SS and Ukrainians to finish up the job and shoot the rest of the people.

They killed the rest of the people. They didn't leave one person alive. The commandant told us to cover them with soil that they had removed from the hole. They gave us shovels and equipment. While I was standing near the hole I saw that many of the people were still alive. One young girl stretched her hand out and asked to be taken out of the hole. I heard screaming and the Hebrew words, "Shema Israel." I still remember the sight and asked myself why God had forgotten us Jews. There was no one to help us.

They made us work faster and faster. It took us more than three hours to replace the soil in the hole and cover all the dead. We worked fast and hard. They watched us the whole time until we finished. After we finished, they let us rest for a few minutes. A little tender came and took us to the kitchen of the new Plaszow Arbeitslager, which they were building. The SS commandant who had picked out the ten young Jews was named Goeth. We were given soup to eat. After we finished they gave us bread.

They said that this was once a Jewish cemetery. We saw the stones with the Hebrew names. They had made a path out of the stones to walk on. I almost fainted when I saw that. We noticed new barracks. They were not finished. They had many Poles working there. Also there were Jewish carpenters and plumbers working with them. The Poles told us that the commandant's name was Amon Goeth. We didn't know what they were going to do with us once we finished eating. We thought they were going to kill us because there was no place for us to sleep. We waited for our destiny. They had given us an hour for lunch.

All the building material was on the ground. The same tender came and took us ten Jews. We were scared. They drove for about a half hour when I saw the Krakow ghetto. My heart felt a little easier. I couldn't believe I was still alive. It was unbelievable. It was so terrible what they did and how they had killed men, women and children. They didn't shoot the little children; they just threw them in the deep hole alive.

When we got to the gate of the ghetto, we jumped from the tender and they turned us over to the German guards. They told us to go to the Jewish Center for new identity cards because the old one was left at the jail. I told Henek that it was a miracle from God that we were still alive that we shouldn't lose our faith. We shouldn't be depressed but we had to fight. We went back to our place; we called it "Hotel Wendzy Poza Wieniedzy, or Poor Hotel Without Money." I told Henek that I wanted to talk to Commandant Shapiro because I had spoken to him on Rosh Hashanah. He had told me that after the holiday I should go to see him at his office in the police station and say to the guard that he told me to come. He said that he would try to help me. He might be able to get me a good steady job. I told Henek that I would speak to the commandant about getting him a steady job, too.

The next morning I went to the Jewish police where I saw the sign that said "Jewish Police Command. Two policemen were standing outside the entrance and I told them that Commandant told me to go there to see him. They asked me my name. I told my name and that my father was Symcha Frydman and he was the Badchen at weddings. One of the policemen was from Krakow and he told me he had known my father. He asked about my father. Tears came to my eyes and I told him that he had been shot in Dzialoszyce. The policeman went inside to the commandant office. He came back a few minutes later and said the commandant couldn't see me today because he was busy all day. I was told to come back in the morning around nine o'clock.

I went back to my place and then went to the Jewish Center and told them what had happened to me and that they had kept my card at the jail. I told them I was afraid to walk in the streets without a card. They asked me questions and gave me a new card, but I had to have a job. Henek also went to the Jewish Center to get another card so we could walk outside the ghetto.

The next day Henek went to the place where they picked us up for work. At a quarter to nine I went to the police station to see Commandant Shapiro. They told me to come back the next day because he was too busy to see me. I was afraid to walk in the streets so I went to the hospital and asked to see a doctor because my leg was hurting me. I told the doctor that I had been cutting trees and one hit my leg and it was hard for me to walk. The doctor looked at my leg and said it was a little swollen. He gave me aspirin to take three times a day and told me to rest for three day. I didn't have to go to work. He also gave me powder to soak my leg. The doctor signed my paper and sent me home. I was very happy. At lunchtime I went for the soup, but the soup was just cooked water and a small piece of potato. I was very hungry and decided to go see my Aunt Zelda and the whole family.

When I got there, my Uncle David was at work and my aunt asked me what had happened. She remembered that I had left the ghetto with my friend and I was supposed to be living with a Polish family on a farm. Aunt Zelda asked, "What happened?" I told her everything that happened to Henek and me, and that now I was very hungry. She told me that the family already had lunch and she was saving my uncle's for his return from work. She said to sit at the table and she gave me my uncle's food. She prepared something else for him. After that I wasn't hungry any more.

I told my aunt that it was a miracle that I had come away alive from my experience. When my uncle came home at five thirty he was surprised to see me and asked me what had happened. He thanked God that I was there. Aunt Zelda prepared food for him. When he finished eating he asked me to tell him what had happened to both Henek and me. I told my uncle how we had taken the streetcar to the Polish family's apartment and how they were so glad to see us. They had treated us kindly and gave us three meals. We were very happy to be at their apartment. They were supposed to take us to the Polish man's parent's farm the next day. It was not far from Krakow. They had promised us good things and said we would be safe. Then in the middle of the night three Gestapo woke us up and told us to get dressed. They took us by car to the Monte Lupi criminal place. They questioned us separately. They then took us by tender where there were hundreds of Jews being killed. The SS, Gestapo and Ukrainians had the men, women and children surrounded and told them to get undressed. It was very cold. We had heard the hollering to get undressed fast. The soldiers had guns and bayonets. After the people were shot they fell into a very deep hole. My uncle asked me how I had survived. I told him how Henek and I kept moving to the back of the line because they kept bringing in more and more people to kill. I had already said my last prayer. We were almost the last of approximately 500 Jews. We had pushed ourselves to the end of the line. I then saw somebody on a horse coming toward us. He told the soldiers to stop the killing. He was an SS obersturmfuhrer and with his loud speaker he asked for ten young men to come forward. We went, still naked, to where he was standing. I had told my friend that we didn't have anything to lose because they were going to kill us anyway.

It was the end of October and very cold. The SS Obersturmfuher told us to get dressed and fast. He told the SS and the Ukrainians to finish up the killing. They then killed the rest of the people who were screaming and crying. After we got dressed with clothing and shoes that didn't fit, we filled the hole with dirt. It took us four hours. When we finished the commandant told us he was from the Plaszow Arbeitslager. They took us by truck to a kitchen for lunch, which consisted of soup and bread. When we finished eating they took us back to the ghetto. It was still unbelievable to me that this had happened in our century. My aunt and uncle looked at me at began to cry. We kissed and I said goodbye to them and went back to my place.

Henek was there and told me he had a terrible day at work. It was a factory making war materials. The manager was an SS man, a murderer. He was beating up all his workers on their backs with a stick. Henek showed me the marks on his back from the beating. He told me I was lucky that I hadn't had to go to work that day. After that we went for our food. I wasn't hungry so I gave Henek my bread. I told him I had gone to the doctor and had been released from work for three days and from there had visited my aunt and uncle.

Henek told me that the Polish man had called the Gestapo because that was what most of the Poles were doing. He said we were very lucky to be alive and he thanked me for my portion of bread. He asked me why I hadn't kept the bread for the next day. I told him I could wait until tomorrow. I had two free days where I didn't have to go to work. I told him I was going to see Commandant Shapiro. We then went to sleep.

I got up early and prayed even though I didn't have the Tefillin. After I had my black coffee I walked from the ghetto to the police station. I saw hungry young boys about 10 or 12 years old walking around the streets. They asked me for money. They were dirty and wearing torn clothing. I gave them some money. Their faces were pale and their bodies were very thin. They were skin and bone. The Jewish police warned them that if a German truck or car came along they would pick them up, take them to the woods and kill them.

When I came to the police entrance, I told the policeman that I wanted to see Commandant Shapiro and he had told me to come back today. They took me to his office. He was in full uniform. I said good morning to him. He looked at me for a while and I got really scared because he had changed a lot. He was very skinny, wore glasses and had a black beard. He used to work at making glasses for windows and doors. That was his profession. He was a very religious man. He said that he remembered my father and how I had always walked with him. He asked where my family was now. I told him that we had lived in Dzialoszyce for two years and my older brother, Moshe, was with my sister in Russia. It had been three and a half months since the ouszidlung. I told him how they had taken my father and killed him and I was now alone. I said that they had pulled my father out of line and that I couldn't hold on to him. One of the Ukrainians has hit me in the chest with this gun. My mother had hollered that he was a murderer and should leave my father alone. After that they put my father and about 1600 other people in wagons. Some people were shot and some were buried alive. I remembered the dream where my father told me how he had been shot. After my story, the commandant told me my father was a great man, a genius and how he had remembered the whole Torah by heart. He didn't ever need a bible. He said that my father had been at his sister's wedding and everyone remarked about how a blind man could have such talent. They wondered how he could remember everything. The commandant said he loved my father very much, that they had been friends. He had gone to the commandant house many times. He knew that my father had been studying to become a rabbi until he started to go blind.

The commandant said that now the main thing was to help me. I told him I would like to have a steady job, a decent place to live and enough food to eat not like the ghetto. I said how I was always hungry. The only food was watery soup and bread with margarine and black coffee. Every day I was picked up to work at a different location. Sometime they beat you at work and many times people never returned from their job and no one ever knew what happened to them. It was a terrible life and the work was very hard. I said, "Dear commandant, the only thing I want from you is a decent steady job and a better place to live." He asked me about my profession. I told him that before the war I had a small factory where I made luggage. I had my sister and three people working with me. Thanks to this job I made a living and was able to help support my family. During the war I had learned carpentry. He told me that carpentry was a better profession.

He told me he wanted to help me to get a good steady job. He proposed that I become a Jewish policeman. It would be a steady job with a good living and I wouldn't have to work so hard. I would live in a house with three meals a day. I would have a clean suit, underwear and live a normal life. He said that a handsome boy like me would be respected as a policeman and my life would be different. He told me he had many applications from people begging for the policemen jobs. He said that no one knew what tomorrow was going to bring. We should live today like a mentsh. I would then have many friends and be respected. He said that he believed it would be the best job for me. He reminded me that I was a single man with no family responsibilities. It was wartime and the only one I had to care about was myself. If I became a policeman I would have fresh clothing and hot meals.

He told me he had pity on me especially since I had lost my father and I had been very good to him. He remembered that he had heard my father praying and had listened to the songs my father had composed himself. He said that while my father was at his sister's wedding he composed a song for them on the spot. It was a song about their biography and it rhymed. He told me he was trying to make my life easier and what more could he do for me, his friend's son? He said I didn't have to give him an answer now but to think it over and to let him know my decision later. I thanked him very much for his friendship and for his help. He handed me 500 zloty and told me to buy food with the money. He said he expected my answer in five days. I said goodbye to him. I hugged and kissed him and he did the same. He told me not to worry that everything was going to be okay. I walked out of the police station and went home.

I got a little dizzy and asked myself what to do. I thought about my life now and how I had to go to work every day. My life was in jeopardy. Maybe one day I wouldn't return from work at all. I'd be finished. As a Jewish policeman maybe I could help the Jewish people and I would be around other Jewish policemen. I would be in a clean uniform and would have respect. I could with intelligent Jewish people, which would be the good side of being a policeman.

I would also have to be ready to obey the laws when the Germans went to the Jewish houses. We had an underground organization in the ghetto. They were preparing a revolution in the ghetto so the Gestapo engaged Jewish people like the F.B.I. They paid them wages and promised them they would be safe until the war ended. The Gestapo wanted to find out who the leaders and organizer were. The top man was Mr. Spitz. Everybody knew him in the ghetto. Someone pointed him out to me once. He was elegantly dressed in new boots and everybody was afraid of him.

One time the Gestapo came in the middle of the night looking for weapons. They didn't find anything, but the next day we found out they had taken 600 people away who had been planning the uprising. They had taken them, including doctors and lawyers to Monte Lupi. None of them ever returned. They had taken them to the woods and killed them. It reminded me of the Dzialoszyce ouszidlung. The Jewish police told us not to worry that they were taking the people to work and we would be together with our families. That was why all the people went to the market place. They were in it with the German Gestapo. They found out where the Jews where hiding and pulled them from their hiding places in the basements and bunkers. They were shot before the eyes of the Jewish police. I thought that if I became a Jewish policeman, I would have to do the same thing. That would mean I would have to be an executioner helping the Gestapo to kill Jews. I would be forced to do what they asked. The Jewish police had finished all the Jews in Dzialoszyce. I could not obey that law. I would become a saboteur and then they would kill me. How could I face the Jewish people just because I wanted to have a good normal life? I would become a partner of the Germans killing Jews.

On the way home I bought bread for Henek and me with the money the commandant had given me. When I got home I went for my allotment of soup and ate the bread I had bought. I thought I would tell Henek what the commandant had proposed and get his opinion. When Henek came home I gave him the bread I had bought and he was very happy. He had a good day and didn't have to work so hard as usual. I explained to him about my conversation with the commandant, and how he wanted me to become a policeman. I would then lead a normal live with clean clothes and food every day. Every week I would get fresh underwear and a new uniform. I would live with four single intelligent policemen in one room. I wouldn't be hungry any longer and would have good friends and good company. They had a special kitchen for the policemen and they ate three meals a day. It would be a normal life. I would also be paid for the job.

I was supposed to let the commandant know in a week whether I was going to accept the job. I asked Henek what he thought about the proposition. After thinking for a few minutes he said he thought it was a very good opportunity to be offered such a good job. He reminded me that the work we had to do now every day at different locations was too hard. We were even beaten at work and we never knew if we were going to return. He said I had noting to lose but more to win. I explained to him the bad side of the job and how I had seen what the Jewish police had done to the people in Dzialoszyce. How the Jewish police had helped the Gestapo find the Jews who had been hiding. The Gestapo had shot men, women and children on the spot when they were discovered. The Jewish police had helped the Germans send people to Auschwitz, Treblinka and Belzec. Also, the Jewish police had spies in the ghetto working for them trying to find out about the uprising. They caught all the underground and their leaders and killed them. They then took the Jewish police to the woods and shot them. I thought is it worth it? Then Henek started to think differently about the prospect of me becoming a policeman. He told me I was right and that I had to do what my heart told me.

Five days later I went to Commandant Shapiro to give him my answer. I was afraid to walk the street even for one day without an identity card with a signature from an employer. But I had to do what my heart told me. If it was my destiny to remain alive after the war, I didn't want people pointing their fingers at me and saying that I was a Jewish policeman and had helped the Germans kill the Jews. I couldn't do it. My conscience would bother me. If God let me live until the end of the war, I had to do the right thing.

At nine o'clock in the morning I went to the police station. Every time I went there was a different policeman at the entrance. I showed him my identity card and he took me to the commandant. I said good morning to him and he answered me. He asked me what I had decided. I told him that I felt he treated me like a father or as if I was his son. I told him I knew he didn't want me to suffer any longer or to be hungry again but that I couldn't take the job as a policeman. I wasn't prepared for it. I didn't have the courage and I felt I would be unable to fulfill all the laws that a policeman had to obey. I asked the commandant to forgive me but I only wanted a steady job as a carpenter so I wouldn't have to run to a different job everyday. I also didn't know whether I would return from work each day. I said that I would be a better carpenter than a policeman. I felt that everyone knew his own feelings and what they wanted to do.

I told him I thought I would be a better carpenter than a policeman. Police work required discipline and I didn't believe I had that. I asked him not to be mad at me and hoped he understood my feelings since he was such a good friend of my fathers. I asked him not to be insulted and to please find a different job for me. I told him if he could get me a different job, I would be very thankful and remember it all my life. I hoped that God would bring us peace and end the war. I then would tell my friends what he had done for me in patience.

The Commandant didn't interrupt me the whole time I talked to him. When I was finished he said, "My dear Kalme I understand your position very much. Each person has his own feelings about what they want to do or not do. According to my thinking it would be the best thing for you, but if your heart is telling you not to take the job, I won't force it on you. You are right. Not everyone is cut out to be a policeman. Now I have to think about finding you a day-by-day steady job as a carpenter. I am interested in trying to find you a job that you will like and one that is good for you. I will try my best to help you." He told me to come back in a week because he had to wait for a job opportunity to open. He might be able to find a special carpentry shop where they needed professional people to work every day. I asked him to give me a signed slip showing I had been there to see him. The commandant said that if he found a job for me, he would send a message with one of the policemen. He asked for my address and said a friendly goodbye. I again thanked him for everything, including the money he had given me.

I went straight home from the police station because I was afraid to walk around in the streets. When I got home I sat on my bed and kept thinking whether it was good or bad that I did not take the job opportunity. I knew that people paid money to get the police job. When Henek came home from work I told him the whole story about meeting with Commandant Shapiro. I told him I hadn't asked the commandant about him because I wanted to see what kind of a job he would get for me. Once I got a job, I would then talk to the commandant about Henek. I would tell him how we were good buddies and we would like to stay together.

The next morning I went with Henek to work. The Germans took us to load big boxes. We were six people and worked very hard. We had to load the boxes onto trucks and then they took us to the railroad station. From there we unloaded the boxes from the trucks onto railroad cars. We both came home very tired.

After eight days, I still hadn't heard from the commandant. I thought that he had forgotten about me or maybe he didn't want to be bothered. He probably had more important things to do. We didn't have a telephone either. I told Henek that I would wait one more day that I had to have patience and that it was wartime. After a while I went to the office where I lived and asked if I had a letter from the police. She gave me a letter from Commandant Shapiro. I opened the letter and it said I should go to see him the next day about a job.

As instructed, I went to the commandant's office at nine o'clock. I was very happy. When the policeman escorted me into the commandant's office, he told me that he had found me a job. He said that he hoped I would be happy as a carpenter. There were three other men working at this military place on the Wawel. Who didn't know were the Wawel Castle was. He said that I would work with the three men every day. I would work for Governor Frank and the company was called "SS Viking." This place was where Polish kings were at rest. He told me that at seven thirty every morning I was to meet the others at the Judenrat and they would take me back and forth to work. I thanked him very much and apologized for not taking the job as a policeman. He wished me good luck in my new job and accompanied me to the entrance door. I smiled and said goodbye to him. I was amazed at how nice he had treated me.

I didn't want to talk to him about Henek because I didn't want to aggravate him. First I wanted to find out about the job and how it would accommodate me. I didn't know yet whether I would like it or if they would like me. Later I would try to get him a job at the same place so that we could work together. If everything went well, after two or three weeks I would try to help Henek. I thought about the commandant becoming angry at me if I went to talk to him about getting a job for someone else.

I received permission to leave the ghetto to go see my Aunt Zelda. While I was walking, I only saw the Jewish police and German soldiers. There were not too many people in the street. I did see many children standing near the buildings asking for bread or money. They were very skinny and dressed in old clothes. The Jewish police told them to go home before the Germans took them away and killed them. I saw a wagon going around picking up dead people from the streets and buildings. The Chevrah Kedusha sent them to pick up those dead so they could have a religious funeral and buried in the cemetery. After they cleaned them, they took them to the Jewish cemetery.

I went to Aunt Zelda to tell her that I had a job as a carpenter thanks to the commandant of the police. When I arrived, my uncle was at work. The job was at the Wawel starting the next day and I hoped that it would be a steady job. I asked her if she might have a suit or a jacket and pants that would fit me because her son was about my size. I was still wearing the clothes that I had picked up in Plaszow that were too big for me. I looked very sloppy. She brought me a suit and it was a perfect fit. She also gave me a pair of shoes that fit, three shirts, three pair of underwear, and a few handkerchiefs. I had breakfast there, and I was very happy. I took all the clothes and said goodbye to my aunt. I said, "God should keep you and your whole family and give you health and happiness. I will never forget how much you and Uncle David did for me." I kissed everyone and left with all my clothes. I was not afraid to walk in the streets because I had a slip from the police.

When I walked through the streets in the ghetto, a Jewish policeman asked me what I was carrying and if I had an identity card in order to walk around. He asked me why I was not working. I took out my note from the police and showed it to him. He walked with me to my place and he told me that the German SS commandos were looking for weapons. They thought that the Jews in the ghetto were going to have an uprising against the Germans. He told me that sometimes when they took people to the commandos, even though they were not guilty, sometimes they just disappeared. While I was walking with him, I saw people dying by the hundreds. I saw 20 wagons pull up to a building and carry out dead bodies. Children were walking around half dead from hunger. They were skin and bones. It was like a cemetery.

The policeman told me he was from a small town near Krakow, called Wieliczka. He had lost his parents and was alone. He became a policeman because now he had everything he needed and also some money. I didn't want to tell him my story about the offer I had received to become a policeman. He took me to my place and waited until I went inside. I went straight to bed and thought to myself that I had done the right thing by not becoming a policeman. I couldn't help the Germans destroy the Jewish people. I couldn't be selfish. I felt that I had done the right thing. I was happy and thinking about my new job in the morning.

The next morning I again went for a walk. I saw unshaved people asking for bread or money. They wore torn clothing. I saw trucks with Germans picking up men, women, and children and taking them away forever. The people who worked for the Germans received better rations such as butter, eggs, and sugar even though they were small portions. If you had money, you could buy anything because professional Poles came to the ghetto to work. They brought in everything because they didn't check these people. The people in the ghetto sold the Poles gold, diamonds, clothing, and things from their houses such as new shoes, suits, underwear, and bedding. They had to sell these items just to stay alive.

The Poles knew what was going on in the ghetto every day. They also knew that the Germans could liquidate them, but what could they do? They had families with small children. Sometimes the Gestapo did check the Poles and would find salami, cheese, and bread. They took them away and sent them to the concentration camps. I was very nervous about what I saw happening in the ghetto. It was a terrible situation for the Jews of Krakow.

I waited for my friend, Henek to come back from work. He was tired and also nervous. He told me about his job. There were eight people and they took them to a warehouse where they had new furniture. The furniture was very heavy. They had to carry it to the second floor. Henek was very tired and hungry. After he ate his soup and bread, he told me the SS beat the workers with a stick. He was lucky not to be one of those beaten. He was very happy to get away from the German murderer when the workday ended and he was returned to the ghetto. He then went to bed so I didn't have chance to talk to him about my day. I, too, then went to bed because I knew that tomorrow I was starting my new job and I was hoping for good luck.

The next morning I told Henek about my new job at the Wawel and how three other people were going with me. If I liked the job, I was going to talk to them about getting him a job there, too. I didn't want to ask the commandant before because I wasn't sure the job would work out for me. My friend looked very worried because he didn't want to be separated from me. I said my prayers and took a shower. I put on my fresh clothes that my aunt had given me. When Henek saw me, he asked where I had gotten the new shoes and clothes. I told him how my aunt had given me my cousin's clothes and shoes so I could wear them to my new job.

The First Day on my Job at SS Viking

After I drank my black coffee, I went to the place where I stood and waited with other people who were standing and talking to each other. After 15 minutes, a car with two SS men pulled up, and three men who had been standing with me went over to the vehicle. I ran after them and said good morning to them. I took out the letter from the commandant of the Jewish police. The SS man looked over the letter and told me it was okay and to get in. While driving to the job, I introduced myself. About 18 minutes, we came to the Wawel, which was surrounded by a thick wall where Polish kings, including Marshal Josef Pilsudski, are buried. It was like a museum. Hundreds of people from all over the world come to see this place with its beautiful paintings. The walls around the building are red brick. It is a beautiful museum with beautiful antiques. Governor Frank, an anti Semite and a Jew killer, lived there. He was the one who made all the special laws against the Jewish people. He was one of the biggest murderers.

As they drove up to the building, I recognized it right away because I had gone there many times while on school trips. They stopped the vehicle and let the four of us off. They took us to a carpentry shop that had very modern electric power machines. It was a big shop with all kinds of equipment. The spokesman from our group was Mr. Sheidl, a German Jew. He was a short friendly guy. I introduced myself. He was not a professional carpenter. I found out later that he had a restaurant in Berlin. He showed me what to do. He told me to cut the pieces of trees in order to make boxes for parts. The parts were for airplanes, trucks, and cars. He gave me the measurements for the length, width, and depth. I was not accustomed to working with electric machines, but he showed me how to do it. He worked with me a while. The other guys had finished their boxes and were filling them with parts for airplanes. I worked with them to learn more about the machinery. Later I was on my own. It took me a long time to make the first box from my measurements, but I was catching on. Mr. Sheidl told me not to worry because it was a nice place to work. The main thing was to make a perfect box. He said it took time. My first box wasn't too good but I asked him to give me more time. He agreed.

I noticed that the personnel liked him because he spoke their language, which was perfect German. He was a good cook. He made them special sunny side up eggs when he worked in the kitchen and then he worked with us. At noontime, I introduced myself to the other workers. They gave us soup and a piece of bread. We had an hour for lunch and had time to talk. One man was Mr. Wolf from Podlasie. (His sister lives in Haifa, Israel and is our best friend). He lived in Krakow and was single. Another worker was Mr. Goldstein. He was from Krakow and was single also. They told me that everyday we could go to the store and buy food like bread. If you had money, you could buy anything. I still had some money that the commandant had given me. Mr. Sheidl gave me coffee from this thermos. He was in his forties and a very nice man. All the workers lived in the ghetto. After lunch, we all went back to work.

At the SS Viking, they had a big hall where they brought parts for their airplanes, trucks, and cars. From there, we packed them into medium sized boxes we had made from wood in the carpentry shop. After we packed the boxes with these parts, we covered and nailed the box shut. A soldier then came with a paintbrush and painted the address on the cover for shipment to different places. The next day they would load the boxes with a forklift onto trucks. Four of us helped with the loading. Some of the boxes went to the Russian and other front lines.

Then Obersturmfuhrer Hoppe introduced himself and told us he was in charge of us. If we needed anything, we had to tell Mr. Sheidl and then he would speak to the Obersturmfuhrer. He was standing near me and looked at my work and he showed me how he wanted it done. He asked me about my profession. I told him I was a carpenter. He stood near me for about 20 minutes and was very friendly toward me. When he asked me my name, I told him it was Schumacher Kalme because in Poland you only took Chuppah by a Rabbi and not by a magistrate. I was written in school as Cheuder Chaim Kalme Schumacher. All day we made new boxes because they needed a lot of boxes. At five o'clock, we finished the job. We washed up and got ready to go back to the ghetto.

When I came home from work, Henek was already there. He wanted to know all about my job. I told him about SS Viking and making boxes. It was all right, but lifting the boxes onto the trucks was very hard work. I told him that after I had been working there awhile, I would talk to them getting him a job because it would be a good, steady job for him. Afterward we both went to sleep.

The next morning Henek and I were waiting at the same place to be picked up for work. I again promised him that when I became more acquainted with the people at work, I would speak to them about getting him a job there, but he had to be patient. I had my portion of bread and margarine with me. When I was picked up, I was quiet during the ride because I didn't know the people very well.

When we arrived, they called me into the office. I was scared. The girl in the office gave me an envelope and I left. I opened the envelope and smiled because in the envelope was my identity card with the signature from SS Viking. It stated that I was employed at the company as a professional carpenter and I was not available for any other work. I was very happy.

At lunchtime we were still allowed time to buy food. I asked Mr. Sheidl if I could go to get food and he said that I could. He told me that most of the workers brought food from home. Mr. Sheidl explained where the grocery store was located. I still had the 500 zloty that the commandant had given me. The store was approximately 200 meters from where I worked. I bought bread, margarine, and two apples. The prices were much cheaper than in the ghetto.

They told me I would be paid in two weeks but I had spent all my money on food and now I was very hungry and didn't have any money. I was ashamed to ask the people at work for food so I went from door to door asking the Poles for bread but no one would give me any food. They just opened the door and then closed and locked it. It was the first time in my life that I had to ask for bread.

The next day I asked Mr. Sheidl if I could borrow some money to buy food. He gave me a hundred zloty. At lunchtime, I went to the little store and bought a small salami, bread, and margarine. I ate some of the food at lunch and saved some to take home.

After lunch, I went back to my job making boxes from wood and packing the parts as I had done the day before. I learned more and more about the work and it came easier. I was happy that I had steady work and thought about getting Henek a job. I talked to Mr. Sheidl about Henek and whether it was possible to hire him. Unfortunately, I saw in his face that he was not happy about my request. He told me he didn't think they needed any more people unless they became desperate for workers. When I got back from work, I took the small salami that I had hung on my shoulder and hid it in my coat because I didn't want anyone to see it. I was happy that I had a job and would be paid three times as much. I got my portion of soup, bread, and margarine.

There was a slip for me in the office that said they had changed my place. I packed my things. I felt very bad that I now was going to be separated from my friend, Henek. I told him that I had spoken to Mr. Sheidl about getting him a job there, but he had said it was too early to ask about anyone else since it wasn't even a week since I started to work. I promised him I would ask Mr. Sheidl about him again. Henek helped me carry my belongings. I didn't have very much and it wasn't too heavy. I hoped I would like the new place. When we got there, it was almost the same thing with lots of people, but it was much nicer and cleaner. They gave me a room with four other people but I had a place for myself with a door. The bed was much cleaner and Hench said that he believed it was a nice change. I saw the tears in his eyes when he said goodbye. I found someone from Krakow named Janek Frenkel. He was a little older than me. After we finished talking, I went to bed. It had two pillows and two blankets because it was wintertime. I slept very well.

In the morning, I got up at six o'clock and took a shower. Even that was much nicer and better because it had hot water. At seven o'clock and after I had my black coffee, I waited for my ride with the three other guys. I started working much better and also faster. I wanted to get a good name at work. It wasn't an easy job because every day the trucks came with the parts for the airplanes, trucks, and cars, and we had to load them after packing them into boxes.

In the morning, Mr. Sheidl was always busy in the kitchen and when we finished loading, we went to the carpentry shop and made more boxes. Every day Obersturmfuhrer Hoppe gave us a list with the size and number of boxes required. For airplane parts, we needed large boxes. For the cars and trucks, we needed smaller boxes. Some times, we would get a rush order that had to be finished that same day. Day by day, we worked faster and better. I now knew what to do and liked the work. I was not afraid that every day they were going to take me to another place where they beat the workers. The loading was hard, but I got used to it. The carpentry was a pleasure. I was happy to have a steady job.

At lunchtime, I went to the little store and bought food for myself. If some of the workers asked me, I would buy food for them, too. Every day I bought salami to bring back to the ghetto. Sometimes I sold it and made double the price. My friends didn't know I was doing that. I wasn't hungry anymore. I had enough money to pay back Mr. Sheidl the one hundred zloty.

When I went home each day, I thanked God and the commandant for my job. I was also thankful that I hadn't taken the job as policeman. I hadn't forgotten by friend Henek. He was very good to me and became like a brother. It was a different life for me now. After work, I went to my new home. It was an apartment owned by an older Jewish woman. We were five men in two rooms and a kitchen. It had a toilet and a shower. We made our own beds, but every month a lady from the house changed the bedding. I didn't have monthly payments for living there, but I had to supply my own food and support myself.

I had started work in October. After two weeks, I received my first payment. It was not enough money for my needs. When I went to the grocery store and bought a small piece of salami or other food, I would hide it in my clothes. They never checked our clothes only any bags that we carried back and forth. I sold the food in the ghetto. I then had enough money to buy myself more food. I was not hungry any longer because I had many customers who wanted to buy the food. When we didn't have to load trucks at work, we did the carpentry work making the different size boxes. Mr. Hoppe would then come, inspect the boxes, and have a man write the address. Then at five o'clock we would be taken back to our place. Sometimes a vehicle was not available so we walked on foot to our place with an SS soldier.

One morning when we were picked up for work, there were two soldiers. One of them was Russian, and his name was Sasha Beshwilly. He was supposed to guard us. He was very friendly and we started to talk to him in Polish. The Germans had brought him from the front and he wore an SS uniform. Sometimes they sent him to take us to the ghetto. We showed him the way and it took us almost an hour. We tried to understand each other as best we could because he only spoke Russian. He had volunteered in the German Army. I thought that when we became better acquainted, I would ask him to take me to where I used to live. I wanted to ask the manager of the building if he knew anything about my family. I was hoping that some of my family was still alive or perhaps there was a letter there from my brother in Russia.

One day, I heard the Obersturmfuhrer talking to Sasha and telling him that he had to walk us back home to the ghetto after work. I had someone translate my Polish into Russian. I wanted him to know that I was born in Krakow and begged him to take me to Miodowa 39 where I had lived with my parents. I was hoping that either there was a letter there from my brother or sister or perhaps a message from my family that they were still alive. Sasha understood and said he would take me to the caretaker of the building. I was so happy and thanked him for his kindness. When we finished work, he took us from the Wawel to walk in the streets.

He was dressed in his SS uniform and was carrying a rifle and a revolver. We marched through the streets of Krakow until we came to Miodowa. I saw someone standing at the entrance to our building. It was maybe 200 meters to the house. My heart started to beat very fast. It reminded me that this was the house where I lived with my whole family. I remembered my father, mother, brother, and sisters. I then recognized the man as Mr. Bomba. I went up to him and said good morning in Polish. I asked him if he remember me, Kalme Freedman the son of Symcha Frydman and we had lived on the fourth floor. He looked at me in an angry way and didn't answer me. I asked him if he had heard from my mother, brother, or sisters. He looked at me with wild eyes and said, "Yes, I do recognize you and go to the devil. They have killed all the Jews. How come you are still alive? Go to the devil from here in Poland." I became hysterical. It was a shock to hear such a mean angry anti Semitic remark. My face was burning. It gave me a pain in my stomach and I became very nervous. If I had a revolver in my hand, I would have shot him. Although he couldn't understand me, I shouted in a strong voice for Sasha to shoot him because he was a murderer. Sasha put the Uzi right in his face and I told him to kill him that he was a bandit, a killer. I told Sasha one more time to please kill him. He had his finger on the trigger. Mr. Bomba opened the door of the building, ran inside, and locked the door. We tried to open the door but couldn't. I ran to the back door but it was locked. We just stood in the street. I wanted to go into the apartment but both doors were locked. Mr. Sheidl said it was getting late and Sasha had to walk back to his place after he took us to the ghetto. We had to go.

Mr. Goldstein then explained to Sasha in Russian that the caretaker from our building was an anti Semite and what he had said to me about the Jews. He told him it was lucky that he had run away. Mr. Wolf said that we couldn't trust the Poles because they were more anti-Semitic than the Germans. Some Poles were glad that the Germans were killing the Jews. I thought to myself that I never would want to visit Poland if I lived through the war because my heart was hurt. While we were walking through the streets of Krakow, I passed by the corner of Kraskowska Street where I remembered living with my parents.

When we came to my new place, I took the salami from my shoulder and hid it my jacket because I intended to sell it. I had to live and this helped me because now I had steady customers for the food. I started to make more friends in the ghetto. I went to see my friend, Mr. Korngold. I hadn't forgotten him. I told him about seeing the caretaker from our building. Afterwards, I went to bed. I couldn't sleep. I couldn't stop thinking about the caretaker who was a bastard and had no right to talk to me the way he did. I was very nervous and must have only slept for two hours.

The next day they picked us up for work. Now the four of us had a very good relationship, and we became friends, thanks to Mr. Sheidl. Because he prepared breakfast for the Germans, they liked him. He was a very friendly man. Because of him, we enjoyed our work and we were treated well, but things changed when the Germans started losing the war on the Russian front. Mr. Sheidl told me that the Russian surrounded a German regiment of approximately ten thousand men during the winter months. They were without food and the whole regiment froze to death.

Our bosses were nervous and they started to holler at us. They told us we were too slow and because the Russians took much of the equipment sent to the German regiment we had to hurry up and send new ones to the front. We had to work overtime every day and it was nighttime when they brought us home. We felt how nervous they were and they took it out on us. The worst one was Obersturmfuhrer Hoppe, our manager. There was a higher-ranking officer there named Wallheimer. He was more understanding. During this nervous time, we tried to work faster. We heard that they might send all the soldiers from this area to the front and they didn't want to go. Here they had a good life and didn't want to go to the Russian front. For me, this was a terrific job, but in one way, I was very happy that they were loosing. I thought maybe now the war would come to an end.

At lunchtime, I went to the store to get my salami and I bought one for Henek and one for my Uncle David. When I gave it to them they both wanted to pay me, but I did not take any money from them. I again spoke to Mr. Sheidl about Henek and whether he could get him a job with us. But nothing came of it because, we didn't know whether we would still be working at SS Viking or how long we would be working at the Wawel since the troops might be sent to the Russian front. We kept up on information about the Russian front from a young SS solider friend of Mr. Sheidl from Berlin. The soldier warned him about the goings on in the ghetto. Around five o'clock the same young SS soldier drove us to the ghetto.

Now that I had a better place to sleep, I thought about going to Commandant Shapiro to thank him for what he had done for me. Maybe I would write him a letter.

On Sunday, we didn't work but sometimes they did come for us. They didn't pay us overtime for Sunday. Overtime did not exist. One day it was snowing very hard and we couldn't go to work. I went to visit my Uncle David. They were very happy to see me and prepared a good dinner. I didn't ask whether it was Kosher because during these times I was just happy to have a piece of meat. I told them about my new job and about the new place where I lived with four other men. They were happy to hear the good news. I asked my uncle if he could let me have a winter jacket, hat, and underwear because I worked outside and didn't have any warm clothing. My Aunt Zelda gave me a winter jacket, a hat that covered my ears and underwear. I gave her the salami but she didn't want to take it. She wanted me to sell it to buy myself food for the whole week.

Rafuel and his wife came for a visit while I was there. They were very nice people. When I told him about my new job, he invited me to go to his house because he had some warm clothing I could use. Later in the day, I went to his house where they treated me very nice and gave me a sweater, winter underwear, and warm socks. The shoes they had were too big. I thanked them very much and went home.

The next day I thanked God that I had warm clothing to wear. They picked us up for work as usual where we did the same work making boxes and filling them with parts for the Russian front. At lunchtime, I went to the store to get my food because we weren't getting any soup or bread while on the job. We had to bring our own food. I always bought salami and sometimes I bought hard cheese.

I planned to buy a pair of new winter shoes with my own money. In the ghetto, there were people who had stores before the war and had hidden their merchandise. Most of the goods were very expensive. They only sold the merchandise through a Broker, a guy they could trust. You had to buy all your goods through him and he took twenty percent for himself. Otherwise, you couldn't buy anything. On Sunday, I bought myself a pair of new winter shoes and I was very happy. Everyone had to be very careful because some Jews in the ghetto worked for the Gestapo. If the Germans found out about the merchandise such as shoes, suits, dresses, or shirts, they would kill the person with the goods. The people took chances because some of them had young children and needed the money to buy food. I spent most of my money but had enough left over to buy bread and salami.

One Sunday I met Henek and told him about my job. I told him that I was going to make an appointment to see Commandant Shapiro. I spent a few hours with Henek and told him that I would have salami for him next week. I told him about selling the salami in order to have money for food. We were very happy to see each other.

The next day at work and at lunchtime we were told that half of the personnel at the Viking had been sent to the Russian front. The rest were very worried because they were afraid. We tried to work faster and better to show them that we wanted to help them. We knew that if they sent all of them away, we would lose our job. That would be a disaster for us. In five weeks time they all came back and there was a different atmosphere. We started to get big orders for the front. We worked faster and faster and one hour overtime. We had an order for sixty small, medium, and large boxes. We had to work overtime every day and when the work was finished, it was transported to the Russian front. One day while talking with Mr. Sheidl at lunchtime, he told us that something was going to happen at the Warsaw ghetto. The German government felt there was going to be an uprising. After work, we went back to the ghetto.

After working there for about five months, we tried harder and harder to work faster so they would be happy with us. Mr. Sheidl told us very quietly that one of the soldiers he was acquainted with told him that the Germans were going to start checking everyone for weapons. This was going to happen in the ghetto very soon. The Germans also had a problem at the Warsaw ghetto and didn't want a problem in the Krakow ghetto. They didn't want an uprising. After hearing this, we were scared. We didn't know what to do.

After about five weeks, it got quiet and the situation at work was not in order. They gave us new identity cards with an official signature stating we worked as professional carpenters at Viking. They wanted us to have this card in case something happened at the ghetto. We knew now that something was going to happen but we didn't know when. The chairman told Mr. Sheidl that if something happened to just show them the card.

On Sunday, I went to see my Uncle David and told him what I had heard. They invited me to dinner. I showed my uncle the new card they had given me. I hoped that they were only checking for weapons, but I didn't know exactly what was going to happen. My uncle told me that he had heard about something like that at his job. My uncle said that we were in God's hands. What could we do? A lot of people had prepared bunkers in their basements or attics. Everyone in the ghetto was nervous. It was a hard winter and very cold.

Then, the Gestapo along with the Jewish police came in the middle of the night looking for weapons. When they came to my place at two o'clock in the morning, we had to leave while they checked under the mattress and bed. Thank God, they didn't find anything. They looked in the basement. They were also looking for furs because it was so cold outside. When they found something suspicious, they took that person away and they were never seen again. The Jewish police also went to every house in the ghetto. They, too, were looking for people hidden by the Poles or for people without papers. It was terrible that Jews would help the Germans to kill their brothers for money. In the end, the Gestapo killed all of them.

People were afraid to talk to one another because they didn't trust anyone. It was unclear what was going to happen to everyone in the ghetto. They were trying to prepare special food for the small children. People were building bunkers in the basement. They tried to do everything to save their lives. They thought maybe once they were finished looking for weapons and hidden people, life would return to normal. At that time, many from the community were sent to Auschwitz or Treblinka. Everyone was very nervous because everything was closed to the Jews. We thought because we had the identity from the Viking that we might be saved because they had trained us and needed us for the work.

On Friday, March 13, 1943, at 7:30 in the morning SS soldiers, storm troopers, Gestapo and Ukrainians in German uniforms, surrounded the ghetto. That day I got up at six o'clock and got ready to go to work. Then over the loud speaker, everyone was told to come out. All the men, women, children, the old, and young were told to go to the market place. People were told to take all their belonging with them. No one was to stay in his or her home. They were told to form a line with 10 persons. The Jewish police were there to help them get all the people out of their homes and in line. They shouted orders in German and Polish. Anyone who didn't obey would be shot.

I hurried and put on my winter clothing and my new shoes because I remembered that the same thing happened in Dzialoszyce. It was eight months ago that I had lost my whole family and never saw them again. I knew now what they were going to do. I saw thousands of Jewish people, men, women, and children with whole families standing together. I stood alone with my bundle in my hands. Over the loud speaker, the Jewish police said the same thing as before. They said that all the people were being sent away to work in factories for the Germans. The ghetto was being liquidated, but I knew the truth. They were sending the people to their death like they did to my parents and sisters.

As we were standing in the huge market place, we were told to stay in line. They had the Jewish police keeping order. They again said that anyone who remained hiding in his home and were found later would be shot. I had lost my whole family this way. Whole families were coming from all over the ghetto with bundles in their hands. They didn't know what was going to happen to them. When I looked around, I saw many people that I knew. I saw Cantor Kaufman from the Kuper Shul with his family.

We all stood there for an hour when over the loud speaker they said to start marching in fives out of the ghetto through the main gate. Outside there were hundred of trucks waiting to take the people away. I took out my identity card and held in up as I passed through the gate. The Gestapo was looking for people who had jobs. When one of the Gestapo examined my card, I told him I worked for SS Viking at the Wawel and I was a professional carpenter. I told him to call them to verify that I worked there. He took me out of line and told me to follow him. He had me sit on the ground not far away from the main door. I was the first one and I saw other young people doing what I had done. They had them sit next to me and our group got larger and larger. The rest of the people were loaded in trucks and taken to Auschwitz and Treblinka.

The police and soldiers surrounded us. I saw the Gestapo roaming from house to house and looking in the basements and bunkers for hidden Jews. I heard women and children screaming and crying. I saw children from eight to ten years old alone without their parents walking in the streets hiding between buildings in the ghetto. The Gestapo picked them up like animals and put them in the trucks.

When they finished, we waited for our destiny and wondered what they were going to do with us. I saw the Gestapo holding little babies who were about eight or ten months old and throwing them to the ground from the fifth floor. The soldiers then took the dead babies like little toys and threw them onto the trucks. I almost fainted. I asked myself how such intelligent people like the Germans could do such horrible things just because they were Jews. What was the world coming to?

Far away, I saw my cousin Monieh. His father Hershel was my mother's brother. He was six years old and standing alone behind a building. I couldn't leave to help him. I started to cry. The Gestapo came and picked up those children. They threw them like animals into the trucks. I saw the Gestapo and the Jewish police picking up people from the bunkers, basements, and attics and putting them into the trucks. Some were shot on the spot.

They took people from our group to clean up the dead bodies. It looked like a cemetery. They were not finished. Again, they went from building to building looking for more Jews. We heard shooting. The young people were put on the trucks and the children and the old people were killed on the spot. I saw so many people walking through the gate who were then sent away. We heard hollering from the Gestapo and crying mothers and children. They killed about one thousand people right there. About twenty of us helped to pick up the dead bodies that were put into the trucks and taken to the cemetery. I will always remember that horrible day.

Then they told our group to stand up and make a line of six people. After they counted us, they took us to the showers. They brought trucks for about one thousand of the people who were left from over the 20,000 people in the ghetto. When we got in the trucks, we didn't know where they were taking us. I prayed and asked God that we needed Him to help us, to punish our enemies, and to save the children.

There were about 25 trucks in our line. When they stopped, they started hollering for us to hurry. We jumped from the trucks and we had to stay in line where they counted us again. I saw a sign that said "Plaszow Arbeitslager" on the bottom was written, "Work makes your life sweet." The SS who drove us there gave a report to the commandant. He told him how many people were there who previously had jobs. I saw that we were marching on Hebrew marble monuments with Hebrew lettering. It was from the Jewish cemetery in Krakow. The Germans had made a path out of the monuments. As my feet touched the stones, I started to shiver.

They again took us to the showers. It took about two hours. We had to leave our clothing and they cut off our hair. They gave us underwear and a striped criminal-like suit. Everybody had to give away any money, gold, or diamonds in their possession. They told us that if we didn't turn over our belongings, and if they found any of those things on us, we would either be shot or hanged. I still had the diamond ring my mother had given me. I put it in my mouth and under my tongue and they didn't check me. A lot of the people did the same thing.

They divided the people into different barracks. I went to Barrack No. 18. I thought that 18 meant Chei (to life). There were about 80 to 100 people in the barrack with me from the group. The Jewish police took 20 of us and introduced us to the manager. The manager showed us where we were going to sleep. I took a place right away on the top bunk with a window so I could get more air. The beds had three levels of bund beds. I knew that when they called people to work they usually took the people on the bottom.

My bed was a long sack filled with straw as a mattress, a pillow filled with straw and a blanket. I worked on straightening the bed and prepared to go to sleep. It was around six o'clock in the evening and we were very hungry and tired. We were extremely emotional from the terrible day we had just lived through. I again thought that I would never forget and would keep the picture in my mind of the terrible things they had done to the Jews in the Krakow ghetto. I was very upset.

They started to give everyone his portion of bread with margarine, soup, and two cigarettes. I went to the line and got my portion. I went to my bed, ate the bread and margarine, and kept the cigarettes. Since I didn't smoke, I asked my neighbor if he wanted to exchange the cigarettes for his bread or soup. I was glad that I had listened to my father after my bar mitzvah when he asked me not to smoke. I cried when I remember promising my father I would not smoke. This promise to my father helped save my life while in the camps. I changed my two cigarettes for bread. I saw a lot of people giving away their bread or soup for cigarettes. I then went to sleep.

The Plaszow Camp was just opened a few weeks. When they found food on someone they only took it away. They woke us up the next morning at six o'clock with a whistle. I dressed quickly. They gave us a dish for our soup and aluminum utensils for our food. After they gave us black coffee, they had us form a line, counted us, and sent us to work in groups. Our job was out of the camp and very hard. The Kapo who took care of the job was a Polish guy. He was very strict and not at all friendly.

The First Day in Plaszow Camp

They took us to a place where they built sidewalks for the streets. There were 30 people working together. We had a German manager. He was the chairman who took care of the job. There was a room with all kinds of equipment for the job. Everyone was given a shovel or a broom. They divided us into groups of three. They showed us what to do. They gave us a wagon that we had to fill up with little stones to be put in the streets before they put down the asphalt. After they finished with the asphalt, they had a big machine to press the material together. Five other Jews and I delivered the stones that they spread on the street. I worked very hard the first day. I was not used to doing it so fast. At lunchtime, they gave us hot soup that was better than the soup we got in the camp.

After lunch, we went back to work. My job was hard. I had to fill up the wagon with stones and when I finished, I had to fill it with sand. All day long, our Polish Kapo was roaming around and hollering. He looked at each worker and complained that I was not taking enough material in the wagon. When we finished work, we marched through the streets with 30 people in a line. We came to the camp and to our barrack. We had to stay in line for our portion of the 250 grams of bread, a piece of margarine and two cigarettes. Every day I had a guy give me a half portion of his bread or soup for the two cigarettes. When I finished my meal, I started to look around to see if I could find someone I knew from Krakow. I went to different barracks and found people I knew from my Hebrew School, Talmud Torah. I also met friends of my father and they recognized me. I was still upset about the happenings in the Krakow ghetto. Some of the people told me that my father had sung at their weddings. They asked me if I also could sing a happy song. When I went back to my barrack, everyone was talking about what might happen to all of us. They talked about their parents and asked me about my family. I asked them if they had seen any of my cousins.

Everyday new people came to the camp. Our barrack had about 100 people. I talked to the new people. They were very depressed and nervous. They asked about life in the camp. They were not used to such hard work. I met a young boy that I went to Yeshiva with and he knew my father. They asked me to sing one of my father's songs or to say a few words to make them happy because they were so depressed. I sang one of my father's songs and they seemed to like it. I thought perhaps I should start to write down my father's songs. I had nothing to lose. If my father could write beautiful songs, I decided to try. The bible noted that the children inherit traits from their parents. I then went to sleep with the thought that I should start to write my father's songs.

After being in the Plaszow camp for five days, I was still working at the same job. We asked the Kapo if we could buy food to bring to camp because they didn't check us when we came back from work. A few of us went to buy food and I bought a school book and pencils. When I came back from work, I ate my portion of food. I was so tired from the hard work; I went to bed and fell asleep. The next day I went to work and thought to myself that no matter how tired I was when I went home that I would sit down and start writing. I thought about my father's songs because I remembered the melodies.

When I came home from work the next day I took my portion of bread and margarine. I had an apple to eat. I sat down at the table in the middle of the room and I started writing. The first song I remembered was, "Where Are My Children, Where?" He wrote this song for my brother Moshe and my sister Sara when they left the house for Russia and because he hadn't heard from them. I knew the words and I started to write. Little by little, I remembered my father singing this song. Every living person in the barrack was crying because everybody there had children who had left their home for Russia. The same night I reminded myself of another song. It was "Jew Come to Work" and I knew the melody and the lyrics. I didn't remember all the words so I used my own words.

The next day when I came home from work, I wrote again. It was exiting and gave me the willingness to write. Most of the songs that I remembered were written during the war such as "The War Song" and so every day after work I sat down and tried to remember the songs my father had sung. I was too young to remember the other songs my father had written before the war. I was Symcha Frydman's son and had to try to write the songs as I had remembered.

I told the people in the barrack what I was doing, and they begged to sing one of the songs. I told them that I couldn't sing. They said they would help me if I would try to sing. I started to sing "Where Are My Children, Where", and a group of people helped me sing. Then around 7:30 in the evening, all the people gathered around and started to sing. It was beautiful. They were all crying and I started to cry. It reminded me of my family. The manager of the barrack, who was a German Jew, was standing and listening. He said he liked it very much and wanted to start a choir that could sing here at night, but we would have to have a policeman watching outside.

This was a new camp so they were busy with new comers everyday. We still had to be careful because sometimes they would come to our barrack and check on us. I now had ten beautiful songs written in my book. I never sang solo but I made up my mind that I was going to join the choir because the people in my barrack encouraged me to join. The singing helped with our depression. I started to look around for men with nice voices to sing in the choir. I found four people who said that they used to sing in a choir with a Cantor on the High Holidays. Two of the men were from Krakow and knew my father. They had nice voices. I told them I wasn't going to make money from the singing. It was only for the people who had lost their families and were so broken and depressed. I wanted to make them happy and to help them get on with their lives. The war couldn't last forever. It must come to an end some day. We had to be strong. We had to stay alive until the end of the war. Someone had to live to tell the world what Hitler had done to the Jewish nation and to our dear families.

I picked six people from other barracks with nice voices. I told them what I needed from them and that I had remembered ten songs that my father had written. I told them that we had to practice and they accepted. We started to practice singing together and I taught them the melodies. I was very happy because a few of them knew my father and had heard him sing. I went to the Stubenettester of the barrack and told him what I was proposing. He told me he liked my father's songs and he thought it was a very good idea. He said we had to have a Jewish policeman with us anytime we got together to sing as a choir so the Germans wouldn't find out what we were doing. I thanked him and said that it would be good for the people. They would be happier and more cheerful. He said that he knew a man whose brother was a Jewish policemen living in the camp. He said he would talk to him.

Five days later, the manager said he had spoken to the policeman and he accepted, but he wanted a week's notice before we had a mini-concert. He would also arrange to be there every time we practiced. After we had practiced for two week, we arranged a date for our first concert with the ten men. We practiced every Sunday for five hours.

We advertised in the other barracks about the concert. On the day of the event, all the people from our barrack and many from the other barracks came at 7:30 in the evening. I sang six of my father's songs and two with the choir. They sang a solo with Cantor Kaufman. After that, they asked me to sing more songs. I sang three more songs. The Jewish policeman came to watch. He didn't see any Germans because it was

Sunday and they were out having a good time so he came in to listen to the music. The mini-concert was a big success.

After the concert, I talked to the people and they thanked me very much. Some of them were from Krakow and remembered my father. I told them to be strong, to hang on and not be depressed. That's want out enemies wanted, but we were still young and had to stay alive until the end of the war. We had to live with hope and not fall into a panic. I tried to give new life to the people. The Jewish policeman was from Krakow, shook my hand, and said he remembered my father. He told me that the next time we organized a concert, to have the manager tell him so that he could come and watch for any Germans. The choir and I were very happy that the people liked the music and were so enthusiastic.

The next day we worked in the camp and had a better Kapo to work for. We were putting in pipes for the new barracks. When we were finished, they gave us a new Kapo. He was Polish and not very nice to us. He didn't like our work and said it was no good. He had a gun in his hand and he was always hollering. The work was very hard, and I tried to avoid getting a beating. At lunch, they brought a can with hot soup. The soup was no good because it was only water with beet and carrot tops. All of us complained about the soup. It was terrible. When we went back to work after lunch, the Kapo treated us badly. He was a monster and made us suffer.

We finished work at five o'clock and went back to our barrack. I went for my portion of bread, margarine, and the two cigarettes. I was very hungry and exchanged the two cigarettes for more bread. After I ate, I started to write more of my father's songs that I remembered. I was surprised that I could remember so many of his songs. It was as though my father was sitting next to me and telling me what to write. Meantime, the manager of the barrack came to me and I asked him what he wanted. He said that the manager in the next barrack wanted to have a concert there the next Sunday because the people from that barrack were very impressed with our singing. He begged me not to refuse his request because the people in that barrack were very depressed and worried. He wanted to cheer them and give them more courage to live. They needed hope. I promised him that we would go there the next Sunday. I asked him to bring the same policeman to watch for the Germans while we sang.

The choir began to practice for the next concert and I wrote down more of my father's songs. Some of the melodies I remembered but not the word so I used my own words. I was reminded of the humorous Jewish stories that my father used to tell to make people laugh. I started to write down the songs and the religious stories from the bible. While writing,

I also practiced with the choir. Then every Sunday we were invited to another barrack to sing and tell stories. This went on for six weeks.

One morning when I was standing in line for my coffee, the Kapo took me out of line and asked me to stay inside. I got scared and wondered what they wanted. I thought maybe I had done something wrong. I waited about a half hour when a Jewish policeman came and asked me my name. He had a list in his hand and he took me to the main gate. I was shivering and worried about what they wanted from me. He didn't tell me anything. When we came to the main gate there was a vehicle parked and I saw three people waiting. I recognized them and they were happy to see that I was still alive after what happened at the Krakow ghetto. I hadn't seen them before because there were 30 barracks at Plaszow with over thirty thousand people. One of the men was Mr. Sheidl.

They were taking us back to work at Wawel. Mr. Sheidl was thankful because he said he couldn't have hung on much longer. When Obersturmfuhrer Hoppe saw us, he was very happy. He took us to the work shop where we had built those boxes for the Russian front. It looked as though they hadn't brought in any other workers to do our job because everything was the way we had left it. We started to make the boxes. Soon Obersturmfuhrer Hoppe asked Mr. Sheidl to make them breakfast. There was a different attitude toward us here. It was not the same as in Plaszow. At Viking, they treated us like people and professional carpenters. In Plaszow, we were treated like criminals sentenced to hard labor and eventual death. There they gave us bad food and beat us while we worked. We never knew who was going to be sacrificed or who would be shot to death or hanged.

We had a lot of work left to do and we worked very fast because we were happy to be there. At lunch, I went to the grocery store to buy some food with the little money I had left. I also bought food for the other workers because I knew about the prices. It was a risk because I had to take off the band on my arm and the star on my chest in order to go to the store. The store wasn't too far from where we worked. No one bothered me and I became friends with the Polish owner of the store. Many times when he saw the German or Jewish police, he was afraid. He would tell me to go into the other room in case they came into the store.

We brought the food into camp because they didn't check us and we could make a little money from selling the food. I now was not so hungry with the extra food I was able to buy. The people in the barrack asked me to buy food for them. I told them I would buy the food but only if was for them to eat and not to sell. I was risking my life every time I went to the grocery store. Sometimes they did check people at the main gate and if they found food, they would just take it away and divide it among them. They didn't punish us. Everyday when I came back from work people were waiting for me so they could buy my food. We now were not so hungry.

I started to look for my friend, Henek Korngold. I asked around in many of the barracks but I couldn't find him. Because there were so many people living in the camp, it was hard to find someone. Every morning when I went to work, I thought about Henek and wanted to try to find him. It would have been nice if he had a job here with me. He was a true friend and had a good heart. He helped me in so many ways. Because he didn't have a steady job and a proper identity card saying that he worked at one place, he may not have survived. I hoped that he wasn't transported to Auschwitz or Treblinka when they were finished closing the Krakow ghetto. Every night I looked in a different barrack for Henek. I asked people about him, but I couldn't find him. I then thought that maybe after the war I would find him and we would be together again. (After the war, I looked for him but I couldn't find him.)

Everyday at 7:30 in the morning a vehicle with an SS soldier pulled up to the main gate of the Plaszow camp and picked four of us up to go to work at SS Viking in the Wawel. At 5:30 in the evening, they brought us back to Plaszow. We did the same thing every day building many of the wooden boxes. We packed the boxes with parts for airplanes, cars, and trucks. We were very happy to have this job. They were very satisfied with our work. At the time when we weren't there, they had Poles working for them, but they were not satisfied with their work.

When we went to work the next day, Mr. Sheidl told us that while he was making breakfast, an SS soldier he knew from Berlin said that there was an uprising at the Warsaw ghetto. It was surrounded by German troops. We noticed that the SS at our place were very nervous. Many of the Warsaw ghetto soldiers had been killed when they went into the ghetto. They sent some of the troops from our place to Warsaw. We noticed a change at work. We heard them say, "Die Jew." They told us to work faster because they needed the material for the Warsaw action. This went on for five weeks and now they were afraid they were going to have to go to the ghetto. We were happy to hear that five hundred German soldiers had been killed. We wondered what was going to happen.

We saw a big change at Plaszow. There were a lot of killings. They were going wild beating people at work. The commandant at Plaszow was riding around on his horse and shooting people. Everyday it got worst. We heard that many Jews were being killed every day.

After five week and on the second day of Passover, the Germans bombed buildings in the Warsaw ghetto. All the buildings were in flames. It was unbelievable how the Jews fought against the Nazis in the ghetto.

Before the bombing, the Germans went from house to house and the Jews, with their last strength killed many Germans. It was a street fight, but because they had no food, they had to give up. They were taken and loaded on trucks to be sent to Auschwitz or Treblinka. There was not one house or building left in the ghetto. Mr. Sheidl was told how the Jews had fought against the strong Germans and how they were able to kill so many of the enemy. They were heroes. After that uprising, it got worst for the Jews in our camp because the Germans were afraid of another uprising.

After the Warsaw uprising, Governor Frank instituted a law saying that from this day forward no Jew could go from his place alone. If Jews from Plaszow were caught in the street, they would be shot or hanged. I hadn't yet heard about this law. If I had known about the new law, I never would have gone to the grocery store to buy food for Mr. Sheidl, Mr. Wolf, and myself, but I didn't want to refuse them. When I got back to the Wawel I put on my armband and the star, I saw the Obersturmfuhrer coming toward me, and I got scared. I couldn't avoid him. He saw the bag I was carrying and he stopped me and asked me what I had in the bag. I told him about buying food for my group. He said, "Dog, don't you know that there is a new German government law from Governor Frank that a Jew cannot go outside alone to shop? If a Jew is caught alone in the street, he would be turned over to Commandant Goeth from Plaszow to be shot or hanged." I told him I was sorry and didn't know about the law and would not do it anymore. He pulled out his revolver from his pocket and hit me on my right ear. I thought he had shot me. I fell to the floor and the groceries fell out of the bag onto the floor. At that time, I lost my hearing on the right side. He told me to lie there because I was going to be shot anyway and he left. I touched my ear and it was very bloody. I sat upright on the floor and I was mixed up, everything was going around like a carousel.

I didn't know what to do. Many of the German military walked passed and saw me sitting there. I thought maybe it was a dream. After twenty minutes, two SS from Viking came and told me to get up. I knew them from work and they took me down to the basement. They opened a door and told me to go in. They told me that after work I was to be given over to the Plaszow commandant. They locked the door when they left. I remained standing and looked around. It was very dark in the room. There was a little window with an iron bar. I couldn't run away. On the floor, there were pieces of iron, broken chains, and a small wooden box. I took the box to the window and sat down. My face was on fire from the pain all over my head. I felt my left ear with my finger and knew I was deaf in that ear. I thanked God that I was still alive.

While I sat on the box, I thought to myself that it was probably my last day. Tomorrow they were going to hang me. I knew I had to say a prayer, called Vydy. I started to say all the prayers that I remembered from Hebrew School. I remembered the two prayers from King David that my Grandma had taught me. She had said that I was very good at remembering the prayers. At two o'clock, I was still sitting in the room and knew what was going to happen to me the next day. I was fighting to stay alive until now. I wanted to stay alive to tell the world what the Germans had done to us just because we were Jews.

While I was there, big rats were running passed me. They came from outside through the small window. I was so mixed up that I didn't care. I just sat there and thought about my troubles and the situation I was now in. I was thinking about my parent and our house and how the Germans had taken us all away. That was the last day I was with my parents and sisters. Before we left the house, my mother had given me the diamond ring. It was my grandmother's and a great Rabbi had blessed her while she wore the ring. She thought that by giving me the ring it would help me in a life or death situation. I had hidden it in my mouth every time I changed my clothing. No one knew about the ring that I kept in my pants. I thought that this would be a good time to use it. I might be able to give it to the guy who would be taking me back to camp. What can I lose? I had my sentence, but I believed in God all the time. I had a feeling that I was going to live and that God would help me. I wanted to live. Maybe Mr. Sheidl could talk to them because he had a connection with the Germans.

After four and a half hours, I was still sitting on the small box, but it felt like a month. I started to talk to myself as if I was talking to my father, mother, and God. I asked them to help me because I wanted a life. I didn't know what was going to happen to me. I saw before my eyes the angel of death. I thought that tomorrow they were going to hang me in front of thirty thousand people. There was no one to cry for me or say the Kaddish for me. There was no one to remember me. I remained sitting in the dark basement with the rats running back and forth, but I didn't care. I pretended not to see them.

At 5:30 in the evening, the door opened and a young man in his twenties called Fritz came in. He was a quiet, nice man and told me to go with him. I walked with him through the corridors of the Wawel to a waiting vehicle. I was very, very nervous on the way. While we were walking, I asked him where he was taking me. He told me that Obersturmfuhrer Hoppe gave him a letter and that he had to give it to Commandant Amon Goeth, the well known murderer, and Jew killer at Plaszow. I started to talk to him and told him they were going to hang me. I showed him my mother's diamond ring that had been blessed by a great Rabbi, a holy man. I told him the story about my mother giving me the ring because she thought it would save me in times of danger. She felt that the ring would save my life. He said he didn't know what to do because he had the letter to deliver to Commandant Goeth from Obersturmfuhrer Hoppe. He stopped talking and didn't say anything. I didn't know what he was thinking. Before we got into the waiting vehicle, I asked him again to take the ring, that I was going to be dead tomorrow and didn't need it. You could use it to save your life and go back to your family. He didn't say anything and I still had the ring in my hand. Then, before we got into the vehicle, he took the ring from my hand, but he didn't say anything.

Mr. Sheidl asked me what had happened and where I had been. I told everyone in the vehicle what had happened and where I had been all day long. I said that the driver had a letter for Commandant Goeth from Obersturmfuhrer Hoppe and that I probably would be shot or hanged in the morning. They had pity for me and I couldn't talk anymore. I had tears in my eyes and became very nervous. I asked them to try to give my story to a Jewish organization so that my brother Moshe or Sara from Russia would know what had happened to me. I wanted to be remembered by them with yearly prayers. I asked Mr. Sheidl to talk to the driver, but I didn't tell him about giving the driver my mother's ring. I asked him to tell the driver to say that he waited and waited for Commandant Goeth, but he must have been busy so he was unable to give him the letter. Then he could take the letter back to Obersturmfuhrer Hoppe and he wouldn't be punished.

It was a thirty minute drive and the whole time Mr. Sheidl prevailed upon the driver to help me. He talked from the heart. Mr. Fritz listened the whole time but didn't say anything. I had a feeling that he would do something to help me. With God's help, I would be saved. When I had given him the ring, I saw that he felt sorry for me. Mr. Sheidl did a wonderful job with the story the driver should use when he went back to the Wawel so that he wouldn't be punished. Mr. Sheidl told me not to lose hope. Mr. Fritz still didn't say a word. I knew that all the German SS at Viking liked Mr. Sheidl. He was a good man and the driver respected him because every morning he made them breakfast.

When we came to the main gate at Plaszow, my heart was broken, I was depressed, and my heart was beating fast. I thought I was having a heart attack, but I knew I had to be strong and I prayed to God that the commandant was not there as usual. He was at the main gate in the morning and at night because a lot of Polish workers, who were carpenters or plumbers, also worked at the camp. Mr. Fritz jumped from the vehicle and looked around. He didn't know whether to give me over to the commandant or do what Mr. Sheidl had asked him. I saw him go over to one of the guards and talk to him. It looked as if he was asking for the commandant. My heart was jumping while he was talking to the guard. The murderer Goeth was not at the main gate today. He came over to us with a smile on his face and said that the commandant was not there. They were at a party that was to last very late into the evening. He told me with a smile that he couldn't wait to see the commandant and had to go back to Wawel because he had a lot of work to do. He told the guard to let us in and said he would see us again. He didn't hand over the letter to the guard; he still had the letter when he left.

When the group came to the main gate and because of the new law, they found our food and took it away from us. While we were standing there, we found out that this was the last time we would be able to work outside the camp. The guards checked us again from top to bottom. I was afraid that they might have my name, but thank God, they let us go. I was happy when I went to my barrack. I thanked God for saving me. I didn't want to think about the next day. I was afraid that they would come back with the letter. I didn't want to think about it. I thought about what would happen to me if they did bring back the letter from Obersturmfuhrer Hoppe. After a week's time, no one called me to the police about the letter. Little by little, I stopped thinking about it. I prayed every morning and said the Psalm of David. I prayed to God to make them forget about me.

Now no one could go outside to work because of the new law. Every day they took me to a different place to work. It was very hard work. After work, I was tired and hungry. The food was very bad, but at least I was alive. Then I sat down and started to write again. My father's songs and stories came back to me. I remembered the stories he used to tell and the songs he used to sing for brides and grooms. I was so happy that I could remember so quickly. I used to be with my father so much that I wrote what I remembered him telling me. If I remembered the melodies but not the words, I would use my own words. When I helped my father sing on Friday nights or at weddings, sometimes I would have trouble with my throat. I used to have lots of colds and singing was hard for me. That's why I didn't want to sing solo.

I didn't have a chance to say thank you to Mr. Sheidl for what he did for me when the driver took us back from the Wawel. I went looking for him even though there were so many people in the camp including Poles and Gypsies. I finally found him about twenty barracks away from me. I kissed and hugged him and thanked him for what he had done for me. I went to the manager of his barrack, who was a Jew from Berlin, and told him what had happened to me and what Mr. Sheidl had done for me. I told him that he had saved my life. If it weren't for him, I would not be here any longer. I invited him to my barrack for our next concert. He told me that Mr. Wolf and Mr. Goldstein were divided in different barracks. He gave me the numbers of their barracks. Since it was nine o'clock, I went back to my barrack and went to sleep.

The next day I started to look around for the people who had been in the choir. I found five of them, but the rest had been sent to a different camp. There were some groups who still worked outside. When they came back from work they were searched. Over the loud speaker they were told that if they found anything on them, they would be shot or hanged. People then were afraid to bring food into the camp. All we had to eat was soup, 250 grams of bread with margarine. The soup was water with beet and carrot tops with no potatoes. It was very hard to live on it. The people who went outside to work took their clothes with them to sell to the Poles, but they still couldn't bring back any food. The only reason they let some people out was because they could do important work for the Germans.

One Saturday evening over the loud speaker, everyone in the camp was told to go to a big place where there was a little hill called pagorka. The Kapos and the managers had to go too. It was almost dark. They said that no one was to stay in their barrack. No one knew what was happening or why they had called us all together. Thirty thousand people were together in a very high place with music playing. They had searchlight and told us to stay in line. Now we could see what was going on. They had built three places for hangings. Two Jewish policemen were standing nearby and the music was playing very loud. On the other side sat Commandant Amon Goeth with his SS commandos. We were waiting to see what was going to happen. We were scared. I was afraid they were going to call my name. I started to shiver and my heart was beating fast. I thought the hanging was for me.

I saw a vehicle coming toward us. They let out three young girls and they stood together. I heard them say over the loud speaker that the girls had broken the new law. They had been found with food when they were checked at the main gate. Now they were going to be hanged together in front of all the people standing and watching. When I heard that I was afraid I was going to faint. I urged myself to stay strong and I hoped that they wouldn't call my name. I thought that this parade had been for me, but I thanked God that it was not. My thoughts turned to my father and what they had done to him. He never did anything bad. They killed him because he was blind and a Jew. He was a good hearted man. Tears started to run down my face. I was crying with happiness that I still had a life.

They brought the three girls to be hanged. I saw a tall Jewish policeman that I recognized. His name was Lalc. I knew his family and he went to my Hebrew School, Talmud Torah. He went straight to the three girls and put the noose around each of their necks while the music still played very loudly. We heard a shot and the policeman removed the chairs the girls were standing on. The noose on one of the girls broke and she fell down. They brought another stronger noose and they put it around her neck again. While she was hanging, they shot her. I was numb. I said a prayer to God. When the hangings were finished, they announced over the loud speaker again that this was the punishment for bringing food into the camp. They told us to form a line and the Kapo from each barrack took us back. I was in a state of shock. All the people were depressed and walking with their heads down. They talked quietly to each other about it being the end of their life in this camp. They felt that this was just the start. Today it was three girls, tomorrow it will us.

I started to look for my choir. I had nine people and I started to prepare for the Sunday concert. I knew that after horror of the day, the people needed a concert because they were depressed and needed something to lift their spirits. I asked our manager to get in touch with Mr. Orenstein, the Yiddish policeman to watch for Germans while we conducted our concert. In the group, we had a guy named David Verdiger. He had a beautiful voice. I asked him to sing something cheerful. He prepared to sing in Polish and in Hebrew. We all practiced together.

We got together in our barrack at 7:30 p.m. When the policeman came, he was happy to see me and said he would do his best to guard against the Germans so nothing bad would happen. I knew what kind of an impression the hangings had on the people. To see those three girls killed in such a miserable way was terrible. I thanked him for his kindness. It was good for the people in the barrack to have a little happiness and to give them hope. Perhaps the bad things would come to an end and we all would live to see our freedom.

Before we started the mini-concert, I asked for a minute of silence for the three Jewish girls who had been killed. Life must go on and we had to be strong and patient. We will overcome our depression. We had to remain alive to tell the world what had been done to the Jewish people and we hoped to see our families together again. Our first song was, "Where Are My Children, Where." The choir and the people were singing together with me. We were crying while we sang, "Never worry that you are going the last way." I sang one of my father's songs in Yiddish. I also sang the war song that my father had written. We sang for an hour and the people were very happy and had smiles on their faces. When we finished, the policeman went away and we went to sleep.

In the morning, the same thing happened. We stood in line to be counted after they gave us the black coffee. The Kapo took twenty people to work to dig ditches because they were building new barracks. The work was very hard. The people warned me that Commandant Goeth was riding around on his horse and shooting people at random. It was a sport with him as if the people were animals. He would shoot into a group of people and kill them for pleasure. The Kapo told us to work fast because the commandant liked to shoot people at work. When he galloped past our group, he didn't shoot. We started to breath again. We also heard that not far from where we worked near the main gate, they were shooting people they had found with food. When they caught Jews in the streets of the city that were given over to them by the Poles, they also were shot. The Poles were getting a kilo of sugar for each Jew they turned over to the Germans. They brought them to the pagorka and buried them there. It was five months ago that Henek and I stood there and almost got shot. We had been saved by a miracle when they took us out of line and had us bury the dead. Plaszow was not ready to take in more people because the barracks were not finished. If you were taken to the pagorka, it meant you would be shot.

When I went home from work, I started to write down more of my father's songs that I remembered. I tried to remember the songs that he had written before the war. I was busy every Sunday with the choir because all the other barracks wanted us to come and sing for them. During the concert, the policeman, Mr. Orenstein, would come and watch at the different barrack where we were scheduled to sing. I didn't want to do anything during the week because the Germans were always there and it would be dangerous. We only had concerts on Sunday.

Five weeks later, we heard over the loud speaker that everyone was to come out of the barracks. We were told to form of line of five. They took us to the big place where we remained standing and waiting for orders. We understood that something must have happened again. We waited for about twenty minutes when they told us to march to the pagorka. There were German and Jewish police with us. When we got there, the loud speaker told us that the day before they had caught a group of one hundred Jews with food and other goods in their clothing. They had been taken to the pagorka and Commandant Goeth said that the whole group had been shot. They wanted everyone to know that they were serious. They marched us over to where the dead bodies had been placed. They already had made a hole in the ground for them. As we marched through over one hundred bodies, I saw a fiddle on the ground near a dead person. I recognized David Lessman from Dzialoszyce. He was only about twenty five years old and a very good violinist who used to write the notes when my father created a song. He had a brother Bert and they lived in our house until the war broke out. I screamed when I saw him lying on the ground. I had a cramp in my stomach but I had to move on because the people kept walking. I was broken hearted when I looked into his face. I thought that twice I had been sentenced to die at this place, the pagorka. Thank God for my luck. It was my greatest miracle.

When I went back to my barrack, I found out that the group of one hundred people worked for a German construction company. David Lessman didn't have to do any of the hard labor at the job because he only played the violin for them. He took the violin with him every day. The Obersturmfuhrer had given them the food to take home. Only four or five of the people had food with them but they killed all one hundred. This would have been their last day of work outside the camp. It was a terrible end for them. Everyone was punished because the others had food in their clothing. Their manager was a high ranking officer and he was the one who let them buy food in the grocery store. He was a very good man. It was Commandant Goeth who was standing at the main gate when the hundred people came back. He was the one who gave the orders to shoot all the people.

Terrible days began at Plaszow. Not one day went by without a killing. Commandant Goeth continued to shoot people as he rode by on his horse. At this time, we had to live on a 250 gram portion of bread and margarine for breakfast. At lunch, they gave us a terrible soup with the beet, carrot, or turnip tops. Many people started to become swollen and had diarrhea. The work we did was hard and we were not given enough food. Every day there were people dying in bed so the Germans didn't have to kill them. I was very scared. They were bringing Jews to Plaszow from other camps and then sending them to Auschwitz, Treblinka, or Majdanek. That was their tactic. Everyday more people were killed.

I tried writing down more songs and also practicing with the choir to prepare for the Sunday concerts. When we went to the different barracks, the people were very happy to see us but it was still dangerous. Sometimes when someone had died or went to the hospital and didn't come back the manager would give me that person's food. I then would share it with the choir, so we had it a little better than others. Even with that extra food, we were always hungry because we had to work so hard every day. Now with the new law everybody was hungry because we couldn't buy food or exchange clothing for food. More people were dying from hunger than from the shootings.

One morning after we had our coffee, they sent me to work with a group and we had Mr. Orenstein, the Jewish policeman guarding us. There were pipes on the ground near ditches that had been dug for the new barracks they had just built. They put the pipes in the hole with a forklift. The Kapo who was assigned to the job got sick so we only had the policeman watching us. It was August and very hot at the site. It had to be one hundred degrees. When the pipes were put in the ditch, we had to make sure the pipes were set together before we covered them with dirt. It was very hard work and very hot. The policeman told us to sit down and rest while he watched for the Germans. Sometimes Commandant Goeth would come to the work place on his horse to supervise the work. He would kill many people there for no reason. Mr. Orenstein's cousin was in the work group and lived in our barrack. While he was our guard we didn't have to work as hard, but the heat made us very thirsty. There were no trees or any shade.

At lunchtime, the policeman took us to the kitchen not too far from the site. He told the cook that we were special, professional workers and he was to give us the better soup not just the watery one. After we finished, we asked for more because we were very hungry. They did give us more and we were very happy for the cook's kindness. That was the first time they had treated us so good. We rested again because we had an hour for lunch. I asked the policeman if I could speak to him alone because I knew him very well. He took me to a place where they kept all the equipment. We sat on two wooden boxes and made sure no one saw us. White he ate his lunch; he asked me if I had written down any new songs and where the next concert was going to be held. I told him the number of the barrack where we were going to have our concert on the following Sunday. He said that he would be there.

While sitting there, I told him face to face that conditions at Plaszow were getting worst and worst. It was becoming very dangerous, there was less food, and we couldn't buy any from the outside. It didn't look as if we could hold on much longer because the work was so hard and there wasn't enough food. I was a fighter but I was loosing strength. How much longer could I hold on? I reminded him that our camp was a transit place where people came from other places and then were sent to their deaths. I knew that there were companies on the outside who were looking for new workers. They would come to the Germans and then they would send them workers from the concentration camps. It was the Jewish police who decided which workers to send outside like they did in Krakow. I begged him to put my choir and me on the list. I didn't have anything to lose. I was fighting to stay alive. I tried to give other people hope with my singing, but I myself was falling apart. Every day there were new restriction and laws changing.

He listened to my speech but didn't say anything. He was very quiet. Then he said that he remembered my father at weddings and how he was the Badchen. He sang songs in Yiddish and told stories and we started to laugh. He said that he used to go to many weddings but never got tired of hearing my father's stories. He knew about the pain and suffering of the people in Plaszow. We never knew when Commandant Goeth would kill next. He was a sadist, a murderer. The Jewish police were very afraid of him. Very quietly, he told me he knew the situation was getting worse, but he couldn't do much to help the people. He tried to help as much as he could. In the territory that Hitler occupied, it was very dangerous for all the Jewish people. He took out a small notebook with a pencil and wrote my name, the names of the choir, and the barrack numbers. I couldn't remember all the names of the men in the choir. I told him I would give it to him later. He promised me he would try his best to help us get to the outside. He also hoped that the situation would change in Plaszow.

Every day we saw terrible things happening to the people. Sometimes when people went to the toilet Commandant Goeth, while sitting on his horse, would shoot them just like animals. I continued to remember more of my father's stories or songs and I would write them in my book. Then on Sunday, we would have our concert at a different barrack. The people were able to forget their problems for about an hour. I made more friends especially with the Jewish police because they liked the singing.

One Tuesday Mr. Orenstein told me that the choir and I might have a chance to work on the outside. The day before a man called Oskar Schindler and German commando came to the camp looking for workers for a new factory he had opened in Zablocie, a small town near Krakow. He needed eleven hundred people to work in his shop where they made pots, pans, and other items. They gave the request to the Jewish police but they didn't have any of the details as yet. He said as soon as he found out more information about the work he would let me know and he left.

I was quiet and didn't say anything to anybody not even the choir. I continued to go to work every day. I suffered from hunger. There was not enough food. Our group would have to load old heavy machinery onto trucks. We had to straighten the machines before the forklift could put them on the truck. When we finished that job, they took us to load big stones onto trucks. Every day we had a different job. After work, I could only eat the food they gave us and then I would go to bed. Once in a while, our job was a little easier like sweeping the floor.

I was a new person on Sundays. After lunch, I would practice with the choir and at night, we would go to a different barrack to sing. When the concert was over, I would talk to the people and would encourage them not to lose hope and not to get depressed. The war had to end soon and we would have peace.

I heard that someone was coming for workers and I was on the list. Maybe I was getting out of Plaszow. I always had the will power to live. Three weeks later, the policeman explained that Oskar Schindler had taken over a Jewish factory from a man named Mr. Bachner. He told me this would be a good job for the choir and me and we were on the list and should be prepared. I was not to say anything to anybody because then people would pay to be included on the list. I didn't even say anything to the choir.

Five days later while I was standing and waiting to be counted, something was different. Over the loud speaker, they asked everyone to be quiet that they had an announcement. They started to call out names and numbers. Anyone called should get out of line and stand aside to be weighed. They called eleven hundred names and eighteen were from our barrack. They told us to wait. Ten people from the choir were included. After waiting fifteen minutes, another policeman came and marched us to the main gate. Somebody asked where we were going and the name of the Obersturmfuhrer waiting for us. Someone said the man's name was Schindler and that he was taking us to his factory that was not too far from here. We saw him talking to five German officers who went into the building with him. It took about twenty minutes to settle all the formalities saying he was responsible for eleven hundred Jewish slaves. As soon as he came out with his portfolio in his hand, twenty or thirty trucks pulled up and we jumped in. You could see the happiness on everyone's face.

Since there were not enough trucks, they had to get about five more. We didn't know if this trip was going to make our lives better or worst. I started to remember the last five weeks when I saw them hang the young girls and the killings that went on every day. I started praying the daily prayers and the psalm that my grandmother had taught me. I thanked God for my life. I told my friend from the choir that we had done the right thing leaving Plaszow. Also the Jewish police were going with us. The commandant was Mr. Sperling and his helper was Mr. Kuba Nadel. In addition, there was a German commandant with a group of Germans.

About a half hour later, we came to Schindler's factory in Zablocie. All the truck stopped and we remained standing. The Jewish police helped us jump down. They told us to stay in line so that they could count us again. While waiting, I saw a tall, handsome SS Obersturmfuhrer get out of one of the trucks. He said, "Good morning, gentlemen" and introduced himself as Oskar Schindler. In a short speech, he welcomed us to our new job and he talked in a very friendly tone. He said, "My dear Jews, you are not slaves any more. You now will work for me in my factories. I ask that you take care with your work and work as fast as you can because the goods were going to the German Army. I want you to be happy." He then left.

They took us to our barracks. There were about twenty two or twenty four barracks with a wire fence all around. Two German soldiers were standing at the entrance and told everyone where to sleep. Mine was the fourth barrack with a Kapo called Mr. Feldstein who was a German Jew and about fifty years old. He was speaking Polish and Yiddish. I picked the top bunk near the window for more air. Everyone had his own little drawer. I put my thing away. They gave us two blankets. It wasn't like Plaszow where I only had one blanket. The pillow was filled with straw. It was like our other barracks where the beds lined both sides of the building with three bunk beds one on top the other. The atmosphere was different from Plaszow. It was quiet and the air smelled different.

It was lunchtime and we heard a whistle. Our Kapo, Mr. Feldstein, took us to the kitchen across from our barrack. I had my dish and spoon ready for the soup. There was a young blond fellow working in the kitchen was named Maier. He used a ladle to give us our soup. Everyone was very hungry. The soup was thick and had potatoes. Unlike Plaszow's watery soup, this was thick. We looked and smiled at each other. The managers from the barracks gave us each a ticket that we had to give to Maier. We had an hour for lunch. I went back to my barrack and ate my lunch. I told the neighbor next to me that the food was different. After lunch, we heard a whistle. We went out and stood in line and they took us to the factory where we were to work every day.

Who Was Oskar Schindler?

Oscar Schindler belonged to the Nazi organization from 1930 through 1939. In the years from 1939 through 1940, the German government took over all the businesses and factories from the Jews. From 1943 through 1944, Oskar Schindler took over Mr. Bachner's enamel factory, *Deutsche Emailwaren Fabrik*, in Zablocie near Krakow and divided it into two parts. In the enamel factory, they produced pots and pans and in the other part, they repaired radiators from airplanes that were shot down. They divided the people to work in both factories. Half went to the enamel factory where they made the pots and pans and the rest went to the N.K.F. factory to repair the radiators from airplanes or trucks. The manager was Mr. Meiteles and Mr. Bauman was the sub-manager. The main professional was Mr. Meiteles.

Mr. Meiteles took me to a table with a small basin that was filled with water and had a gas burner. I had a piece of lead and a small hammer. It was everything I needed to repair the radiators. He showed me what I had to do. Mr. Bauman took a radiator and put it into the basin of water. The water started to bubble. When he took it out of the water, he marked it with a piece of white chalk. The reason it bubbled was because it had a hole in it. He showed me how to fix the hole. He took a long piece of lead and turned on the gas burner. When the lead melted, he filled the hole. He took another radiator and showed me again what to do. The first day was not very hard for me.

They took all of us back to our barracks. I straightened my drawer and started to write in my book. It was like a vacation for me on this first day. When I looked out the window, I saw a group of boys playing soccer. My heart was full of joy. I wished I could have had my whole family here with me. I found five of the men from the choir who were in different barracks. We got our 250 grams of bread and margarine with two cigarettes. Everyone was talking together and we were happy for the change.

The First Day at Work

At seven o'clock in the morning, we marched together to work in two groups. One group for the enamel and the second went to N.K.F. I knew where I was to work and went to my place. I stood and looked at the equipment on the work table and I asked somebody to help me start the job. Mr. Meiteles helped me put the radiator in the water where it started to bubble. It was from an airplane that had been shot down. He marked the six places with holes and showed me again how to fill up the holes. I had to turn on the gas burner to melt the lead. I then filled up all six holes with the hot lead. Afterward we put the radiator back in the water to see if it had stopped bubbling. Four of them had stopped but two had not. We put the radiator back on the table and melted more lead from the gas burner and filled the two holes. He was with me for about three quarters of an hour. He was very friendly and asked me if I understood what to do. I told him that I did understand. He told me I should start working on another radiator and he would be back in about an hour to check on me. When he came back to inspect my work he told me I had to practice more but that it would be okay. I did that all day long. I practiced and tried to do a good job, but I was very slow. At five o'clock, they sent us back to our barracks.

I got my 250 grams of bread, margarine, and the two cigarettes. I exchanged the cigarettes for bread. The next day was the same. We got up at six o'clock in the morning, got washed, and dressed. I got in line for coffee and they took us to work. I went to my work place where I had all my equipment. I put a radiator on the table and did what Mr. Meiteles had showed me. I saw where the water was bubbling in three places on the radiator, marked it with chalk, melted the lead and filled the holes with the melted lead. I waited for it to cool and put it back into the water and one place was still bubbling. Mr. Meiteles and Mr. Bauman passed by and stopped to see how I was doing. After they both checked it over, they saw that one hole needed to be fixed. They told me I had done a good job. They wanted me to do piecework. I told them that I was not ready to please give me more time. I told them I would do a good job for them but not on piecework. They left me alone.

I wanted to learn and was very interested in the job. I knew right now I couldn't work fast because I was just learning. I didn't want them to send me back to Plaszow so I tried harder. Mr. Schindler passed by and was very friendly. He said that he hoped we were doing our best work. At lunchtime, I met Mr. Henek Tenenbaum, Fredi Fridner and others. Mr. Meiteles was a genius at the work. He came back to me five times during the day to show me how to do the job easier. I thanked God that I had come out of the Plaszow Hell. That was my first day at N.K.F. with Oskar Schindler.

The First Night at the Barracks

When I came home from work, I was very tired from doing a job that I was just learning. I exchanged my two cigarettes for more bread. It was like a market place with so many people exchanging bread or soup for cigarettes. Most of the people there were from Krakow and a lot of Poles came to work there from the outside. They had connections and they brought food in to sell for clothing such as men's shirts, dresses or sheets. It was not like Plaszow. The German guards didn't check the Poles to find out what they brought into the buildings. They had salami, cheese, bread, butter, and rolls. Whoever had money could get anything he wanted. There was no more hunger among the people. We were not afraid that they would shoot us for bringing in food. It was a different atmosphere. Those people who had money lived much better. I didn't have any money when I went to Plaszow because they had taken everything from me even the money Commandant Shapiro had given me.

Some people didn't think about tomorrow. They lived for now. There were eighty people in each barrack. After a week, we all started to get acquainted. We were like brothers who cared about each other and some people knew me from Plaszow when I sang and told stories from barrack to barrack. They wanted me to start a mini-concert and get the choir together. I began to think about it. It was nine o'clock and we had to go to bed.

At six o'clock in the morning, the bell rang and we all jumped out of bed to get dressed and get in line. We had to be on the job at seven o'clock so we marched together to the factory. Everybody went to his job. I went to my work place. It was a little easier and I knew what I was doing but I needed more experience. I asked some of the workers if they knew an easier way to do my job. During the work day, the managers came by to check on my work. They told us they didn't want any monkey business and wanted us to do our best job. They said that we should obey all the rules or we would be sent back to Plaszow. If we tried to run away and were caught, they would send us back to Plaszow to be shot.

At lunch, I was lucky to get the scraping from the bottom for my soup. It was very thick. It was still a hard day for me. I had to learn more to make the job better and faster. They did understand and gave me more time to learn. I tried my best because I didn't want to go back to Plaszow.

We had to meet a quota but it was impossible not only for me but all the other workers. Mr. Meiteles showed me how to work better and faster. After that, I improved and did a better job a little faster.

We didn't have to work on Sunday because the factory was closed. The difference from Plaszow to Schindler's factory was like from hell to paradise. At Schindler's factory, you were a worker not a slave to be shot at any time. In addition, the Poles came to the factory to work as carpenters, plumbers, or electricians. They were not afraid to bring in food so I started to deal with them. I first talked to them at lunchtime and told them I wanted to do business. I ordered fifty sweet rolls and told one of the boys that he would get twenty percent of those he sold. In the evening when we went home, I gave 15 pieces to the boy to sell. It took about a half hour and he sold all of them. He kept five sweet rolls for himself. He brought me the money and I gave him twenty percent of the profits. I had paid my debt because I had borrowed the money from Mr. Fried.

Sundays we still had to get up and be counted. After we had our coffee, we were free to do whatever we wanted. People read books that they had brought with them. Some took naps. I started to write in my book. I tried to remember more of the four hundred songs my father had composed. I remembered the melodies better than the words. I wrote down two beautiful songs, one was "Want, Want the Wailing Wall" and "Shabbat Saturday." I wanted to get the choir together and have a mini-concert. When I finished working, I saw a group playing soccer and my heart was full of joy, but I still missed my whole family. I also saw families with small children. We had special soup on Sunday; it was sweet like Farina and very thick. When I finished, I went to the kitchen for more but the cook didn't know me and wouldn't give me any more. I went back to my barrack and went to sleep.

After sleeping for an hours I jumped down and went to the next barrack to try to find someone I knew and I was looking for the members of the choir. I found two people, Israel Yungewirt and David Verdiger. I was very happy to see them and they asked me what I thought about organizing a choir. We decided to look for more of our choir. I went back to my barrack for my bread and cigarettes. I had a steady customer for the cigarettes. He gave me half of his bread that I ate it on the spot. He had been a very rich man and had connections on the outside. Every week someone sent him money and he was able to get salami, cheese, and butter. If someone had money, he could buy anything. Apples, pears, prunes, and other fruit were available. Then it was time for bed.

It was a different life here and I started to do business. I asked people what they had to sell and at lunchtime, we had contact with the Poles.

Then we could exchange merchandise. I started to organize a choir with my friend, Cantor David Verdiger, who had a beautiful tenor voice. (He now lives in Borough Park in New York and on one of his records; he sings one of my father's songs, "Kotel Hamaoroir" ("Wand-Wand"). I met the two brothers, Israel and Nute Yungewirt and others who used to sing with me at Plaszow. I put a nice choir together. Every night I talked to the manager of the barrack and asked him for permission to practice and he said it was okay with him but I would have to get permission from Mr. Feldstein or the commandant of the Jewish police before scheduling a mini-concert.

When I came back from work I spoke with Mr. Feldstein. He was as short fellow and talked very fast. Sometimes he talked so fast that I couldn't understand him. I asked him if we could have our concert next Sunday in the first barracks because it was the biggest. It would make the people happier and that I had done the same thing while in Plaszow. He said he would have to talk to the commandant about it first. We continued to practice in my barracks. Since some of the choir lived in other barracks, they used to come to my barracks. Soon Mr. Feldstein said that the commandant would allow the concert but to be quiet about it because we were only there a short time.

The first concert started Sunday at seven thirty in the evening. Five hundred people showed up in the first barracks for the concert. It was packed and it was a big success. We couldn't believe that it would be so successful. The people were impressed. Mr. Feldstein and the manager from the barracks told me the next day that they would like us to have another one the following Sunday. Mr. Feldstein asked me to compose a special song. He wanted it to be about how he was trying to protect us. He said that he would give me a couple of hours off from work in order to work on the poem. I composed a song about him, which told about his goodness towards us, and that he was a special Kapo. I also praised the commandant of the police, Mr. Sperling and Mr. Meiteles because they also were good to us and we were fortunate to have them as our leaders.

We started to prepare for the next concert. The choir and I got together to practice every night from seven thirty until nine o'clock at night. At the same time people were busy selling things like soup, bread, salami, cheese, sardines and different foods that the Poles brought in. It was at lunchtime that people made connections with the Poles, who were working there. They could bring anything in through the main gate because no one searched them.

One time when I came back from work, a German guard said that he heard I spoke Yiddish. He said he was a Romanian Jew and was wearing a German uniform. He said that a lot of Jews were in the German Army and he was sent here to guard us.

Everything was going well and nobody was hungry. We almost forgot our lives in Plaszow. Everyday I got to know more and more people. At Christmas time, Mr. Feldstein told me that the German commando wanted to see me. I got very scared because I didn't know what he wanted or if I had done something wrong. I was worrying all day long but said to myself that I believed in God and He had helped me before and He will help me again. Mr. Feldstein came to my barracks and said that he thought they wanted me to do some entertaining. He asked me if I was the only one who took care of the singing. I told him that I was. They wanted the choir to sing at a party they were going to have for the New Year's holiday. When I went to see the commandant, Oskar Schindler was sitting with the SS man. I told him that I used to sing with my father and that he was a composer of Yiddish songs. I told him we had a Cantor who sang beautifully. They wanted me to bring the choir to perform at the party on the evening of December 31st. I said I would and left. When I left, I was shivering but I thanked God that was all they had wanted.

I went to work right away because there wasn't much time to prepare. I called the choir together and informed them that we were going to sing for the German commandos at the holiday party and Commandant Goeth from Plaszow was going to attend. They also got scared and said they were afraid to go there, but I told them not to worry. I had talked to them and they were very friendly. This will be good for us. They decided to do it and started practicing.

At lunchtime, we continued to get together with the Poles so we could buy food from them. Day by day, I improved at my job. I still couldn't make the quota because it was too much. No one could have done it. It was too much. When Mr. Bauman came by and checked my work he said it was good but we had to try to make more. He didn't want the Germans to complain. I promised him I would try harder. I became very good friends with a guy named Fred Tredi. The time was flying by. I wasn't going around hungry any longer because I was buying and selling food. I didn't have to live on the soup, bread, margarine, and hot coffee that they gave us. I even had some fruit along with cheese and sardines, and I bought bread for myself.

Almost every Sunday we had a mini-concert in the first barracks. I now knew Maier who worked in the kitchen because he never missed a concert. He really liked my music and always thanked me after the concert. He wanted me to know how much the people appreciated my work and that I was giving them life and hope. He told me he had lost his family. I told him not to worry but to hold on. From then on he gave me more soup and bread. Every night the choir practiced together and I told Mr. Verdiger to prepare the songs that he liked to sing.

On December 31st at seven o'clock in the evening, twelve of us were waiting for Mr. Feldstein to take us to the party. Two Jewish policemen were waiting outside and all the people got scared when they saw us with them. They took us to the German commando and my heart was beating very fast. I didn't believe the Germans and what they wanted us to do. When we went into the place it was decorated with flowers and a long table was set with a tablecloth. Around the table sat German women, SS and Gestapo. The men were all in uniform, smiling and laughing together. Oskar Schindler was sitting there with a woman. I didn't know whether it was his wife.

Oskar Schindler stood up first and said that we were Jews who worked for him in the factories. He said that we were amateurs and not professional singers. We were going to sing and make everybody happy. First, they gave us good food and drinks. After we finished eating, we started singing. I started to sing one of my father's songs "Jew Come, Jew Come to Work." The song lyrics were about us walking in the streets and the trucks running after us and catching us for work. The Cantor sang "Srejubune Beith Hamudash"—that a new temple would be built in Jerusalem. The next song I sung was "Where Are My Children, Where? When will I see them back?" We sang for over an hour. After each song, the people clapped and cheered. It looked as though they enjoyed the songs, but I think they all were drunk. When we finished, we said goodbye and Mr. Feldstein took us to the kitchen and gave everyone a loaf of bread. Mr. Feldstein told us that we had done a terrific job. They had liked our performance. When we got back to our barracks, we divided the bread among the people. It was nine o'clock and we had to go to sleep

After we were at our new job a while, we were told that Commandant Goeth, the murderer from Plaszow was coming to check up on us. This was the end of February and he wanted us to be counted to make sure none of us had run away.

Commandant Goeth from Plaszow

On a Friday morning in February 1943, Mr. Schindler let us know that Goeth was coming for an inspection and we were prepared for it, but everybody was scared. We knew he couldn't be trusted because he was a murderer. Wherever he was there was death. We were shivering. After breakfast, we left the barracks and stood in line. There were women and children standing in line with us. It was winter and cold. I had a winter jacket but some people didn't have warm clothing. Even though it was very cold, we didn't have any choice but to wait. We all stood there shivering from the cold and scared. We didn't know why he was coming or how many people he would shoot. We remembered him riding around on his horse shooting people while they worked. Who knew whether he would do the same thing here?

We stood there for two and a half hours. I stood in the second line among eleven hundred people. I saw a vehicle coming with Goeth and his helper, an SS commando. They jumped out of the vehicle and Oskar Schindler greeted them. There were four other SS men with them in uniform. They all walked toward us and with a wild holler he said, "Heil Hitler!" Goeth and Schindler walked slowly through the rows of eleven hundred people. Every five steps they stopped and Goeth looked in the eyes of the people in the front line. I really don't know if they were really counting us. Goeth walked with Schindler behind him. Suddenly, Goeth stopped and pulled a guy standing in the second line. I was standing near him. I was very scared and shivering, and I'm sure everyone felt the same way. He looked into the man's face as if he didn't like him. He told him to walk a little but then to remain standing. He became angry and pulled out his revolver and held it as if to shoot the man. Behind Goeth, Schindler grabbed his hand holding the revolver and told him to leave this dog alone. I will finish him. They both continued to count the people. When they were finished, they stood together awhile. Schindler told Goeth to accompany him to his office for a drink.

After an hour or so Goeth, and his men left and we saw that he was drunk. Two of his men took him to his vehicle and they left with Schindler to go to Plaszow. When Schindler came back after about an hour, he told the manager the whole story. Goeth had come to kill at least ten people but Schindler told him that he needed them for work at the factories. At about 10:30 in the morning we were marched to the factory and back to work. All of us were very nervous. I thanked God that we were all safe and there had been no killings. It was like a miracle.

After work, we received our rations and two cigarettes and people started to exchange their cigarettes for food. Soon after they started to check the Poles and it was harder for them to bring in food. That happened after Goeth had come to our place. After a while, it became easier and they were able to bring in food. After Goeth had been there, we were still worried and didn't know when he would come back. I still thought about my parents, sisters, and brother. I wondered if they were still alive or if I would ever see them again. I remembered the last time I had seen my family in Dzialoszyce and remembered my mother's face.

One night Mr. Goldstein asked me again to write a song praising him for his kindness towards the workers, and I was to sing it at the concert on Sunday. He wanted to be remembered by them. I told him he would have to give me time off from work to compose the song. This way no one was there to bother me and I could concentrate better. At night, there were too many people around and there was too much noise. The next day he took me out of work, so I could work on the song. He was a good man and a good Kapo and everybody liked him. The German's thought he was very strict with us, but when they weren't looking, he told us not to worry.

I composed a beautiful song about him. When I sang it on the following Sunday, he was very happy. This action helped me a lot with the food and at work. Sometimes we had to load trucks with heavy things like cement blocks and heavy machines. He took me out of the group doing that work. He told the Germans that he needed me to do a special job.

Before Purim, Mr. Goldstein told me to take the young man from the kitchen and give him a part in the choir. I taught Maier a comedy skit called "Shadchan Goilem, Shadchan the Stupid." I was the matchmaker and he was the stupid groom. My father used to do this skit at weddings. He liked it and learned his part quickly. I was the matchmaker trying to find him a bride and he was the stupid groom.

During one of the performances, people filled the barracks and people were still coming. The police had to stop them because there wasn't any more room. Maier and I performed our skit and the choir sang. All the people joined in the singing. Afterwards, everyone clapped for about five minutes. They were very enthusiastic. I talked to many of the people afterwards. I told them to live in hope that the war had to end one day and all bad things would come to an end. I told them that we would overcome and would be able to start a new life. We would build a home, get married, and have children and grandchildren. I felt that the time wasn't too far away. While I spoke with the people, they were crying.

Meanwhile I was writing my biography about my experiences and how Oskar Schindler saved my life. I told people that our lives were better now that we were out of Plaszow. We now lived in paradise compared with Plaszow. Oskar Schindler had taken us from Hell to this paradise.

The next day at work, I found a trick that would help me fix the radiators. Everyday I got better and better at the job. The managers were happy. I now had a connection in the kitchen where I could get as much soup as I wanted. I gave some of my slips for the soup to the members of the choir. Many times Mr. Feldstein gave me time off during the day to write about our Sunday performances.

Christmas Time 1944

Time passed and it was Christmas 1944. We didn't have to work so I spent time with my friends, Zechiel Winer (he is alive now and a New York doctor) his brother Israel and Henek Lichtenstein. I would write for a few hours and then talk to David about practicing for a while. Cantor Verdiger was singing Chason music and the choir helped him with the singing.

The next day Mr. Feldstein told me that the SS commandos were having a party again and wanted the choir to entertain as we had done last year. He said to prepare a nice program with my best singers. Oskar Schindler was going to attend along with Commandant Goeth from Plaszow. I shivered at the mention of Goeth's name. I asked him why he hadn't given us more notice so we could have practiced. He told me to the best we could. He told me he would give me time off during the day so no one could disturb me while I prepared the program.

Mr. Feldstein took me out of work and back to my barracks. I wrote down the songs I wanted to sing. When everyone came home from work, I got together with the choir and Cantor David Verdiger and explained the whole program. We had five nights to prepare. The 15-man choir and I had been together for over a year and everyone knew the songs. It didn't take long for them to learn the new ones.

On the evening of December 31st Mr. Feldstein and two Jewish policemen marched us to the German commando. It was only five minutes away. Mr. Feldstein introduced us and Oskar Schindler got up and told the guests that we were his workers and we had come to entertain them. He smiled at us and told us to have a soda. There was a long table with a beautiful tablecloth and flowers. Sitting at the table were about ten people in SS uniforms with their wives or friends. There were twelve Kapos with their spouses. I didn't see Commandant Goeth. He might have come after our program. I sang, "Jude Come to der Arbeit, Jew Come to Work." It was very cold outside so I sang one of my father's songs, "Cold, Cold, Cold, It is Cold, Cold." Then Cantor Verdiger sang a beautiful Chason song from an opera. We sang for a half hour when we stopped for a drink. There was a lot of food on the table. They had bread, sardines, caviar, fruit, and nuts. You would never know there was a war with all the food on that table. When we finished the second half, the people clapped and shouted, "Bravo, Bravo." We were given a loaf of bread and we said goodbye.

On the way to our barracks, Mr. Feldstein told us that we had sung much better tonight than last year. We thanked God that we got out alive. The people asked us if the murderer Goeth from Plaszow was at the party. I told him that I hadn't seen him.

During this winter, it was very cold. I was glad I had the clothing my uncle had given me. Every Sunday we continued with our concerts in the large barracks. Everyone was there, the barracks was full, and Commandant Sperling and his helper Kuba Nadel were very good to us. I thought maybe Oskar Schindler told them not to bother us.

In the factory, I improved at my job. I was able to work faster but I still could not make the quota that they gave me. I was not punished but the manager encouraged me to work faster. I told him I would try. Everyday the managers would stop and inspect my work and talk to the workers and me. They were very friendly and not forceful. I was not afraid to talk to them. We worked like normal people on a job not like a slave. We had enough food and those people with money could buy more. They also could buy clothing.

There was a man in a bunk near me named Mr. Hofer who was about fifty. He had a full mouth of golden teeth. He was a very intelligent man. He would take out one of his golden teeth and show it to me. He had been a dentist. He would take one of his teeth out and sell it to the Polish workers when he needed food or clothing. He said that if God let him live through the war he could always make himself more teeth. I told him he was one hundred percent right to sell his teeth. I would have done the same thing. He said the teeth were 24 carat gold. (After the war I went to Landsberg from Theresienstadt in the American Zone. It was a camp for the Holocaust survivors. We didn't know where to go because we didn't have a home. I didn't want to go back to Krakow because I had heard what the A-K in Poland had done. There was a pogrom in Kielce. They killed Jews all over Poland. I never wanted to go back to Poland once I left. One day as I was walking around and I met Mr. Hofer. He said how thankful he was to be alive. He had sold all his teeth and he already had new ones that were even better than the old. We were very happy to see each other. We had been the lucky ones to work for Oskar Schindler. He did a lot for his workers.)

While working for Oskar Schindler, we tried our best to do a good job because we didn't want to be sent back to Plaszow. I knew about five people who were sent back because they weren't satisfied with their work. We never found out what happened to them, but everybody got scared. I went back to my job and tried to improve on my work. After a while, we heard that Schindler was thinking of moving his factory. All the workers were worried because we didn't know what would happen to us. We wondered if he would take us with him or send us back to Plaszow.

Mr. Feldstein was writing down names. He told me that we were going to have to move, but he didn't say when or where. He wrote down my name and number. (I found out later that workers had paid to have their names included on his list.)

Carl (Kalmen) approximately age 14
with his father Rabbi Symcha Frydman,
Krakow, Poland 1934

Carl's mother, sisters and aunt.
Back row L to R: half-sister Sara, Ryvka, Chana
Front row L to R: Aunt Chava, Mother Beila Ruchel Frydman

Youngest sister Mira and Ryvka

Carl and brother Moshe, Stuttgart, Germany 1947

Ruth Wisniak working at Post Office, Displaced Persons Camp, Stuttgart 1946

Carl Freedman ca. 1947

Carl Freedman and Ruth Wisniak on their wedding day in 1950.

Carl and Ruth in August 2002 with children and children's children:
Back Row L to R: Mel Freedman, Shelley Higgins Freedman, Jonah and Zachary Freedman, Shai Ofer, Rosalie Freedman Ofer, Dov "Dubi" Brosh
Front Row L to R: Alona and Hanni Brosh, Carl Freedman, Ben Brosh, Ruth Freedman, Niva Ofer, Shelli Frydman Brosh

The Liquidation of Schindler's Factories

At the beginning of April 1944 Oskar Schindler decided to take all his machinery to Brinnlitz, Czechoslovakia. They organized a group of workers to work outside. The main Kapo of the group was a Polish guy with one leg. His helper was a young Polish guy. They were both big anti-Semites. I can see them even now. Every day they came inside the factory and picked up workers for job outside. They worked the people very hard. The mechanics dismantled the machinery and we had to help load in on the trucks. When the trucks were full, we had to set the heavy machinery in place. Some people tried to hide so they wouldn't have to do this work, but their names were on the list. When they finished with the machinery, they started to dismantle the buildings that they had built.

Two men, one was Janck Haubenstock and the other one was Inzinuer Kraudis, worked loading and setting up the equipment in the trucks. While they worked, they were singing and whistling Russian songs. The two Polish Kapos were standing and listening while they worked. When they finished working, the Poles went to the SS Rottenfuhrer and SS Sturmbannfuhrer and told them that they had been singing and whistling Russian songs. They told the Poles that they would take care of them. The next day they were questioned and sent back to Plaszow. We heard that they had been hanged. During the hanging, the noose broke on one of them and he fell to the floor so they shot him. It was very painful for us when we found out about our friends.

After that, we were very careful not to say a word when those two Kapos were around. When we worked outside with them guarding us, we didn't open our mouths. After a short time, they started to send workers away. We didn't know where they had gone. We heard that many had been sent to either Mauthausen or Lundz in Austria or back to Plaszow. There were about 150 workers in the last barracks. We were scared because we didn't know what they were going to do with the rest of us. I heard that people were giving money so that their name would be put on the list for Brinnlitz. I knew that Mr. Feldstein had put my name on the list. I just knew that all the machinery and the parts from the buildings had been sent by truck to Brinnlitz. I heard that they had sent about two hundred of the workers to Auschwitz. Everything was a secret.

Every week the rest were sent to work on the outside with the two Folksdoutche Polish men. Nobody opened their mouths when they were around. The workers looked at them with hate in their eyes. All of us worked hard and fast, so they wouldn't have any reason to report us to the Germans. It took them almost five months to dismantle the machinery and the buildings.

It now was the Jewish Holiday of Rosh Hashanah and Yom Kippur. A group of religious Jews were worried about whether they would make us work on the holidays. We spoke to our manager and asked him to help us about work on the holidays. We wanted to prepare so that we wouldn't have to work. I remembered that on one of the holidays, I told them I was sick so I wouldn't have to work. Mr. Feldstein said he would try to help us, but after a week, we still hadn't heard anything. A week before Rosh Hashanah, I again spoke about it to Mr. Goldstein. I told him I would compose a special song about him and sing it at one of the concerts. It would be about what a good man and a wonderful Kapo he was. He did get me out of work by telling them that he had something else for me to do. On Yom Kippur, I fasted all day long. I only had to work for two hours. The next Sunday I sang the song that I had composed about him. He was very happy and he thanked me.

They were still dismantling the buildings and sending the furniture to Lundz, Austria. Everybody was shivering and afraid. Now it was harder for the Poles to bring in food. We didn't know what was going to happen next.

An Australian airplane was shot down on November 2, 1944 in the middle of the night. Everybody was sleeping when we heard a noise outside. We jumped from our beds and didn't have time to get dressed except for our shoes. We grabbed our blankets and went outside. Outside I saw something burning. There was a lot of fire and smoke near the last barracks. We were shivering from the cold. I was standing near my friend, Zechiel Winer. The fire got larger and larger because the barrack was burning. Suddenly a German commando told us he was taking us to the woods. It was about one o'clock in the morning and very cold. There was frost on the ground and we hadn't had time to put on our clothes. As we marched from the camp, the German commandos and the SS surrounded us. I was wearing shoes; a night shirt and I had a blanket around me. After a half hour, we came to the woods and stood in line. They told us to sit down on the grass. I sat close to Zechiel to try to keep warm. The trees were very thick so we couldn't see any light. It was very dark. One of the SS started to speak. He said that they took us from the camp to save our lives because they were responsible for us. They told us no one was to leave or try to escape. If anyone escaped and was caught, he would be shot. We sat, shivered, and wondered what was going to happen next. I thought about escaping into the woods to the town of Zablocie. I might be able to take a chance and hide or maybe it was suicide. I talked it over with Zechiel because now that the camp had burned, they might send us back to Commandant Goeth. From there, we would be finished. It would be a death sentence because they worked you so hard there. Plaszow was terrible and there was a lot of killing. I thought that because we had no clothes, the Poles wouldn't take us in especially in the middle of the night. We didn't know anyone in Zablocie and we would have to go to Krakow. That was too far away. Either the German or Polish police would catch us, and send us back to Plaszow where we probably would be shot.

Meanwhile, we didn't know what time it was. People were coughing and shaking. They kept saying, "Oi, vai oi, vai, I am so cold." I couldn't stand it much longer. Over the loud speaker, the German said any one who ran away would be shot. It felt like a month's time. I thought it would never end. We asked each other what was going to happen. If the whole barracks and the factory burned, they must be going to send us to Plaszow to Commandant Goeth. We waited impatiently for the morning and hoped we could go back to our barracks. I thought about the things I had left and hoped they were still there. We couldn't fall asleep because it was too cold and we were shivering too much. Day light soon appeared. We all tried to squeeze together to keep warm, but we were still shivering. Luckily, there was no snow on the ground. The people started to stand up to look around to try to find out what was going on.

We stood up and started massaging each other to get some warmth because our bodies felt like iron. I never spent such a horrible cold night. We massaged our arms and feet to try to get the circulation back in our bodies. I heard a whistle and over the loud speaker a German voice tell us to get up and stand in line. Everyone stood up and formed a line. The commandant of the camp who was an SS man counted us to make sure we were all there. They said that two people were missing. They counted us again. Then Mr. Feldstein came to us and said that we were going back to the barracks. Meanwhile we were still standing in line trying to get warm. I started clapping my hands and massaging my arms, legs, and my back. Everything was frozen. I also massaged my friend Zechiel. We kept stomping our feet. Another whistle blew and they started to count us again.

We continued to stand and shiver from the cold. We were all very tired since we hadn't slept at all. Mr. Feldstein was in front marching us back to the barracks and to the factory. As we marched back, the Poles stood and watched us. We could still see the fire and the cloud of smoke in the air, and we started to cough and choke.

The Burned Airplane

We came to a burned airplane that was spread over the ground. I asked Mr. Feldstein what had happened. He said that an Australian airplane wanted to bombard the factory, but the German's had shot him down and two barracks had completely burned. It was a miracle that there were no people in the barracks that burned because they had just evacuated 200 of them to Auschwitz, Lundz, Austria, or Plaszow. Those people were very lucky that Oskar Schindler had sent them to other places. There was very little left of the airplane, and it was scattered over five hundred meters. Mostly I saw metal parts from the plane but the rest was burned. I could see a burned person sitting in the plane at the wheel. He was burned like a big goose. That was the first time in my life I had ever seen a burned body. The body was whole but small; I could see his head, hands, and legs but little else. I saw a bible that had not burned near the Australian pilot. Another whistle blew and they told us to stay in line. It was almost seven o'clock in the morning when they counted us again. The two people were still missing.

Oskar Schindler showed up and talked to Mr. Sperling the manager of the enamel factory, Mr. Meiteles and Mr. Bauman from the N.K.F. He told them not to worry that we were going to be transported to Brinnlitz. He left and we walked to the kitchen to get black coffee. They told us to go back to the barracks.

When we got back to the barracks, we all checked to see if everything was all right. Nothing had happened to our barracks while we were gone. Everything was in the same place. About an hour later, we heard another whistle. We formed a line and Mr. Feldstein took us back to work. Everyone was very tired because we hadn't slept the night before. I couldn't stand because as hard as I tried, I couldn't keep my eyes opened. I went to the bathroom and sat down and I closed my eyes for five or ten minutes. I went back to work and tried to fix a hole in the radiator but I couldn't finish. Every chance I could, I went to the bathroom to rest. This day felt like a whole week. Thank God, the work day came to an end. At six o'clock, they marched us back to the barracks. I was very happy to get into bed. I asked my neighbor to wake me up when they were passing out the bread portions.

My neighbor woke me up after about an hour, and I got my bread, margarine, and two cigarettes. I felt like a new person. I ate my bread and exchanged my cigarettes for the half portion of bread from my customer. I had my body back. I went back to bed about eight o'clock and slept all night.

At six o'clock the next morning, they woke us up. I was still tired from the night before. After the black coffee, they marched us to work as usual. We passed by the burned pilot and his plane. I heard that they found the two guys who had run away. They were sent to Plaszow. I never found out what happened to them. I thought about the terrible night, the burned pilot and his plane and our night in the woods and the terrible cold. It was a miracle we were still at our job and not in the hospital with pneumonia. I thought about how I might have run away but the German and Jewish police surrounded us. Two people walking through the streets of Zablocie wrapped in a blanket would never have made it. We didn't know anyone and we couldn't trust the Poles. If we knocked on someone's door and didn't have money, they would have called the Gestapo. I was glad we decided not to run away. It was our destiny. God would give us life after the war. I had to live with hope and to have patience to be ready for the good or bad times. I knew for sure that the Germans would lose the war. They and the other murderers would be prosecuted when the war came to an end. I would then tell the world all about the Germans and what they did to the Jewish people.

It was my turn to work outside. I didn't like working outside because I was afraid of the two Poles. The work was not easy because we had to lift heavy machinery into the trucks. The forklift put wooded boxes filled with parts into the trucks that Schindler needed for his new factory in Brinnlitz. I was on the list to go to work there even though I had not given Mr. Feldstein any money. A lot of people paid to be put on the list, everything was done very quietly. They had connections with the Poles and had brought money and diamonds to Schindler's camp. There was a lot of speculation about the new factory. Mr. Feldstein told me my name remained on the list and that I was lucky that he had taken care of me.

Later things changed because people were paying to be included on Mr. Feldstein's list. I heard that many of the workers were being sent to Plaszow or to Auschwitz. There were less and less people in camp with about six or seven hundred people left. I didn't know my destiny. Day by day, I worried and wondered what they were going to do to us.

Meanwhile we did our job inside the factory and people were sent to work outside. I tried to work better because I wanted to go to Brinnlitz. We stopped conducting the mini-concerts on Sunday because most of the choir had left. Oskar Schindler told Mr. Feldstein to tell us not to worry that we were going to be taken to Brinnlitz and we believed him. I felt better and thought I would be going to Brinnlitz, too.

The Last Transport

At the beginning of December, we felt that something was happening. Any day we would be finished with work because most of the machinery and bricks from the buildings had been sent to Brinnlitz. There was nothing left to do but clean up. On December 15, 1944, we were standing outside waiting to be counted. Mr. Feldstein called the names of those who were to be transported. Thirty people were left inside to clean up. Six hundred people filled up about 20 trucks. I didn't know where they were taking us. We had German commandos and Jewish police with us. Then I saw a sign, "Plaszow Arbeitslager." I was not happy because I was afraid to go back there and to Commandant Goeth, the murderer, but I had no choice. We stopped at the main gate. Mr. Feldstein told us to get out of the trucks and to stay in line at the main gate. I saw two SS standing at the gate. Mr. Goldstein told us that Oskar Schindler said not to worry that he had to bring us back to Plaszow temporarily. Schindler was going to send for us and take us to Brinnlitz.

When we went into the camp, Mr. Feldstein was not with us. I went to Barracks 18 and was a stranger. My good days with Schindler had come to an end and it looked like they had broken their promises. I felt very strange here but I couldn't do anything. Five people from the factory came here with me. They put me in a work group and it was much worst than before. I had heard stories bout what was going on in Plaszow. There were killings and hangings every day. It was like Hell. When I looked at the faces of the people, they were skin and bone and had a wild look in their eyes. They didn't have any strength, and they had lost the will to live. They said they would be better off dead than live at Plaszow. When I started talking to them, they were quiet. They were afraid to talk to me. They had to work hard with little or no food. Many people died every day. They didn't have to shoot people any more because they died from hunger. I got very upset. What kind of life was this? Everyone knew that when Goeth rode his horse he was going to shoot someone.

My neighbor told me he felt sorry for me that they had sent me back. I told him I had come from Paradise to start a miserable life again without food. I missed having the freedom and the mini-concerts every Sunday evening. I was a person, a worker there; here I was a slave awaiting hard labor with no food. I tried to be optimistic and still had a little strength. I hoped that the war would soon end. I decided to fight and hoped things would change.

Whenever someone told me that this was a death sentence, I told everyone not to lose hope that freedom was very near. Outside the Germans were running away. We had to have the will power to live and I tried to give them hope and more optimism. A man named Velvel, who lived in my barracks, said that Hitler was not going to lose the war. He became very agitated, but I told him to be strong and asked him not to be depressed.

(I was married after the war in December 1950. When my wife, Ruth, and I were on our honeymoon in New York, we went to a place where all the survivors had gathered. We went there to see if we could find someone we might know. We went to the office and saw an elegantly dressed man coming toward us. He looked at me and said he knew me from Plaszow that his name was Velvel. Before I could say a word, this man started to hug and kiss me. He said he was alive because of me. I had given up because I didn't want to suffer any longer, but you gave me hope and the courage to try. He had tears in his eyes and said he had me to thank for helping him to survive. He said I had given him a new spirit. He was so happy to see me again. He wanted to give me a hundred dollars, but I didn't take it. I had brought money to the States and had enough for a deposit on three houses. He gave me his address in Zurich, Switzerland and invited us to visit him. He had a wholesale business selling chocolates and coffee. Thank God, he was a very rich man. He took us to a beautiful kosher restaurant in his Cadillac. We spent a wonderful evening with him. He had married and had a child and he asked us again to visit him in Switzerland. As we were saying goodbye, he hugged and kissed me again. It was a wonderful moment in my life. My wife then told me how proud she was of me.)

They took us to Schiowitz

We were in Plaszow a few days. When we were in line one day to be counted, they started to call people from the line that had worked for Schindler. Over a thousand people were there and they put us into trucks. In one way I was happy to get out of Plaszow because I felt that any place was better than here. It took them eight hours to drive us to the railroad station. They made a lot of stops and they gave us food at lunchtime. We heard they were taking us to a factory making tanks at Schiowitz near Dresden. It was November 1944 at night when they stopped at the factory. We climbed down from the trucks and stood in line. They called my number, 22283, and marched me to the factory. I picked an upper bed near the window because I liked having more air. I also had a drawer with my number on it and I put my belongings in it. After that, we had to take a shower. There I met a lot of people from France, Holland, Germany, Hungary, Greece, and Russia. I heard many languages being spoken. After the shower, I went to bed. I was very hungry because they had only given us bread with margarine. I finally fell asleep.

At six o'clock in the morning, the whistle blew and we had to stand in line. I was given black coffee. I was still tired but glad that I had a good night's sleep. They selected the people to work on the tanks. My bosses' names were Mr. Dzuckman and Mr. Puszbach. I introduced myself to them and they were nice to me but strict. The job was very interesting and not too hard. The work was more technical than physical. I had to use my mind. I worked putting parts on the tanks.

I was glad to be inside because it was very cold outside. The work outside entailed digging and there was snow on the ground. It was much worst outside. From time to time, I had to work outside unloading trucks with merchandise from abroad. I was still wearing the striped uniform. When I worked outside for about five hours, I was freezing. I took newspaper and string and wrapped it around my body inside the uniform. That helped to keep me warm.

We had a Kapo named Smith, a German convict who was a murderer. He had been in a Munich jail for twenty years. When he found out someone was wearing newspaper under his uniforms, he reported it to the German commando. They hit that person twenty times on his behind. Some people didn't care about the beating; they kept using the paper rather than freeze and get pneumonia. If someone got sick, he was taken to Flossenburg were there was a crematorium. Twice a month they checked for sick people. Those people were then sent to the crematorium that worked 24 hours a day. We had another convict Kapo named Paul who had been in prison for ten years. He and Smith were murderers and made lots of trouble for us. There were 1,150 workers with me from the different countries. I was more afraid of Smith than Paul. He was without pity. He spied on everyone. If you said something, he didn't understand he would take you into his office and beat you up for nothing. He also was gay. He had a fifteen year old boy with him all the time. At that time, we didn't understand what "gay" meant.

Sundays I used to look out my small window and I could see people walking around. I saw a little dog running back and forth and I envied him his freedom. I was a slave here who was always hungry and waiting for a death sentence.

The first week at the new place there were not enough blankets so we slept three people in one bed. At night, it was very cold because it was wintertime. The man who slept in the middle of the bed was the warmest so every night we would switch places. One night someone took our blanket from us so we put on our uniforms. We were afraid because we didn't want the Kapos to see us sleeping in our uniforms. When we got another blanket the next night, we did not sleep. I saw a Russian guy coming slowly to our bed and he tried to steal our blanket. He couldn't get it because we had tied it to the bed. He ran away, but the guy who was not asleep grabbed him and the Kapo came. There was a lot of trouble but at least we had our blanket.

The next day we found out that the Russian guy had gotten 20 whips to his toches. In a few days, everyone was given his own blanket and I could now sleep in my own bed. The worst situation was the food. Every once in a while, I worked outside shoveling snow, sweeping the streets or unloading merchandise. The cold was terrible and I was afraid to use the newspaper to keep me warm. If I did that and found out, I would have been beaten. I was hoping Oskar Schindler would show up one day and take me to Brinnlitz. That's what Mr. Feldstein had told me when I left Schindler's factory. It was only a dream.

When I came back from work at six o'clock, I was given bread and margarine,. Twice a week I was given two cigarettes which I exchanged for a portion of bread or soup. The soup here was made from carrot or beet tops with no potatoes. I kept the extra bread portion for the morning to give me more strength. The Russians found about the hidden bread and at night, they would try to steal it. With a knife, they would cut someone's night shirt and take the bread. This happened to my neighbor and in the morning, he didn't have his bread. From then on, I ate the bread on the spot that I had exchanged for the cigarettes. I didn't trust the Russians. I was going around hungry. I had been used to the food at Schindler camp, which had been more than enough. It was better food than we got here.

Now there were 1,800 people here working at the factory on the tanks. The people were treated like dogs. I remembered the time when I went from Schindler's factory back to Plaszow and became depressed. Mr. Feldstein had not kept his promised to send me to Brinnlitz. He said the factory was still not ready and that is why we had to go back to Plaszow and to Commandant Goeth. It was a good thing that I had brought a kilo of tobacco that I bought from one of the Poles to Plaszow. I had hid it in my mattress and little by little, I exchanged it for food. No one ever knew about it. My first customer was a man named Leon List and we became good friends. I gave him the tobacco and because he knew the manager, he was able to get soup or bread. He still owed me five portions of soup. (I met Leon after the war at Landsberg. He now lives in New Jersey.)

After work, it was the same thing as in the other camps. People with money could buy bread or soup. Some of the Germans who worked there brought in sandwiches of salami and sold them for money, jewelry, or clothing. None of us could live on the food rations. I exchanged my cigarettes for food.

My job at the factory was to clean and oil the parts for the tanks. Mr. Dzuckman and his helper, Mr. Puszbach worked on the machines. They were tool makers. They didn't talk very much. The factory name was Mille Fabric. They also milled flower to bake. Sometimes they would leave their sandwich at my work station. They didn't say anything so when they left I ate the sandwich. They never hollered at me. As long as I had the tobacco, I was okay. I now had more soup and bread and I wasn't hungry. I was in good shape.

For a full month, I gave Leon List two cigarettes. Sometimes he gave me soup or bread, but sometimes he didn't give me anything because he was my friend. One day someone found out where I kept the cigarettes. They had disappeared. I now didn't have any tobacco. This had been a life saver and I got depressed and wondered who had stolen it. I thought that the tobacco was not as important as the fact that they had taken my whole family from me. I was always a believer in God. I had to go on. The people who stole from me might have been the ones who changed the sheets and pillow cases. I could not report them because I didn't want any one to know I had the cigarettes in the first place. I would have been in big trouble, but it was a big loss for me because now I had no way to get extra food. It was getting impossible to keep going.

Everyday we had to get up at six o'clock in the morning, stand in line while they called our name and number, and gave us our coffee. At seven o'clock, everyone had to go to his job. I still worked cleaning and scraping the parts for the tanks. I worked until lunchtime and then went to get my soup. I had to be lucky to get a potato in the soup.

The cook here was named Meyer. He was a German Jew from Plaszow. I don't know how he found out about me being here but he found me. He said he remembered the concerts in the Plaszow barracks. He wanted me to sing the Yiddish songs that he had heard at the concerts. A boy from Krakow worked with him in the kitchen. Meyer introduced me to him so I could get more food. I was very happy.

I prepared five songs for the 1944 holidays. They had a stage for the performers and it was a big place that held over one thousand people. The workers performed in their language such as French, English, German, or Polish. Meyer organized the affair and asked me to sing in Yiddish as I had done at Plaszow. As a matter of fact, he wanted one of his favorites, "Jude Come der Arbeit" and then some of my other songs. I asked him if I could have more food. He told me there was a guy from Krakow named Munk. He said he would tell him about me and ask him to give me more food. This was two days before the holiday and I felt good and promised him I would be prepared to sing.

On the day of the performance, Mr. Meyer called the performers up to the stage. The hall was full with over one thousand people. I got there at six thirty in the evening and the show started at seven o'clock. First, he called 12 dancers. The music started and they danced beautifully. There was a man who told jokes in German and an Italian opera singer with a beautiful tenor voice. There was a Polish singer and after that, he called me onto the stage. I was a little scared but once I started the music helped me. They were very good musicians. When I finished the place exploded with enthusiasm. I sang two more songs. When I sat down, he thanked me and told me to wait. He then took all the performers to the kitchen and gave them a half loaf of bread. I thanked him. I was so hungry that I ate the whole thing on the spot.

The next day, I remembered that Mr. Meyers told me he would talk to Mr. Munk from Krakow about giving me more food because he worked in the kitchen. At lunchtime, I stood in line for my soup. When I came up to Mr. Munk, I told him my name and that I was from Krakow. I told him that Mr. Meyer was supposed to talk to him about giving me more soup from the bottom of the pot. He didn't say a word and looked at me angrily. I took my portion and left. When I started to eat the soup,

I saw that he had not given me a potato just the carrot and beet tops. I was very mad, but I couldn't do anything. I had no choice but to eat what he had given me. I looked around for Mr. Meyer but I couldn't find him. I thought maybe Mr. Meyer hadn't had a chance to talk to Mr. Munk because of the holiday.

The next day at lunchtime when it was my turn to get my soup, I very quietly told Mr. Munk that yesterday he had give me only the soup from the top. I told him that is was only water with leaves and to please give me soup from the bottom. I asked him if Mr. Meyer had spoken to him about me. He looked at me angrily and hit me over the head with his big kitchen spoon. I fell to the floor and fainted. I woke up in the hospital. My head was bleeding and hurt very badly. I was in the hospital for three days. While I was there I had more soup and bread because if you asked the nurses and you were sick, they would give you more food. After three days, I left the hospital and felt better because I had been given more food.

When I went back to work Mr. Dzuckman asked me what had happened to me. When I told him the story, he couldn't believe it. For the next five days, he brought me sandwiches. He didn't give them to me but just put them where I was standing or working. I had a lot of luck because while I was in the hospital, the Gestapo had taken away many of the sick people. They had taken about twenty people and sent them to Flossenburg Concentration Camp and to the crematorium. No one ever came back from Flossenburg.

Mr. Munk had hit five other people. One of them had died. My first day back from the hospital and at lunchtime while I was getting my soup, I told him that after the war if people he had hit found him, they would have him jailed. He said he was not afraid, that after the war he didn't care if they hanged by the beicim. (One day after the war, I was walking with Leon List in the Fernwald Camp and saw Mr. Munk walking in the street. We recognized him, grabbed him, and forced him to go with us to the Jewish police in the camp. He did not want to go but Leon and I forced him and gave him a few knocks. We brought him to the police and I told him my story and what he done to me and other people. They had a hearing and sent him to our camp in Landsberg where they put him in jail. Everyday I went by and told him now he was paying for everything he had done to others and me. He was in jail for almost a year and I don't know whatever happened to him. I heard that he went to Israel. When I was in Israel, I looked for him all over but I never found him. That is the story of Mr. Munk from Krakow.)

I was still wearing a bandage on my head after I came out of the hospital and my head was still hurting me. Everyday I started to feel better and better. I took the bandage off because the Gestapo also checked the slaves in the factory every week for sick people. I was afraid and worried that if one of the managers complained to them about me not working very well, they would take me away. That's why I was afraid to wear the bandage. Before that, I used to hide in the bathroom if I heard the Gestapo was coming to check for sick people. Mr. Meyer continued to bring sandwiches and leave them for me. Sometimes he would leave an apple, too. I put it in my pocket so no one would see it. If he had been caught giving me food, he would have been jailed. Mr. Dzuckman was a very good man. His food helped me a lot. He never rushed me like the others. He tried to help me because he liked me. He always had a smile on his face. He was very good to me but he was afraid to do anything for me openly. The managers were told not to help us or discuss anything with us. He was different from the other Germans.

It was January 1945 and very cold. They used the workers to clean the snow and cut the ice. I only had my striped uniform to wear. When I went into the toiled I took paper with me to wrap around my body and tied it with string. I had to wear my shoes without socks. It was twenty degrees outside and a cold strong frost. I couldn't take the cold especially when they sent me outside to unload merchandise from the trucks. Whenever a worker got sick they sent him to the hospital and life was very bad.

My friends, Israel Yungewirt from Krakow and Leon List were sitting on my bed next to the window. We looked out and could see people walking their dogs. They were so free while we were in the camp. It was like a jail with not enough food to eat. There was no tomorrow for us, but I tried to stay optimistic. I told my friends that I felt the war would soon end, but maybe it would take six or eight months. We had to hold on. We had to stay strong a little longer so we could tell the world what the Germans had done to us. We were hoping that Oskar Schindler would come back and take out of here to Brinnlitz. It was over two months and we were still waiting. We all remembered about our choir and how it had given a lot of people the desire to live. I felt that money lost was nothing. It was everything else we had lost.

The next morning I was standing in line. Suddenly Kapo Smith came over to me and told me to go to the German Commando. I was scared. I wondered what they were going to do with me or if I would return. I thought I recognized the tall man who was the German commando and he asked me if my name was Kalme Schumacher. He smiled and said he knew me from the barracks in Plaszow. He said that he remembered my singing and stories and how the people were smiling and crying. He was the main cook here from Plaszow. The German commandos were having a New Year's party on the 31st of December and he told them about my choir. They wanted me to entertain on the big stage. I was to organize a choir after work and in two weeks, we were invited to sing at their party. I felt better and was not as nervous. I was very happy and I promised him that I would prepare a special program. I thanked the German commando and left.

When I went back to my bed, I tried to figure out what to do. My neighbors were very scared, but they were happy to see me back alive. I told them that I had to organize a choir for the party. I needed about ten people. I didn't know too many people except the two Yungerwirt brothers. They knew a few other people and when we got together, they gave us a place to practice. Some of the people were not too good but I had no choice but to keep them. Four of the people were from the Schindler choir and they knew my songs. We practiced every night.

On December 31st at seven o'clock in the evening, we got together in the big hall and Mr. Meyer was the master of ceremonies. There were other entertainers from all over the world and some of them were professionals. After the performance, they took us to the kitchen and gave us each a half loaf of bread, 500 grams, a portion of margarine and two cigarettes. Everybody was very happy.

After the party, life went back to working outside in the terrible cold and we didn't have enough food. I was always hungry. I had a friend about my age named Henek Mintcheles who was from a rich family. His bunk was under my bed. He would say he would like to have a whole loaf of bread and if they found it they could shoot him. He talked to himself all the time. He said the same thing in Polish because he didn't know Yiddish. His father was a famous doctor. One day he showed me his legs. They were very swollen and his face, too, was swollen. I told him to go to the hospital, that they would help him. He said he was afraid to go to the hospital because they might send him to Flossenburg and to the crematorium.

About five days later Henek could not get out of bed, he was still sleeping. I touched him and told him it was getting late and we had to get in line to be counted. He was quiet and didn't say anything. I called my neighbor and when we looked again at him, he was dead. I didn't call the Kapo because we were afraid of him. I called the manager from the barracks. He came and verified that Henek was dead. He was only twenty two years old. My heart was aching and I thought the same thing would happen to me because I didn't have enough food. I had to find a way to get more food. I had to find some kind of a business since some people still had money that they had brought from home.

I started to ask people if they had anything to sell like jewelry or diamonds. I would find them a customer to buy their jewelry and diamonds. We worked with German people who lived on the outside. I told the people that I would sell their goods and take ten percent for myself. I met a Russian man named Josel from the Budzin Camp who was from Lemberg. He had left his whole family in Lemberg and when he tried to go back to get them it was too late. His whole family was sent to Auschwitz. They sent him to different camps. They had sent him here from Buderim. While I spoke with him I saw that he had 24 carat gold in his teeth. I told him if I had gold in my teeth, I would take it out and sell it. I told him people were dying every day from hunger and he could help himself by selling the gold. I had customers who would buy the gold and bring him sandwiches from the outside along with other food items. Selling his gold would save his life. He listened and accepted my proposition. I started to work on it. I found a person who said he had plenty of customers who wanted gold, but we would need a dentist to get the gold out of the teeth. It wasn't going to be easy.

After awhile, we found a dentist and explained what we wanted from him. He said he would do it but he didn't have the tools. He knew a German guy who wanted to buy the gold and would get the dentist tools. It took a while to set up the whole thing. When we had the tools and the professional dentist removed the gold from his mouth, the German brought bread and money.

Until that time, I started to get weaker and weaker. One morning I woke up to go to work and my legs were swollen up to the knee. I went to a doctor from Hungary, showed him my legs, and told him I was getting weaker and weaker. I was thinking about my friend, Henek, who had the same thing on his legs and had died. That's why I went to the doctor, because I was afraid the same thing was going to happen to me. The doctor checked my heart and lungs and looked at my legs. He told me if I wanted to live, I would have to go to the hospital. The swelling would travel up to my heart if I didn't go right away. I went back to my place, picked up my belongings, and went to the hospital. I was very scared that they were going to send me to Flossenburg's crematorium. I decided that what will be will be, I had to go to the hospital.

The Hospital at Schiowitz

At the hospital, they had a big room with about twenty five or thirty people in beds where nurses took care of the sick people. A nurse showed me a bed and I got undressed. I weighed 37 kilo and the nurse took my temperature. The doctor came in and told me that if I didn't have a temperature they couldn't keep me. I saw a lot of soup, bread, and margarine that people were too sick to eat. I made sure I had a temperature. At lunchtime, they gave me a Farina type soup with milk. It was also sweet. I was so hungry that I ate it very fast. I looked around at the people who were too sick to eat their food. I asked the nurse if I could have their food because they couldn't eat and I didn't want them to throw it away. I asked her to please let me have it. When I finished the soup, she asked me if I wanted more. I said, "Yes!" She brought me more. I enjoyed it very much, and started to feel the difference.

While I was lying there, I saw many people die. I was scared. They gave me some medicine to take and I fell asleep. After a couple of hours, I went down for them to take my temperature again. I rubbed the bottom of the thermometer with my finger to make it register higher so I would be able to stay in the hospital. I knew I needed more food and not medicine to get my strength back. If I could stay here a week, I knew I would be myself. In the evening, they gave everybody his portion of food. The man in the next bed was too sick to eat his food so the nurse gave it to me. I was still so hungry I ate it in a hurry. She brought me another portion of bread with margarine and I blessed her in Hebrew. I told her to be careful. I didn't want anything to happen to her because she was very good to me. I told her God would be good to her and she looked at me and smiled. That was my first day in the hospital.

I slept very well the first night. In the morning, I didn't have to get up early. At eight o'clock in the morning, two doctors came in to check everyone. Because I was a new patient, they looked at my portfolio and started to check my heart and lungs. They asked me where I hurt. I told them that my stomach and legs hurt. After they check my legs, they told the nurse that I should keep my legs elevated and to stay in bed. I didn't listen to them because I knew that the Gestapo checked the hospital and sent people to Flossenburg. I knew that my only problem was that I was undernourished. I just needed more food than the soup and bread I was given. In the hospital, I had an opportunity to get more food from what they served me and from the sick people who couldn't eat.

The third day that I was in the hospital, I started to gain weight and the swelling on my legs went down. I started to feel much stronger. I didn't want to go back to work yet. I hoped to stay in the hospital at least two weeks because once I was discharged I would not have enough food. I would be hungry again. At the end of the week, I was due for another checkup. The nurse came to take my temperature so I cheated again. I rubbed the bottom of the thermometer to raise my temperature. It registered one hundred degrees. When the doctors checked me, he said I looked much better and had gained weight, but he saw that I still had a temperature. I complained that I still didn't feel well and he told me I had to stay in the hospital for another five days. I remained there until the next check up. The doctor then told me I was to be released because the doctors from Flossenburg were due for their checkup. They would decide who lived or who died. I thanked the doctor for helping me in my situation. He had seen that I only wanted to stay n the hospital to gain strength.

While I was in the hospital, I befriended people and asked them if they had anything to sell such as jewelry or gold. I tried to help the sick people, too. If they needed a nurse or wanted to go to the toilet, I would call the nurse for them or walk them to the bathroom. I tried to help the nurses as much as I could by taking the patients to get their x-rays or other tests. After I had been at the hospital for twelve days, I felt stronger but I still complained about my head hurting me. They gave me pills, but I didn't use them.

One morning about eight o'clock, the doctors from Flossenburg came in and checked every bed. When they came to my bed and looked at me, my doctor explained to them that I was being discharged next week. They picked out six people that were to be taken from the hospital to Flossenburg. I knew they would never come back.

I met a guy in the hospital and we became good friends. He had a brother that worked with us in the factory. He wanted to give me a small package to deliver to his brother. He gave me his brother's name and who he worked for and where his bed was located. He asked me to be sure no one saw me give his brother the package. God forbid that anyone would catch me with whatever was in the package. He then told me the package held dollars and a letter for his brother. I accepted to deliver the package, but I knew it was very risky. I was feeling much better and stronger. I really didn't want to leave the hospital yet. I knew what to expect when I went back to work. The work was hard and there was no food. I wasn't in a hurry to leave. During my next exam, the doctor told me I looked fine, had gained nine pounds and the swelling in my legs had gone down. He said he had to discharge me from the hospital. This doctor was a Jew from Hungary and he told me to come back to see him if I had any more problems. I felt like a new born man.

Saturday at twelve o'clock before I left the hospital, I met with the gentleman who wanted me to take a package to his brother. I tied the package to my right leg. I didn't want to put it in my pocket in case I was searched. I said goodbye to the doctors and thanked them, especially the Hungarian doctor. I wished him long life. I said goodbye to the nurses and to the patients. I wished them well and hoped to see them when they were released from the hospital. Some of them were crying because they were very sick and couldn't walk. The man who gave me the package told me to be careful. He suggested that a safe place to give his brother the package was in the bathroom. He was going to talk to his brother about me because he wanted him to know how nice I had been to him and everyone in the hospital. I said goodbye to him.

At lunchtime, I didn't open the package. I never knew how much money was there. I went to look for the man's brother in the factory. When I found him I told him how I had met his brother in the hospital and that he looked good and was due to be released in about a week and he shouldn't worry about him. He was getting enough food and was resting. I told him I had a package for him but I couldn't give it to him on the factory floor because it was a big risk for me. I told him that all I wanted was a little money to buy extra soup and bread. He looked very nervous and was shaking. He promised that he would take care of me. We went to the men's room when no one else was there. I gave him the package and he thanked me. I asked him not to forget what I had done for his brother and him. I didn't know how much money to ask him for and he didn't tell me how much he was going to give me. I guess that was a little stupid of me. He left first and after a while, I left.

Five days later, I saw him and asked him how much he was going to give me for delivering his package. He told me not to keep asking him and that I shouldn't worry. He was going to take care of me but he didn't want people to notice us together. The following week he told me to meet him in the bathroom. I figured he was going to give me some money but I didn't know how much. When we went into the men's room no one else was there. He said that someone had stolen his package from his bed and he started to cry because it wasn't his money. It was his brother's money and he didn't know what to do. I looked in his eyes and knew he was bluffing but I couldn't say anything. I couldn't go to the police about a fellow Jew. I left and thought that I had done something for a brother Jew. That was the most important thing for me. I wanted health and I wanted to come out of the war alive.

I started to look for a business. I met Mr. Josel with his teeth. He told me that while I was in the hospital he had two of his golden teeth removed and he had sold the gold for food. He was very happy. He also was a very honest man. When he sold more of the gold from his teeth, he would bring me a half portion of the soup or bread as long as we were together. (After the war, I met Mr. Josel at Landsberg and we remained friends. We talked about him selling the gold from his teeth and how it had saved our lives. He thanked me for it because I had advised him to do it. He told me he had already made arrangements to have new teeth made by a dentist in Munich.)

It was a big struggle to get enough food. Even with the deals I was able to make, I was still going around hungry. Leon List and I would go to the area around the kitchen where they discarded food and try to find potato skins or something. There was a big German shepherd dog tied up with a chain behind the kitchen. Near him was a box where they put all kinds of discarded food even cooked meat. We saw how much food they gave to the dog. He couldn't even eat it all. The dog looked at us and I was scared that Kapos Smith or Paul would see us. We were so hungry that we decided we had to do something to get the food from the dog. We had to make a plan for the next time.

A few days later, we looked to see if the dog was in a better mood when we went back. The dog was lying down and very quiet. Leon and I walked towards him as if we wanted to play with him. We gave him some of the food. I was afraid and while Leon held the dog, he told me to get the box of food. I grabbed it and put it away behind the kitchen. We cleaned out the box and put it back where it had been. We ate the food and the meat was very good. It was much better than the food they were giving to us. I asked Leon why he wasn't afraid of the dog and was able to hold him. He told me he came from a big farm in Lvov and he had five dogs that he took care of and played with. He said he was not afraid of dogs. I tried to sell some of the food I didn't eat for dollars or jewelry because now I felt much stronger since I had come from the hospital.

From time to time Mr. Dzuckman left a sandwich. It consisted of two slices of bread, butter, and cheese. Sometimes he also left an apple. It helped me a little. I was a good worker and he liked me. He still had to be careful because he would have been punished if they found out he was helping me. Most of the managers were not like him; they were rude and harsh to the workers.

The Americans Bombard the Factory

At the end of February in the middle of the night when everyone was sleeping, we heard a knock like a bomb exploding. It woke all of us up. It was very dark. There was no light. I got up and asked Leon if he knew anything. I didn't know what had happened and neither did Leon. We heard crushing as if the whole factory was falling apart. Then it sounded as if another bomb had fallen on the factory. I grabbed my blanket and put on my shoes. I heard people hollering that they were being killed. I couldn't see anything but heard people walking towards the door. I followed and felt the walls splitting. I told Leon that we had to get out but it was hard because it was so dark and debris was falling everywhere. I could hear people hollering and crying that they were finished and being killed. I came to a place where I couldn't go forward because there was a hole. Everyone was pushing one another. There were no steps and people were jumping into the hole. Leon and I held each other and jumped into the hole like everyone else. We had to jump because we couldn't stay where we were with all the debris falling. Leon jumped first and I jumped after him. We came to the third floor and I heard him calling my name. I couldn't find him because it was dark and people were on top of one another.

A bomb had split the factory in pieces and I still couldn't find Leon but I could hear his voice. I noticed that people were jumping down to the second floor. I heard people saying that they were dying, that they couldn't breath and to please help them. I jumped to the second floor and it was the same thing. People were falling on one another and me. I felt it was the end for me. I started to scream at the people to free themselves or we would all die. One very strong man was on top of me and pushed the people away who were coming down on top of us. He freed himself and carried me from that place. I started to breathe again. I couldn't see who had freed me. I was almost killed. After fifteen minutes, I knew I had to get to the first floor. I got up and looked for the bottom floor. I crawled on my hands and knees and people were lying on one another, screaming, and hollering that they couldn't breath. It was so dark that no one could do anything. I called Leon about five times but he didn't answer.

I got up in the darkness and looked for the broken wall and a place to jump or slide down. I felt I had to get down otherwise I was finished.

I continued to crawl on all fours and reminded myself that no matter what kind of a predicament I found myself in I always got out alive. I found a wall that was divided and I did the same thing as I had done in the upper floors. I slid down into a big hole. There was a lot of flying dust, stones, cement, and debris. I only had my blanket and shoes on. I found out later that 258 people were killed in the building. Out of 1,758 workers, there were only about fifteen hundred left.

    Leon and I finally found each other, and we felt lucky to be alive. It was very cold outside with frost on the ground. We saw a big fire in the kitchen. I saw a man wrapped in his blanket run into the kitchen and grab a loaf of bread and came out of the kitchen eating the bread. The blanket around him was burning. He didn't care he just stood there and ate the bread. Five guys grabbed a couple of blankets from people, threw him to the ground, and tried to save his life by putting out the fire. Meanwhile people grabbed his bread and started to eat it. His life was saved.

    It was the middle of the night and we stood there not knowing what they were going to do with us. Kapos Smith and Paul blew a whistle and told us to get in line. They started to count us and it was then that they found out that 258 people had been killed. We started to march away from the factory, but we didn't know where we were being taken. Over a loud speaker, they said that anyone who tried to escape would be shot. All of us were covered with soot, cement dust, and stones. I tried to clean myself off. I could see that the fire in the kitchen was getting bigger and bigger. I was in line with Leon and we were both cold and shivering. I wondered what they were going to do with us. Leon and I discussed how we slid from floor to floor to get out of the building and how lucky we were to be alive. Leon asked me if we should run away and hide because we both felt the war was coming to an end. I didn't know if they would let us live. I told him we had no where to go. Who would help us? They would probably only call the Gestapo and we would be shot because the German police did not like Jews.

    We saw Kapos Smith and Paul with an SS commandant coming from the direction of the factory. The commandant told us about the factory fire and that they were trying to put out the fire and that they were going to take us to the woods until morning. In the morning, they were going to return us to the factory and none of us had better run away. If someone tried to escape and was caught, he would be shot. Shortly a whole group of SS troops surrounded us and they marched us to the woods. Leon thought they were going to take us to the woods and kill us. I told him that we were in God's hands and had to live in hope. We had to be optimistic. We had to wait for the liberation. They marched us through the streets in the middle of the night. The Germans were worried because Dresden and the surrounding cities were being bombed and in flames.

When we got to the woods, they said over the loud speaker that we were going to stay here and that we were surrounded by troops. We were to sit down on the ground. In the morning, they said that we were going to be taken back to the factory. I wrapped the blanket around me while I sat on the cold ground. We talked to each other very quietly and remembered our home and our parents. I told the story about how I had gone through the same thing at Schindler's factory when it had been bombed when a plane was shot down and burned. At that time, they had also taken us to the woods at night in the cold.

The next morning, I was still shivering from the cold. I stood up to straighten my bones. I still didn't know what they were going to do with us. While waiting, I heard a whistle and over the loud speaker, we were told to get up and stay in line. It was about six o'clock in the morning when they marched us out of the woods and counted us. While marching through the streets, the people from the town were looking at us through the windows of their homes. No one even gave us so much as a piece of bread. It took almost an hour to reach the factory. I saw that the fire department was just leaving. I saw steam coming from the factory. Half of the factory was smashed with water running from it. The Obersturmfuhrer in charge of the factory said that those people who had run from the factory after it was bombed had 24-hours to return. After that if they were caught, they would be shot or sent to Flossenburg.

Before we went into the factory, they counted us again. They called our name and number and we had to respond, "Yes." We went inside and saw that everything was smashed. All the walls were cracked and tons of debris was on the floor. Almost all the machinery was smashed. Parts were all over the place. The factory had been split in half. I didn't recognize it at all. They took us to the basement where there were small bottles of soda like Coca Cola but it had a different German name. Everybody grabbed two or three bottles and started to drink the soda. When Kapos Smith and Paul came in and saw us drinking the soda everybody put the soda back. The soda was cold because it was freezing in the basement. They gave us black coffee that they had brought in from the outside. When we finished, they divided us into groups of eight or ten to clean the debris and to check the machines. All the parts from the machinery were put aside. The cement and stones were brought outside. We had shovels to work with and small wagons to fill with the debris. It was very hard work taking the stones from the basement. Some pieces weighed about 150 or 200 pounds. They also used a forklift to remove the stones. The Kapos were running around and hollering for us to work faster. I was very tired from being in the woods all night. I hadn't been able to sleep.

When we were sent to where our beds were located and I found my clothing, I got dressed. Some of the beds had disappeared. Half of them were gone or were loaded with stones and dust from the debris. We didn't know where we were going to sleep that night.

At lunchtime, they took us to a place that had already been cleaned. They told us to sit on the floor. I sat on the blanket I still had with me. They brought in big pots of soup with a portion of bread and margarine. The food gave me new life. We had an hour to rest. When the whistle blew, we returned to work. The work was so hard. We had to carry those big pieces of cement from the walls that had been bombed. They were very heavy. We worked until six o'clock.

We couldn't go back to our place so they let us know that we had to sleep on the floor. Luckily, I had my blanket. They sent someone to sleep with me because he didn't have a blanket. Leon also had a blanket so four people had to sleep together with two blankets. We tied the blanket to us with string so that no one would steal them during the night. We were afraid of the Russians because we knew they stole things from us while we slept.

During the night while we were sleeping, I felt somebody pulling on our blankets. I woke up and because we had tied the blankets, they couldn't get them it from us. I fell back to sleep again because I was very tired from the night in the woods.

In the morning, they woke us. I washed and went to the line for the black coffee. After they counted us, we went to work in the basement. I again saw all the bottles of soda that were there for the German commandos. They had lemon and strawberry soda. I drank some of the sweet and cold soda. Some people got sick from drinking so much. Leon and I took two bottles with us but we only drank one.

We continued working on cleaning the basement. We found dead people mixed in with the debris. We called Kapos Smith and Paul and they brought the Red Cross workers to take out the bodies. We had to help them. We found part of the steps and we worked on clearing them for about three days, because the building had four floors.

Later they brought in professional people to check the machinery and the parts. They dismantled the machinery because most of them were broken. When the Kapos came to check on us, they treated us badly. They said our work was no good, but we really had done a good job. It was very bad because we kept finding dead bodies.

Again, we were told that we would have to sleep on the floor with nothing but a blanket while they repaired our building. After such a hard and terrible day, we had nowhere to sleep. After working, they only gave us bread and margarine to eat. We had to guard against the Russians stealing our blankets so we tied them to ourselves. We suffered a lot because they were still trying to repair the kitchen, too. People were running around the city going from house to house asking for food. The Germans called the Gestapo and they brought about twelve of them to us.

At lunchtime while we were standing in line for our food, we were told that the twelve people, who were surrounded by the SS, had broken the law. They had been sentenced to death and were being sent to Flossenburg. I looked at them and saw that they were already half dead. They were skin and bones. They looked very frightened. Then they took them away. Conditions in the factory were terrible. There was no food, just cleaning and working outside in the cold. From time to time, we had to shovel the snow and chop the ice from the sidewalks. I was shivering. I put newspaper under my uniform. It was illegal but I took a chance because without the newspaper, I would have not lasted one hour outside in the cold. I thought that it was better to take a chance. I thanked God that they never checked me. My friend, Leon, did the same thing. I think they were a little lenient with us because they figured that the whole world was against them. The Americans and English were coming at them from one side and the Russians were pushing them from the other side.

We March to Theresienstadt

They could not repair the factory. Ninety percent of the machinery was broken. They needed completely new machines and the building was in ruins, it would have to be rebuilt. Food had to be brought in from the outside because the kitchen was demolished. They had no choice but to take us to Theresienstadt. I heard that thirty five thousand Germans had been killed in the bombing of Dresden. I didn't know that the war was ending.

On March 28, 1945 at six o'clock in the morning as we stood to be counted. Kapo Paul told us that we were leaving for Theresienstadt to work in the factory. We were given black coffee. Everybody took their utensils and their belongings in a small package that was not too heavy to carry. There were 1,255 persons. I made a mistake when I said it was 1,555. Between us, there were Russians, French, Belgians, and German slaves. Gestapo, German soldiers, and the SS surrounded us. Our last march was from the *Deutsche Mulle Fabrik* at eight o'clock in the morning. The sun was shining but it was still very cold.

I walked in a line of eight with my friend Leon. This was going to be our last trip and I encouraged him not to lose hope. I told him if he felt weak to let me know and I would help him and if I felt weak, I'm sure he would help me. All of us received a portion of bread with margarine. Leon and I ate it on the spot because we knew the Russians would steal it. They didn't tell us where we were going. As we walked through the streets, people going to and from work looked at us. People looked at us from the windows of their homes. No one threw us a sandwich or bread. They had no pity. They saw us and knew the war was coming to and end but they still were cold hearted. I told Leon that the German people were selfish. They did not care about anyone. As we marched out of the city through the villages, five trucks with food pulled up. At twelve o'clock, we rested. We had walked for four hours without stopping. After we had eaten, they gave us water to drink. As the sun started to set, we were still walking through fields and woods.

Before dark about 20 kilometers from Schiowitz, we came to a farm. It was a very big farm with large barns. They opened the barn doors and it was filled with straw and hay for the cows. Leon and I sat down on the straw. Over the loud speaker, they reminded us that if we tried to escape and were caught, we would be shot. We were not given any food or water. I fell asleep. It was much better than sleeping on the floor of the factory. The barn was locked for the night.

At six o'clock in the morning, we heard a whistle. We stood in line while they counted us and no one was missing. They brought in bread with margarine, black coffee, and water. Leon and I tried to eat as much as we could for the long march ahead of us. We had no idea where we were going or how long it was going to take. The soldiers still surrounded us. At seven o'clock, we walked away from the farm. The sun was shining but it was still cold as we walked through fields, woods, and villages.

At twelve o'clock, we rested. We were given water to drink. I asked if anyone knew where we were going. Someone told me that he had heard a German soldier say we were going to Theresienstadt. We started to walk again until we came to another farm that evening. They had hundreds of cows. We were told to go into the barns again. They gave us some water but nothing to eat. I was very tired and hungry. The lights were turned off and I went to sleep in my clothes on the straw.

We got up again at six o'clock in the morning and they gave us bread with margarine and coffee. This was the third day and we had to live on bread and margarine. We started to march again, but the older people were very weak and were having trouble walking. They started to holler at them to walk. Those who could not walk were shot. There were young and old alike. Someone tried to help a young man but he couldn't walk and two soldiers shot him. As I walked, I saw the people who had been shot. From time to time, I heard hollering and shooting. I knew that people were being killed because they couldn't walk any longer. I was worried and scared. I had to go on because I knew the war was coming to an end. I walked and walked until noon.

We rested in a field at lunchtime. I saw little leaves that looked like double hearts on the ground and ate them. They were a little sour but I was so hungry I ate them anyway. We sat there for about an hour and during that time I picked the leaves and put them in my pocket. I was very thirsty. There was no water to drink.

We started off again passing through small towns and woods as night was falling. As we got to the woods, I was afraid because I didn't know what they were going to do with us. Leon and I talked about them killing us or that we might die on the way. They hadn't given us any food and we were starving. I told Leon that now was not the time to die. We had to stay alive. I had some water left in my pot and I ate the leaves that I had picked from the ground. We stayed there and slept all night.

In the morning, we stood in line as they counted us. We were given a portion of bread with margarine but no coffee. Every day it got worst as we marched. I saw a lot of military trucks with soldiers and in the city whole families were walking together. I saw buildings burning as we passed through the streets. We were in Czechoslovakia. I saw trucks loaded with the dead from our march. We were taken to the woods where they gave us shovels to dig holes. We had to bury the workers from our factory that had been shot or died along the way. The bodies were thrown in the holes. Soon trucks with food for the soldiers came but they only gave us bread and margarine once a day. As we came into one of the Czechoslovakian villages we heard them talking in their language. We were taken to another farm where we slept in the barn on straw.

On the sixth day, we stood in line to be counted. I had not been able to take a shower in six days. This day we were missing over two hundred people who had died. We were given cooked hot water and hot black coffee. We started to walk again through the cities of Czechoslovakia. I can't remember the names of the cities but I saw big buildings. Some had been bombed and were on fire. They were falling apart. It looked as though the whole world was on fire. I walked with my last strength between the flames and the bombed out houses and buildings. I didn't think I was going to get out of there alive. I was afraid they took us here to be burned or to finish us up. We had about one hundred meters to go and I was very scared. We continued to march between the debris from the houses and buildings.

Soon we came to a village and over the hill, we saw a waterfall. The water looked very clear and crystal clean. Everyone started to run towards the water for a drink. Leon and I did the same thing. I ran to the water and started to drink. The water did me a lot of good because I hadn't had a bowel movement in over six days. I went inside and cleaned myself. I was a new man. We were given a portion of bread with margarine. I went back to the waterfall and drank again. It tasted so good. It was so refreshing. I felt like a newborn. I felt very weak before coming to the waterfall but now I felt different. I had more hope and more strength. I still had the leaves in my pocket and started eating them even though they were sour. We slept on the grass that night.

In the morning, we got in line to be counted. Half the people were now gone. They hadn't made it. After all the water, I walked better and felt better. Before we left the factory, I remembered the commandant warning me that those people who couldn't work because they were sick or if they tried to escape and were caught would be shot. We left and started marching through more villages and cities. I tried to hold on after ten days of walking. As I passed through the fields, I picked up the sour leaves from the ground. As I walked, I ate the leaves. There was a young boy walking near Leon and me who was getting weaker. We tried holding him because he was having trouble walking. I tried talking to him and told him he should not lose hope. He was only eighteen years old and he wanted to live. I told him to try and stay in line, and that Leon and I would help him. We couldn't hold on to him any longer. He fell to the ground. We tried to pick him up even though we were putting our own lives on the line, but we had to leave him. He was thrown onto a truck. When we came to the woods, the soldiers shot all those people who could no longer walk and buried them in the woods.

It was just a miracle that Leon and I were still on our feet. Two days before we came to Litomerice, just five kilometers from Theresienstadt, they gave us bread with margarine and water. We had walked two days without food. I lived on the leaves that I picked. I told Leon that the end was coming. I couldn't live much longer without food. Five hundred people had died during those two days.

The next night on a farm, we were given water and black coffee. The next day we reached Litomerice, a camp for about five thousand people. When I arrived at the Arbeitslager (work camp), I was half dead. If I had to go any further, I never would have made it. Here they gave me a bigger portion of bread with margarine and hot coffee. I felt that I was alive again. I took a hot shower and felt better. I went to sleep on the cement floor because there were no free beds.

I was so weak but I hadn't lost hope. Because I was a believer in God, I felt I would live to see the end of the war. It was only a matter of days or weeks. Throughout my ordeal, I was always an optimist. The main reason I had to live was someone had to tell the world about the German murderers and they must be punished. I fell asleep on the cement floor.

The next morning at the count, there were only 321 people left out of more than fifteen hundred that had marched from Schiowitz, Germany to Theresienstadt, Czechoslovakia. Most had died on the way. They gave us black coffee and we started to walk. After about four hours we came to a town and I saw a sign that said, "Awa Arbeitslager Theresienstadt Macht dos Leben Zis" or "Work Make Life Sweet." I thought maybe I would find my mother and sisters here because in 1942 they told us that we were all going to Theresienstadt to work. At least, that was what the Jewish police had told us when they separated us in Dzialoszyce where we had lived. That was how the German murderers had cheated us. If we had known that we were being taken to death camps, we would not have gone so fast. We would have fought back with whatever we had like knives or other weapons. We would not have gone so freely. We just thought that because it was wartime, they needed workers in the defense factories. Instead, we went like sheep to the slaughter.

At one o'clock, we reached the main gate of Theresienstadt. When I walked in, I saw hundreds of people working inside. We looked at each other and I was nervous and shivering. I hoped to find my mother and sisters. I heard a whistle and everyone was told to get undressed. The men and women had all their hair cut off with a machine like a Remington Razor. Afterwards we all took hot showers. We were given fresh underwear, a suit, and a hat. We were told to stand in line for food. The soup was good, it had potatoes and vegetables. I asked Leon if it was really the two of us and were we still alive. I couldn't believe that we had overcome this horrible march.

After lunch, I heard a whistle and was told to get in line. They then divided us into different barracks. Leon and I stayed together in a tent-like barracks. The food here was a little better, but it was still not enough. I was still going around hungry. I kept looking around for someone from my family. Maybe my mother or my sister, Chana, would be here.

On the first day, I did not have to go to work. I asked the people there what kind of work they had to do, was it hard, and how was the food. Someone told me that there were over thirty thousand people in the camp from all over. From here, people were sent to the crematorium. I saw many people who were sent outside to work. There were also women and children. At six o'clock in the evening, I was given a portion of bread with margarine. I was very hungry because during the march we hadn't eaten in days.

Soon I found the Yungewirt brothers from Krakow. Israel had been in my choir at Schindler's factory and there my bed had been behind Israel's bed. I was very happy to see them. They had been there about three weeks. They told me that the crematorium worked twenty-four hours a day. The German's brought all the sick people here to be killed. The German government used to invite dignitaries from all over the world to inspect this camp to show them how well they treated the Jews. They told the visitors that here people were given better food. When the dignitaries came, the people were given different food. The kitchen was part of the tour and they were shown the good food. The next day people didn't get the good food. They even brought in artists and opened a theater to show the dignitaries. Some people had been here for over two years.

The next day I got up at six o'clock in the morning, got in line to be counted and was given hot black coffee with saccharine. Over the loud speaker, it was announced that anyone who wanted better food should get out of line. Leon and I immediately moved to that group. They sent us to work helping sick people to the hospital. There were many sick people there with typhus. The Red Cross would take them in their buses.

I worked there for about five weeks. Thousands of people were taken out and they gave us the sick people's food. It was a double portion of bread with margarine. I needed the food and shared it with my friend Israel Yungewirt. Now I had more food and I started to become stronger. I had to have strength to carry the sick people. I heard that the Germans were ready to get rid of the thirty thousand people in camp, but I didn't know when or how. I couldn't do anything as they continued to bring in people from other camps.

I was in the "Medic Group" helping to separate the sick from healthy people. Some of the sick were sent to the hospital and some were sent to the crematorium. Many of the workers contracted typhus and they were sent to the crematorium. I was very scared. I tried to get another job because I didn't want to get sick.

The next morning while I was standing in line, I had the chills and I was shivering but felt hot. I thought maybe I just had a cold. I found another job sweeping the barracks. I also helped the caretaker and I did anything he asked me. I still felt sick, had a temperature, and didn't have an appetite. I was afraid to go to bed and afraid to tell anyone I was sick. That night I felt hot and cold and I had a head ache. The next morning while I stood in line for the hot coffee and after I swept the floors, Leon and Israel saw that I was sick. I told them it was just a cold and I worked all day. Luckily, I didn't have to work outside.

It was April 1945 and I tried to have strength. I knew that I was sick and had a temperature, but I didn't want to go to the doctor. I was afraid. Day by day, I walked around, tried to work, and tried to rest in bed for a while. I couldn't stay in bed for long because I didn't want anyone to catch me. I knew my temperature was high. I knew that if I had typhus, they would send me to the crematorium. I worked with the high temperature and continued to try to eat the bread even though I didn't have an appetite. I knew I had to eat to stay alive.

Leon spoke to the Kapo about my situation and asked him to help me so he let me rest in bed. When he saw a German coming, he told me to get up and start working. Every day I felt worse and I was losing strength but I continued to work. Something new was going on. I heard that the Russian Army was coming from one side and the Americans and English were coming from the other side. I didn't see any German soldiers in the camp only the Kapos. I went to the manager of the barracks to try to find out what was happening. The manager asked me if I was sick. I told him I had a cold but that I felt better. I had been going around for eight days with a high temperature, chills, and a head ache. I was trying to hold on because I thought the war was coming to an end and I had to keep going. Every day I got weaker and weaker.

On May 8, 1945 at six o'clock in the morning, I heard that there were no more Germans left at Theresienstadt. They had all disappeared. When I went to be counted with Leon, I saw people running to the walls that were two meters high. People were sitting on top of the wall. Leon helped me to climb to the top where I sat down. I saw German soldiers marching with their hands up and the Russian Army with their guns marching and guarding them. They were singing Russian songs. When I saw this, I started to cry with happiness. I remembered my brother and sister that had gone to Russia. I thought maybe my brother had joined the Russian Army. I started to yell, "Moshe, Moshe, it's your brother Kalmen!." I was so excited watching the parade, and I knew that it was the end of the war. I had a life, but I started to get dizzy, fainted and fell to the ground. Leon called the Kapo, and he had me picked up by the Red Cross. I was very lucky because if that had happened on the 8th of May, I wouldn't have survived. Also it's a good thing I had fallen on the camp side rather than the other side of the wall, because it was about eighteen or twenty meters high. I saw before me my mother, father, brother, and sister.

I had been unconscious for eight days. When I woke up I saw a doctor who spoke to me in Russian. I told him that I didn't speak Russian that I spoke Polish, German, or Yiddish. He told me he was a Jew. I was happy. He asked me what had happened to me. I told him I had been sick for two weeks with chills and a head ache and I had a fever of 104. He told me I had typhus fever but that I was going to be okay.

My Time in the Hospital

I was in the hospital at Theresienstadt. It was a big brick building and was modern and comfortable. The other hospital was in the barracks. Everyday other "slaves" from all over came here. There were many doctors and nurses with sick people all around me. A doctor and nurse came to my bed and started to talk to me, but I didn't understand their language. The doctor spoke German and the nurse spoke the Czechoslovakian language. I was still very hot with a high temperature. I felt as if I were on fire. When they took my temperature, it was still 104 or 105 degrees. I asked for water because I was very thirsty. I pointed to my mouth when the doctor started to speak in German. The nurse understood a little Polish. She brought me water, but I couldn't keep my head up so she helped me drink the water. The doctor gave me pills to take three times a day and to drink plenty of water for the typhus fever. He told me that if I wanted to live I had to start eating. He was a very friendly man and the nurse was good, too. Since I couldn't eat, I was fed intravenously. I thanked them both for their kindness and I told them I would try to eat something. I couldn't get up from the bed because I was so weak.

The nurse fed me my first breakfast. I was very well taken care of by the doctors and nurses. They took good care of all the sick people. Mr. Bachner, the former owner of the enamel factory was in the next bed. He also was very sick from typhus fever. He was unconscious. I tried to eat more but every time I tried I would vomit, and I had diarrhea. Day by day, I started to feel a little better. I forced myself to eat but it only made me sick. After about two weeks in bed, I could still only drink. When the Russian Jewish doctor came for an inspection with two younger doctors, I still had a 105 degree fever. I told the doctors that I still couldn't eat without becoming sick. He told me in a very strict voice that I had to eat even if it made me sick. At least something would remain in my stomach. He said he would give me medicine for my stomach to relieve the vomiting and diarrhea and pills to reduce the fever. He told me that I was still young and had to fight in order to get well. He said he knew what I had gone through under the Hitler regime.

I thought about what the doctor had told me and since I was always an optimist, I told myself that I had to fight to stay alive. I had to force myself to eat and do what the doctor told me. I started very slowly. The nurse had to give me a bed pan. Later, when I was able to get up, I ate my breakfast and then with the nurses help walked to the toilet. After five days, it got a little easier; I could walk alone to the toilet. I still forced myself to eat and my temperature started to go down. I remember one day they put me on the scale and I weighed 37 kilos or 76 pounds. I was a skeleton, all skin, and bones.

On June 10, 1945 and after being in the hospital for about a month, I started to walk around by holding onto the beds. I was like a little boy just learning to walk. I still had a temperature and my head hurt me. One day around lunchtime, I opened my eyes and saw someone standing near my bed. It was my Aunt Zelda my Uncle David's wife. We looked at each other and the nurse came along and told her it was too dangerous for her to be there because of the typhus. She had to leave. I wondered why they had let her in at all. I was told that she had sneaked in on her own. I got up and slowly walked to the waiting room where she was waiting. I told her not to come too close because I still had a temperature. Someone had told her that I had typhus and was still contagious. I saw that she was very happy to see me.

Tearfully, she told me that she hadn't found any of the family. I started to cry. It was hard for Aunt Zelda to talk but she told me that she had been looking for the family. She hoped that she would find her older son who had run away to Russia. She told me that she had been in many of the camps. She reminded me about the time when I was a five month old baby, they had to take my mother to the hospital because she had gotten very sick when her brother died at nineteen. She had a nervous breakdown. She had been nursing me when it happened. That was the first time I had ever heard that story about my mother. I felt very lucky to find a member of my family, but I started to get very weak. I couldn't sit there any longer and I couldn't hold my head up. I asked her to remain at Theresienstadt until I was better so that we could leave together to look for our families. I asked one of the nurses to get her a nice room and they put her in a room with another woman. I excused myself and told my aunt I would see her the next day.

Everyday my aunt came to visit me and we talked about our lives during the war. I reminded her of our times in the Krakow ghetto when she and my uncle were so good to me. The food I was given and the holiday dinners were such good times for me. She also had given me my cousin's clothing. I told her how we had lived in Dzialoszyce with my Aunt Chava and her daughter and children. My aunt told me that she had lost her husband and children and was alone.

I started to feel better and gained a lot of weight. I gained 20 kilos. When I was released from the hospital, they gave me some clothing and shoes and other things that I needed such as documentation that I had been in the hospital at Theresienstadt. My aunt wanted to go back to Krakow, Poland to try to find out what had happened to our families. She thought that those who had gone to Russia would come back to Poland. I found out that we could go back to Poland or to Landsberg, an occupation camp run by the Americans. I knew if my brother, sister, and my aunt's son came back from Russia, they probably would go to Krakow. I felt I was still too weak from typhus fever to make a trip back to Poland. I didn't have a nickel to my name. I had no money at all. I needed a good vacation, a rest, and someone to take care of me. I also knew that the Polish people were anti-Semitic, they hated Jews. I was afraid of them. I told my aunt that it would be much better to go to the Jewish camp in the American Zone. We found out that in Theresienstadt they called it the American Jewish Organization or the "Joint Distribution Committee." It was for the liberated Jews who now lived in Theresienstadt. People in the hospital gave us an address where we could get more information.

My aunt and I took a streetcar to the address of the Joint Distribution Committee in order to register. I showed them my papers from the hospital and we registered ourselves to go to Landsberg near Munich, Germany. They told us that if we had relatives in American such as an aunt, uncle or cousin, we should get in touch with them immediately. We might be able to find out from them if any of our family was alive. My aunt had family in New York. We answered the questions and told them where we wanted to go. I gave them the names of the people I was looking for, my mother, father, brother, and sisters. After we completed the formalities, they told us they didn't know how long it would take before we might be able to be transported to Landsberg. We were told not to worry. They were going to give us a place to live and enough food, but we had to have patience.

At this time, Czechoslovakia was occupied by Russia, and they treated us well. The Czech's are very good people. The Joint Distribution Committee gave us clothing and shoes, not new but in good condition. I was still very weak and walked slowly. I didn't have my strength back yet. My aunt and I had plenty of time to talk about how we had come through the war. (After the war, I met my cousin Zacharieh in Stuttgart where he had married a lady named Rosa. They had a little girl and in 1948, they went to Israel.) We reminisced about March of 1943 when they closed the Krakow ghetto and divided families. My aunt was sent to one camp and my uncle and the children were sent to Treblinka or Belzec. She hoped that they were still alive. I told her about my life during the past five years and how they had separated us at Dzialoszyce and sent whole families to Belzec. I told her about my sister, Chana, disappearing at that time. (Afterwards, I found out she had lived through the war. When my wife Ruth and I discussed our lives during wartime, I found out that Ruth had encountered Chana in Leipzig. She recognized Chana from a photo that I had.)

Three weeks later, my aunt and I were transported to Landsberg, Germany. It was August 18th at seven o'clock in the morning. After breakfast, I was told to go with 28 other people to a meeting place. I was given a signed document saying that I was authorized to leave Czechoslovakia. I was taken to the railroad station and still felt very weak. I couldn't walk very well. It had been over five weeks since I left the hospital so they gave me a special bunk because I couldn't sit for long periods. I arrived in Landsberg at 4:30 in the afternoon. Landsberg was a special camp for Jews who had been in concentration camps including those people who had run away to Russia. As soon I got there, I went to the office to register in order to get a room. While I was there, I met my friend Leon List. We were so happy to see each other alive. I told him what had happened since I had last seen him when I was hospitalized after I fell from the wall in Theresienstadt. Leon had been in Landsberg for a few months so he talked to the people in the office and they gave us two rooms, one big room for us, and a small one for my aunt. After two hours, Leon and I were moved in with two other young men. The room was very nice and I received food from the Americans.

Five days later, I got very sick and couldn't walk. I didn't have an appetite even though there was plenty of food and I couldn't gain any weight. I had my tonsils removed and almost chocked from the blood in my mouth. They had trouble stopping the bleeding. I was in terrible pain. A specialist was brought in who was a German doctor. I could only take liquids and could not eat at all. X-rays were taken and I was fed intravenously. Everyday my aunt visited me. My mouth started to heal but I still couldn't walk. The doctors felt it might be my teeth because they had been so neglected. They removed some of them and I got an infection after they removed the teeth.

I asked my aunt to bring me a school notebook so that I could write my father's songs. I still have the notebooks. Little by little, I wrote what I could remember. (I purchased a condo in Florida and one day, I visited Dr. Menings. He asked me many questions and I told him about my six year experience in the concentration camps. He told me he had been in the hospital at Landsberg Camp. He helped take care of patients with another doctor. He was a freshman and helped the other doctor. He felt that it must have been the same doctor who had taken care of me. He had worked there for two years. I was shaken. I told him about my experience in the hospital and how they had taken care of me for two months. I couldn't believe how much of those times I still remembered.)

I was still sick and vomiting but continued to write down my father's songs, melodies and stories that he used to tell at weddings. My father used to have my brother and I perform with him in the skits. One of the stories was about us preparing to go to Israel. There was a scene about dividing Israel for the Arabs and Jews. I put down the story about my father managing Jewish weddings form the start to the end of the ceremony. I had ninety songs and stories that I wanted to have printed. I remembered the poem that I had composed while at Schindler's factory. The poem was written in Yiddish so I started to translate it while at Landsberg Hospital. I couldn't get out of bed so it was good that I had something to do. When I was finally released from the hospital, I had to learn to walk again because I was so weak. Aunt Zelda took good care of me and I started to eat and felt better.

Life at Landsberg Camp

While I was being care for by my aunt and being with my friend, I thought that I needed more than food. I needed nicer clothing because I didn't have any at all. The Joint gave me some used clothing that didn't even fit. While I had been in the hospital Leon and my other friends has gotten beautiful clothes because they had started a business. They brought in food other than what we were getting in the camp like butter, farmers cheese and eggs. They would go to a German farmer and get sour cream. People didn't have much money. They started to buy American cigarettes and sold them to the Germans. It was illegal but they did it anyway. The goods were sold in Berlin on the Russian side. All the professions started to open shops like tailors, shoemakers, and carpenters and they were paid for their work.

I started to live a normal life even though it was without my parents. People started to get married and were given separate apartments with two rooms. I lived at Skavinska 10 and my neighbor, Chaskel Lefkowitz lived at Skavinska 13. We went to Talmud Torah together. (He now lives in Brooklyn with his wife, Miriam.) They were the first to be married in Landsberg with about 200 people in attendance. At their wedding, I recited something from the Torah and sang my fathers songs. It lasted from six o'clock at night until two o'clock in the morning. I believe that the Union sponsored the wedding and wondered where they had gotten the money for the wedding. There was a lot of food and everyone was dressed beautifully. It was unbelievable.

Leon taught me how to dance so we went to many dancing parties. I had to try to make some money so Leon and I used to sell merchandise in our building. We bought men's socks, handkerchiefs, gloves, and ties. I took the merchandise on commission and Leon and I were partners. People started to come and we added food like cheese and butter from the farmer. I was able to buy my first suit. The suit was tailored made with a blue collar and stripes. (I still have pictures of me in this suit.). I had special boots to go with the suit.

I belonged to B'nai Akiva, a modern religious organization like a Kibbutz but I didn't sleep there. Every Friday night I would go for Oneg Shabbat and sing my father's songs. Leon was not religious but we were always together. I bought myself a bike from the money I had saved.

One day I was riding my bike down a hill and I almost hit a tree. I fell on both hands and I still have a scar on my left from the accident. After that, I didn't ride the bike too much. I also shared what I had with my aunt because she lived in our house. She became a saleslady while there. While attending the B'nai Akiva I met a girl named Pola from Hungary. She was very beautiful and lived in the Kibbutz. She wanted to get married but I did not want to marry at that time so we were only friends.

My name in the concentration camps was Kalman Schumacher, my mother's name. I registered at the Joint and the Union under that name. I put my father's name as Kalman Frydman. I did this because I was still looking for my brother, Moshe, and sister Sara. That was our name at home so if they were looking for me, I thought it would be easier to find me. My father had a brother named Josel Frydman. I wanted to make sure they knew I was still alive so I was registered in both names. That was smart because the Union found my Uncle Josel in Boston. They called me into the office and told me they had my uncle's address. They also found a cousin, Carl Frydman from Roxbury at 8 Balsam Street. I wrote them each a letter and received a reply from both of them. They said in the letters that they were so happy to hear that I was still alive. They told me that my brother was in Israel in Kibbutz Degania and they were trying to contact him. I was so happy to hear that my brother was alive. My Uncle Josel promised me he would try to process papers in order to get me to America. Meanwhile I was not in perfect health. It took me five months to recuperate.

Once David Ben-Gurion came to the camp and spoke in the main hall along with speakers from all the organizations in Landsberg. I spoke on behalf of B'nai Akiva about the political situation. Chanukah was coming soon and they asked me to prepare five songs for a party. The president of the Landsberg Camp was Dr. Greenhaus from Vilna. He was a terrific speaker and I used to love to hear him speak. At the party I sang a song called, "President, Yiddish" while the eight candles burned. After the party, Dr. Greenhaus asked me about my experience during the war. He wanted me to tell the Union because he wanted me to go to Paris. There was an organization there that helped people with talent. I thanked him and told him I had to go on with my life.

Leon and I were still in business at our house where we sold household goods because I was trying to make as much money as I could. I started to go to Saltzheim near Frankfurt with cigarettes and used watches. First, I went as a helper and the person paid me for being his helper. After I learned, the next time I did it on my own and made three times as much. During one of the train rides, I met a guy named David Plattner and his partner. Mr. Plattner was from Poland and was living in

Landsberg. He had the same business as mine. We got acquainted and became friends while we sold our merchandise in Saltzheim. He was on the religious side.

I met a girl named Sonia Lachner from Krakow and she lived with Mr. and Mrs. Kurtz. She told me she had been in business selling used watches and cigarettes for five months and had made good money. She said to go to Saltzheim to get the prices before selling the merchandise. This was a good lesson for me. There was a man named Mr. Keinig who was the top business man and he also was from Krakow. He gave me the price list that I should be using for my sales. I found out that Mr. Keinig's daughter was our neighbor. His new wife, Sabrina was a violinist by the name of Berl Lessman and was coming to be with him soon. He was already a very rich man. When Berl Lessman came, she was very happy to see me.

When I went home I told Leon about meeting Mr. Keinig. He said he didn't want to go to Saltzheim any longer. He didn't want to get into any trouble with the police because he said that he would soon be leaving for America. He had an uncle and a cousin in American and they were sponsoring his trip to the States. His cousin was a girl about his age.

I didn't think about get caught selling merchandise because I was a risk-taker. I had to make money. I liked nice clothing and wanted to enjoy life. I would only do it for a little longer. I had promised to visit Sonia when she gave me her address. She was a very nice girl with a pretty face. She was a little younger than I was. I took her dancing even though I was not yet perfect at dancing. Sometimes when Leon and I went dancing, I would step on the girl's feet. I would apologize to the girl and tell her that I was just learning. Most of the girls understood. I enjoyed being with Sonia.

It was about four weeks before Pesach when I asked the Kurtz family what kind of a girl Sonia was. I knew she was not lazy, a good business person, and from a very religious family in Krakow. I just didn't like that such a young girl was doing this illegal business. We had been going together for approximately five months and talking about getting engaged. On Pesach, she gave me a beautiful golden ring and I bought myself a pair of new black shoes.

Then I received a letter from my brother in Israel. He had been in Anders Army using the Polish name, Shumansky (he sent me a photo of himself in uniform). He was very happy that I was still alive and he was trying to get papers so that he could travel from Israel to visit me. I wrote back and asked him about our step-sister, Sara because he hadn't mentioned her in his letter. In his return letter, he told me that Sara was alive and living in Russia. He said he would tell me the whole story when he came for his visit. I was very happy and couldn't wait to see him but life must go on. I prepared myself for my engagement to Sonia. I was still living in the apartment with Leon and my friends when a knock came at the door at around two o'clock in the morning. We all got scared but I opened the door. It was my brother, Moshe. He came in with a big piece of luggage, a backpack, and an accordion. We fell on each other with happiness and both cried. Aunt Zelda came in to greet him. We all sat for hours and talked but had to stop because the other people wanted to sleep. The next morning Aunt Zelda made us breakfast. We looked around the table at each other with happiness.

My brother started to ask me questions about our parents, sisters and Aunt Chava and her family. Of Aunt Chava's eight children, four were still alive. We then went for a walk through the camp to meet the people we knew from Krakow. He met some school friends of his. Each one thanked God that they were still alive. My brother said that we should start looking for our sister in Russia. He had heard that she had married a Russian and had two sons. I was very disappointed and didn't believe it but hoped that she had married a Jew. Moshe had begged her to go with him when they were in Dombos but she went with the Russian. After that, Moshe had not seen her. Moshe told me about his life during the war and I told him about my time in the concentration camps.

I didn't take Moshe with me when I went to sell my merchandise. He told me that he was never a business man because he was in the Army and also got paid for playing the accordion. During his time in the Army they didn't know he was Jewish nor did he look Jewish. He was sent to Teheran, Iran while using the name of Mieczysben Shumansky because they didn't take Jews in the Army. My brother had always been a musician. It looked as though he had money, but he didn't tell me about it and I didn't ask him. He spoke very good English, good Russian, and Hebrew. He told me he had gone to Israel while in the Army in 1944. He then ran away from the Army and went to Kibbutz Degania. He remained there until after the war.

Aunt Zelda found herself a boyfriend and I told my brother that I was becoming engaged. I introduced my brother to Sonia and we used to go dancing together. In the meantime, we were in contact with our cousin, Carl. Carl had lived with us before the war between 1932 and 1936. He had left as a single man to America and had married there.

One day while walking through the camp with my brother, he asked to speak to me about something very important. He told me not to get excited about what he had to say. He said that I had only known Sonia for five months and was already engaged. He said that the same thing had happened to him while he was in Israel. He had a beautiful girlfriend in the kibbutz whose father was a member of Knesset, which is like a senator in the United Stated. She had been a poet and her work was published in the newspaper. When I found out that you were alive, I left her to be with you. Now you are telling me that you are going to marry and we will not have any time together. He told me he didn't want to live with my wife and me. He said that I had plenty of time to get married that we didn't even know yet where we would be living, Israel or America. It was also easier for a single man. A single man is readily accepted whereas a man with a baby has a different responsibility. He asked me to understand that he was the only brother I had. He wanted to be with me all the time.

I listened and didn't say anything. As time passed, I didn't know what to do. I continued to go with the Plattner brothers, David and Shaje, to Saltzheim. One day David told me he had a friend in Stuttgart and he was going there for a visit. When he came back after five days, he told me that they were going to move to Stuttgart. He told me there was a chance for a normal life in Stuttgart not like that in the camp. He wanted me to go together with him for a visit to see if we might consider moving there also. He mentioned us making a partnership and doing business together.

When Moshe and I went there we met our friend, Israel Turner who used to work for me when I had my small luggage shop. We met his wife, baby, and brother-in-law, Motl. His brother in law had a grocery store on Reinsburg Strasse 89 and he wanted me as a partner. He said it was a very profitable business. He knew of a factory making whiskey and vodka where they delivered 200 bottles every week. He had made a special label stating that it had come from Toronto, Canada. They labeled the bottles here and sold it at a big profit. My brother thought that it was much better than going to Saltzheim every day. I had heard that the police were checking up and catching people and putting them in jail for smuggling. This was bad for someone who wanted to go to America. You could not get into America with a police record. Moshe and I decided to go to Stuttgart. If we didn't like it, we could always go back to Landsberg.

When we returned to Landsberg, I told my aunt that we were leaving Landsberg and moving to Stuttgart. She was already living with Mr. Kranz. I didn't like it because they were not married, but they were thinking about marrying. I said goodbye to my friend, Leon List, and I told him how sorry I was to be leaving him. I asked him to go with us, but he said no because his affidavit for his America trip was due any day. I gathered my belongings, said goodbye to Aunt Zelda and she wished me the best of luck. My brother advised me to just say goodbye to Sonia and her family. I told her that if I didn't like it in Stuttgart, I would be coming back to Landsberg.

I rented a place from a German family outside the camp at Reinsburg Strasse. My brother said this was better than the risky business when I had been traveling to Saltzheim smuggling watches and cigarettes. If they had caught me, I would have been in trouble with the law. I started working in the grocery store where we sold not only groceries but the liquor. My brother and I were then partners with Israel Turner and his brother-in-law, Motl Glaswand. They called him der Grober Kopf (big head). My brother also rented a place outside the camp. Everyday we went to work. We wanted to make the business bigger.

While we were working, we met a man from Krakow named Mr. Bucheister. He had two sons and he lived on the same floor as the Turners. My brother and I got acquainted with him because he had a soda factory in the next building where we lived. He had lost his wife in the war. On our floor, there was a bath and shower that was operated with gas. The door was kept locked. One day while Moshe was taking shower, he was in there for a very long time. When I knocked on the locked door, he did not answer. I had Mr. Turner break down the door where we found my brother lying on the floor unconscious from a gas leak. If we had waited another fifteen minutes, he probably would have died from the fumes. An ambulance was called and after being in the hospital for three hours, he was sent home.

Life went on working together with our partners, but I wasn't too excited because there were too many of us in the same business. We just about made a living. I felt I had made a mistake and wanted to find something better. For now, I was just glad to be away from Landsberg. In the same building, there was an older couple with a single daughter in her forties. They were very nice people. My brother had his own apartment in the building.

My Brother Remains

In 1947 at the Bucheister's house, they had a German cleaning lady named Lora who was about 25 or 26 years old. I don't know if she slept there. She was blond and pretty. I didn't notice that my brother was always talking to her and had started dating her, usually after we closed the business at six o'clock in the evening. He had his home and I had my home, what was going on between Lora and him I did not know because he didn't talk to me about her. He had only told me about the girl he had dated in Israel. One day he didn't come to work. There was no telephone at our houses at that time. I thought maybe he had gotten sick with the flu or a cold. I went to his house and knocked on the door. He opened it up and when I came in I saw Lora in his bed. I looked at her and I looked at him and I didn't say anything. I asked him why he hadn't come to work, if he was sick? He said this was a vacation day for him. I smiled and left. I had heard that a lot of Jewish boys were having affairs with German girls. The next day when he came to work and told me he was only going with Lora once in a while and he also had a Jewish girlfriend and showed me her picture, I was happy.

In January 1948, five months before the establishment of the Jewish State, I learned that they were mobilizing all the young people for Israel because of the war with the Arabs. They went from house to house asking the names of all the Jewish families. If there were two brothers, they would take one. When they came to our store, they mobilized my partner, Motl Glaswand. My brother told them that he had come here from Israel and was an officer in Anders Army. They mobilized him and he told me not to join. He said that my time in the concentration camps was enough, that he would go.

One day, Mr. Bucheister came into our store and pulled me away to the side. He said to me "you go right now to the *Standesamt* (marriage license bureau) because your brother and Lora are getting married now!". He gave me the address and I grabbed a taxi and he took me there. It was about 1:00 in the morning. I was very nervous and ran up the stairs. They showed me a room where they held marriage ceremonies. I was told that about a half hour earlier my brother had taken out a marriage license. I was shocked. I fainted on the spot and was taken to the emergency room at the hospital. After about two hours, they let me go home.

After that, I didn't see my brother anymore because he was mobilized and sent to Israel. He was afraid to see me and didn't even say goodbye to anybody. I was shocked and so disappointed. He knew what the Germans had done to our parents, our whole family, and me. He could have married a beautiful Jewish girl. I asked myself why he had done such a thing to me. I got very depressed. Now I didn't have anyone. I was alone because my brother was lost to me. He was the one who had told me to leave Sonia and now he was marrying a German girl. How could he do this to me after such a terrible war? He hadn't even discussed his marriage plans with me. He never once mentioned it. I felt I hadn't anything more to live for.

I found out later that he had married her in the Standesamt. I told the Turners and Motl what had happened. I walked around the store like a drunk. I didn't know what I was doing because I was so depressed. I couldn't eat. I went to bed at night and talked to myself. I didn't want to live any longer. I got up from my bed and went straight to the window. I lived on the fourth floor. I looked down and I said to myself, now comes my end. I don't want to live anymore. I was standing at the window. I went with my right foot up on the open window and then with the other foot. And I was standing just so to jump down and as I was standing in the open window I saw in front of my eyes my Father and I heard a voice coming "Kalmenshi" that's what he always called me, "don't do that. Go down from the window . . . you will build your own family . . . you have to live", I saw before me my father and he gave me a push back. I fell on the floor and I remained lying on the floor. My heart was beating so fast my head was flying. I lay on the floor for twenty minutes, I tried to get up and went to bed. I started to think, who would care if I had jumped and killed myself. My own brother wouldn't care. Maybe he would have a tear in his eyes, but that's all. All he cared about was himself. He had dated the German girl for over six months and never told me about her. She already had a baby from who knows what man. So if he didn't care about me at all, why did *I* want to kill myself? I still have to live and continue our religion's way of life. I, too, had to get married and have children in order to build a new generation. If God gave me life and I lived through such a horrible war, my whole family was killed, my three sisters were killed, my mother and father. Why shouldn't I live? Because my brother did some stupid things? He will suffer later. Don't care anymore about your brother, care about yourself. I said to myself, get up and go to work. You have no brother, nobody, but you have yourself.

I thought about my father telling me not to commit suicide, to marry, get a home, and have children. I lay in bed and suddenly I felt like a newborn starting to walk and to grow. I fell asleep and all night I dreamed about my father, mother, and sisters sitting together and talking, laughing and having a good time. It was a very happy night, a family night, unforgettable.

I got up at six thirty in the morning, took a shower, and got dressed. I felt that I had a lot of strength and hope. In the camps, I was always an optimist. I used to tell the Jewish people not to lose hope and that we would overcome. We would be the ones, the witnesses about Hitler and what he had done to the Jewish people. And now I had gotten so depressed that I wanted to kill myself because my brother did a stupid thing? He will suffer and that is true, he was suffering all his life. And for thirty years I was not in contact with him.

I went to the store which I was a partner in. I didn't tell them anything. I was a different man. I was now thinking from life. I said goodbye to Motl Glaswand because he was mobilized to the Israeli Army and was going to Israel. I remained and continued to take care of the business with Srulek Turner and his wife Shifra and their baby, who lived in the same building on the first floor. I still couldn't forget what happened between my brother and me. How he had talked against the Germans and how he didn't want to get married and talked me out of marrying Sonia. I wondered why I had listened to him especially since he turned around and married a German woman with a child. I knew that he also went with a Jewish girl while he was seeing his secret love. I knew he probably was afraid to tell me. Life must go on.

One day two Jewish business men came into the store and looked around while we were busy with customers. After their inspection, they told us they had a proposition for us. They said that they had connections in Switzerland to bring into Stuttgart chocolate and sacks of coffee that was not ground and they needed a place to store the merchandise. They needed enough space in our basement to store fifteen or twenty tons. First, they wanted to see the basement to make sure they could hide that much merchandise. They spent a half hour looking over the basement and said there was enough room. We told them that when we closed the store at six o'clock, we locked up; we put three cans filled with garbage in front of the door. We knew when the German and American police were coming to inspect so that's when we closed up and put the cans in front of the door.

I told them to come to the house for a discussion. We sat down in Srulek's apartment and they said we would be partners with the chocolate and coffee merchandise being stored in our basement. The split would be 60-40. We didn't have any money to buy the merchandise so the profit would be divided after the merchandise was sold. We would get 40 percent and they would get sixty percent. We prepared and signed the paperwork. They told us they would let us know the exact date of the first shipment.

Srulek and I went and cleaned the basement. I was so busy I tried to forget about my brother. Soon they called to let us know that the shipment was coming. It was a Tuesday and when the load arrived, we had to get help unloading the merchandise. We had to work fast. The load was worth $18,000. They told us it was a lot of money. When we finished unloading and they left, we started to sell the coffee and chocolate. The two partners were sitting all day long in our business. They took the money from the load and we marked the amounts in a book. It was going pretty well. We had many customers from around Stuttgart. Most of them were from the camp because we could not sell to strangers. We sold out in about two weeks.

We ordered another truck load of the same merchandise. Srulek and I made $2,000 each and the other two men made sixty percent of the order. We worked very hard unloading the next shipment because the four of us had to do it ourselves. The business got bigger with Srulek and I making $10,000 each. I told Srulek's wife that I wanted to go to Lora and try to give her money to let my brother be free to leave. I asked her to go to Mr. Bucheister's and find out her address. She found out Lora's address and I went there with Shifra and $5,000 but she wouldn't take it. I told her that in the Jewish religion it is forbidden to marry outside our faith. Nothing helped so I left and went home. I was very nervous but I thought that I was strong enough to overcome this also.

Someone called the German police about our merchandise. After unloading a shipment, locking up, and putting the garbage can in front of the door, we saw German and American Military Police. They had flash lights and could see us through the door. The ten of us ran fast and went to Srulek's house. The bag of money was prepared in the open top drawer but we didn't have time to hide it. When the police came to the house, we told them that we were gathered to pray. They were speaking in English and one of the partners also spoke English. He told them that someone had died and we were gathered as a Minyan. They saw the bags of money but they didn't touch them and left. It was a miracle. They were there about five or ten minutes. They went to the grocery store and didn't find anything. We waited one hour at the house and when everything quieted down, we took the bag with money down. There was almost $20,000 in it. We paid them. The next day we tried to put the merchandise in a different place.

My brother came back from Israel but I didn't want to see him. I received my papers for America. When I went to see Mrs. Levine she told me I would be leaving Stuttgart May 28th on a ship called McArthur. I had made almost $10,000 dollars to take with me to America. The train took me to the seaport. Moshe had come to see me but I didn't want to see him. My heart was beating fast and I was nervous. I sat down away from the window because I didn't want my brother to see me. He had come late and the train started to move so he didn't have a chance to talk to me. I left Germany and came to the Port. I took the accordion with me that my brother had brought from Israel when he left it with Srulek.

They loaded us on the ship where I had a room with five boys. We had a good time on the first day and I made some friends. I sang and continued writing. It was okay but on the second day, I started to get sick. I was vomiting and lost my appetite. I traveled eleven days from May 28th until June 8th. I was very seasick. I couldn't eat anything at all. I forced myself to eat and drink. It was like being in hell.

On June 8th, 1948 I arrived in New York. We walked down from the ship, I hardly walked, not only me but also most people had the same thing, sea-sickness! They took us to a train. I was going to Boston, Dorchester, Balston Street 8, to my cousin Carl Frydman. When we got there, I descended from the train. Nobody was waiting for me, no family, no friends. What should I do now? I couldn't speak English. A lady from the UNRRA (United Nations Refugee Relief Association) asked me if I had any family. I told her that I did and gave her the name, address, and telephone of my cousin. She called them and told them I was in Boston. My cousin told her that I should take a taxi to bring me over and he will pay the driver. I felt bad that no one came to pick me up. Many people I had traveled with had people waiting to greet them. It took approximately three quarters of an hour to get to my cousin's house. I remember it was nine o'clock at night when I got there. When I arrived my cousin Carl kissed me and introduced me to this wife, Sally and his ten year old son, Sammy. They gave me something to eat. We talked for awhile but I was very tired from my trip. They gave me a very nice room with nice furniture and told me to go to sleep.

The next morning around eight o'clock my cousin, Sally, I called her Corke Beily, came into my room with her sister Helen. I was half asleep and they looked into my face. They said in Yiddish, "Look at him, what a handsome boy. He doesn't look as though he's been in a concentration camp. Look at his beautiful face." I pretended to be asleep until they left. Around nine o'clock I got up and went into the kitchen. My cousin Carl had gone to work and their son was at school. Carl's wife was preparing breakfast. I told her I had to pray first. After I finished praying, I sat at the table and spoke in Yiddish to Carl's wife. Luckily she spoke Yiddish. She asked me about my family and I told her that the only ones who remained from my whole family is my brother Moshe, he is now in Israel, my sister Sara, was living in Russia. The rest of the family, the Germans had killed. I told her that it was unbelievable what I had gone through. That I am now alive, believe me, I could write a book! She asked me what I intended to do in America. I told her that I didn't know but that my profession was making luggage and I had a small shop before the war that I had opened when I was seventeen years old, had four workers and my sister Chana working for me and was doing very well. I had merchandise worth about 10,000 zloty that is about $4,000 here. It was a lot of money in Poland. I intended to go to work for someone or in a luggage factory. I knew that it would be different now since there everything was done by hand and here it is done by machinery and much easier. But let me stay here a few days and I will see what I can do here in America.

After five days, my belongings were sent to their home. Everything arrived except the accordion. They kept the accordion because it had been made in Italy and had little sprinkles that looked like diamonds. The accordion was held for a month while they removed the sprinkles because they thought I was smuggling in diamonds.

My cousin Carl was a very good violinist. How did I know? I remembered that when I was ten years old, like his son now, Sammy, he came to Krakow from Chmielnik looking for a job and to play the violin. He stayed in our house and lived with us for two years and worked at Tigner's fur shop. At night, he played the violin at weddings, or any occasion. By the end, when he was supposed to go to America, he was playing at the best night club. The Esplanade. He used write the notes to my father's songs. My father loved him very much. Now he had his own band in America. He played his music at weddings and other occasions and by day he worked in a store.

I was at Carl and Sally's house for five days. During that time, the whole family came to see me and talked to me. Most of the American born didn't speak Yiddish but all my cousins who had come in to American in 1935 did speak Yiddish. My cousin Carl told me that his father, Uncle Josel wanted me to live in his house on Monroe Street. He had his own home with plenty of room. I moved in with my uncle and his wife, Dreisl. I found that my aunt was a sick person. She talked to herself and sometimes she was very depressed. She walked around the house in a nervous state. My uncle told me that since she had come to America, she had changed emotionally. I saw that this was not a place for me to be.

On the next Shabbat, they had a party in their house for the whole family and me. This time I was introduced to everybody, my aunt, and her brother, Israel. He was the owner of six Frydman's bakeries in Dorchester and around Boston. He spoke to me about working in a bakery. If I like the work, he would then hire me in one of his bakeries. They thought that I should not stay in this house, I should be living with younger people so my cousin, Corke Beile (we called her Sally), asked me to live in her house. I was very happy to get out of here. That was on Saturday.

On Sunday, the very next day, Sally and her husband Heime came with a car. They took all my belongings and drove me to Interwell Street near Blue Hill Avenue. There were many young people in their thirties living there and I was very happy.

The next day I went to work at this bakery that Uncle Freedman sent me to. The man at the bakery spoke Yiddish. I told him I had been in a concentration camp and would like to learn the bakery business. I told him I was a very hard worker. It was a big place and he had me sweeping the floors and cleaning the equipment. I did all the dirty work and had to work after the store closed. I didn't like it because he never let me see how the bread or rolls were made. He told me I had to start at the bottom and later he would show me how to bake.

I worked there for two weeks. It was hard work for me. Afterwards he had me work near the furnace throwing coals in the oven. When he told me to throw coal into the oven I thanked him very much and told him I was not in a concentration camp any longer. I didn't come to America to be a slave and said goodbye. He said he would mail me my paycheck and he did.

So I was living with my cousin Corke Beile and her husband, Heime. They had two boys, Jonah and Albert. My cousin Corke Beile was a very nice person and she was very good to me. But they were very poor. I couldn't understand it because Heime worked on the railroad and made good money, but he was a gambler, betting on horses and other things so he was always in the red. He owed the Mafia a lot of money. He would come home with half a paycheck because they waited for him when he cashed his check. After he had paid them, he didn't have enough to support his family. He was afraid to say anything because many times he had come home beaten up from them because he didn't pay them enough. My cousin was a beautiful woman, two nice boys, but she had a miserable life. I told her as soon as I got a job I would pay her for my staying there.

The Girl from Stuttgart

I was looking for a job and I found work in leathergoods. I made at that time, 75 cents an hour, which was 28 dollars a week. I worked overtime also but I had to pay for bus transportation. I paid my cousin 10 dollars a week. I found out that there was a high school on the next street and at night there was school for the immigrants. I went there and registered for the night school. The first night I came to school, I met a family from Krakow, Mr. Sigmund Turner and his wife. We started to talk and he told me we lived on the same street. He invited me to his house. I found out he was a cousin of Srulek Turner, my partner till I left Germany. I was going to school a few nights a week and I made friends there. I became friends with Zigi Turner and his wife, Niuszka. They had two sons. When the High Holidays came, I went to Shul near there.

It was after Yom Kippur. I went to school one night and saw a girl I recognized from Stuttgart. She was very pretty. I looked at her and she looked at me and after the lesson finished, I went to her and asked her if she is from Stuttgart. She said to me, yes, I think I know you, you had a grocery market they called the Chasidim Store. I said, yes, you are right. As a matter of fact, she said, my stepfather Samuel Klaiman told me to give you regards, your name is Kalmen Frydman. I said, yes. I asked her where she lives. She told me she lives far away from here, but she goes by bus home. We talked for a while and then we left. I said to myself, I saw her in Stuttgart sometimes. And I said to myself, if I would find a girl like her, so natural, pretty and nice, I would marry her.

When I went home, I told my cousin about the girl and that I liked her, she told me she had a nice girl she wanted me to meet, one of our cousin's daughters. She said she would make the arrangements. A few days later she said, please, come with me. I went with her to our cousin's for me to meet this girl who was there waiting for me. But I couldn't speak English and she couldn't speak Yiddish, or any other language. So my cousin Sally sat with us and translated our talk. I was sitting there with that girl but thinking about Ruth Wiszniak, the girl from Stuttgart, who I had met a few days ago at school. My cousin noticed that I was not too comfortable so we said goodbye and left. On the way home, my cousin asked me if I had liked the girl. I said I was sorry but I was not interested now. First I have to go to school and learn the language and get a good job, then I can think about dating a girl. The truth is, I really didn't like her. First of all, the girl was very fat and second, she was much older than me. I wanted to go to school first, learn the language, and get a good job. I couldn't think about dating a girl just yet.

I found a job making leather belts in Boston. When I started work there, the manager gave me a sewing machine and showed me how to stitch. It took me about a week to get the hang of it. After being shown how to do the job, I started working piecework (I was paid for each piece I did) on top of 75 cents an hour. I liked the job very much and my manager was a good man who was pleased with my work.

At school, I again met Ruth, the girl from Stuttgart. After the lesson, she told me her history and I told her mine. I asked her if she would like to get a job where I was working. She said she would and I told my manager that I had a friend who needed a job. He told me to bring Ruth in for an interview. She got the job and was shown work similar to mine, stitching belts. It took her a little longer to learn and since it was piecework, she didn't make as much money as I did. After work in the elevator, she thanked me for getting her a job. I gave her a kiss and she didn't say anything. I was very happy.

Ruth and I went to school together. She lived on Seaver Street near a big synagogue. I took her home one day, and the old lady who lived there who started to talk to her. She was very depressed because she had just lost her husband. The lady felt that a young girl living with her in the house and seeing her crying all the time was not good for Ruth. The Joint had given her the room and she didn't have to pay because she had no money. But now she had a job and after a few weeks she got her first paycheck. She was paid every Friday. When we saw the Turners at school one evening, they asked her if she would like a room in their apartment for eight dollars a week. At this time, she only made eighteen dollars a week, but she accepted and moved from her place to the Turner's apartment on Lawrence Avenue. That was a lot of money. The Turners paid forty dollars a month for the whole apartment but we didn't know about rent prices. Out of the eighteen dollars, she had to pay for transportation, rent, and live on the rest, but she was happy. I used to visit her in her new apartment. I fell in love with her, and she seemed very happy with me. We were together a lot because we went to school together, we also worked at the same place, and now we lived on neighboring streets.

One day at school, we were talking with our teacher and she asked me about my profession. I told her that before the war I had a luggage business when I lived in Krakow. She told me that her husband and her father-in-law had a luggage factory and asked if I would be interested in working for them. The next week she told me where to go for an interview. I was hired. The job was very far from where I lived, but it meant more money and a better future and it was my profession. I started on piecework doing the same type of work. Meanwhile, Ruth was still working at the belt factory. Happily, she had heard from her mother and she was coming to Boston.

While I was visiting the Turners, I met a nice blond guy who worked in his cousin's grocery store and had also come to visit the Turners. The grocery store owner had a son, also named Zygi after the same grandfather and another cousin introduced this son to Ruth. He had a beautiful car and took Ruth out for the evening to the theater. I didn't know anything about it until I came to see her after work and she was not at home. I was told she had a date. I got very mad. I stopped going to see Ruth and when I went to school, I didn't sit with her as I used to do. Niuszka and Zygi told me how foolish I was acting because Ruth was not my wife. She was just a friend and could date other boys and I could date other girls. This was a good experience for her and I could do the same thing.

The next day after school, I went to the Turners and Ruth told me about her date. She told me about the theater and the restaurant where they had eaten. Her date only spoke English and he didn't speak any other language so she couldn't understand him very well. He brought her to his parent's house where they spoke to her in Yiddish and German. When his mother said something to him, he got mad and told his mother to shut up. When Ruth heard that she thought, how could he talk to his mother like that. She then told him to please take her home. When I heard the story, I felt a little easier.

One evening we went by bus to a dance. I told Ruth that I thought there would be only old maids and old men at the dance. Ruth didn't think so because it was organized by the Jewish Center and she said there would be a lot of young couples there. I bet her a bottle of Kosher wine that I was right. When we got to the dance there were mostly young couples. She was smiling and said I owed her a bottle of wine. I gave her a kiss and until this day, I still owe her the bottle of wine.

When we got together on Saturday nights I used to bring a schmaltz herring with bagels and the Turners' dressed it up with onions and tomatoes. And we would talk.

Ruth told me her story, how she was in the camps with her mother, how her mother saved her when she had Typhus, how she lost her father and brother. After the war, her mother, a beautiful woman in her forties, married a man that Ruth didn't like. He was very plain. He had a son and they lived together in two rooms. The son was against her, she didn't know why. One time the son threw out her clothes for no reason. She left and went to Paris to stay with her father's brother. She lived with them for ten months. He was a rich man who had a pocketbook factory. She had to go back after several months to her mother's in Germany because her papers to go to America had come through. When she left, her stepfather gave her a roll of dollars but she didn't open it and to this day doesn't know how much was there.

Ruth told me she had a diploma stating she could work in dentistry, but she had lost the diploma or somebody had stolen it. That's why she took the job in the belt factory in Boston. I continued working piecework at the luggage factory where I was making good money. We enjoyed each other's company very much. We got together almost every Saturday night with our friend Rosenberg. Sometimes we went to a movie, but mostly we spent time at Zygi and Niuszka's. We had been going out for about a year when Ruth's parents were finally able came to America

We started to talk about a wedding so we went to Rabbi Jacobson. He was very helpful. Of all the newcomers, we were only the second to be married. The first was a couple named Cyla and Sam Moneta. The Rabbi was very friendly and said he would not charge us for the hall but only for the food. The room where weddings were held was called the Imperial Hall and it was a beautiful place. We had to first make a date and then let him know how many people to expect. We had to go to the municipal magistrate to register and get blood work. After the preparations, we were to go back to the Rabbi.

We spoke to Ruth's parents about our plans. Her stepfather didn't say anything about helping us with the Wedding. Thank God, I didn't need anyone's help. I had enough money for everything. We started to prepare for the wedding because I had a big family. Ruth didn't have anyone but her parents. We set a date for November 26, 1950. We sent out invitations. It was to be a beautiful formal wedding with 265 people. Rabbi Jacobson gave us Chuppah Keddishim, he officiated and didn't take any money, and even gave us ten dollars as a wedding present. Ruth looked stunning, like an empress. She wore a beautiful silk wedding dress with a long train that had been loaned by a very wealthy woman. I wore a Tuxedo and a top hat. I hired a photographer who took beautiful pictures and we had a wedding album made, but back then there was no video. My cousin Carl hired an orchestra and wouldn't take any money for his part. I paid for the rest of the music. My Uncle Carl brought a colored guy with him to sing Kol Nidrei and other Jewish songs. A lot of people brought envelopes with money as presents. Everything was wonderful.

Immediately after the Chuppah (Wedding ceremony), the caterers came to me and demanded their money. I had prepared the money for the food and given it to Israel Turner but he had forgotten to bring it with him. The people wanted to be paid for the food and they took me into a room. All the money that had been given as presents was mostly in my big Tuxedo pocket. I took the money out and counted it. They were afraid they weren't going to get their correct amount. I counted it out for them again to the penny. There was enough to pay them but my pockets were empty. I finally went back to the wedding. Ruth and everyone wanted to know what happened to me, I had been gone for more than an hour but I didn't say anything. When I sat down at the head table with Ruth and my mother-in-law, I told them quietly what had happened. Then I got to celebrate! We made a Mitzvah Dance. I think my Uncle Josel sang. Heimie, Sally Rothman's husband got drunk. My friends Israel Yungewirt and Kalmen Rakover had came to the wedding, as did my boss and managers who came with their wives. Ruth's uncle came from Paris and he brought two couples from Virginia, also family. Helen Chaji Gitele and her husband helped me a lot with the wedding plans. He took care of everything. Helen and her husband also helped by bringing home leftovers from the wedding such as whiskey, food, and cake. It was a beautiful wedding that lasted until one o'clock in the morning. We said goodbye to everyone and Ruth and I went to a hotel for the night. We knew it was the beginning of a better life. And it was.

The End—Part I

**Carl Freedman** was born Chaim Kalmen Frydman in 1920 in Krakow, Poland. After Germany occupied Poland, most of his family was killed by the Nazis. Following the liberation, Mr. Freedman was able to come to the USA where he married Ruth Wisniak, also a survivor. They became successful in business and raised a family in America and in Israel. Carl continued to write and perform his poetry and songs and those of his father. Carl and Ruth have been married for almost sixty years and have six grandchildren. The couple have been interviewed by the Spielberg film crew for the non-profit Shoah Project and have lectured to many groups. They currently reside in Florida where they are active in the Jewish community.

Lightning Source UK Ltd.
Milton Keynes UK
UKHW011554070223
416598UK00001B/295